PRACTICAL
PHOTOJOURNALISM

Titles in the series

Series editor: F. W. Hodgson

PRACTICAL
PHOTOJOURNALISM
A professional guide

Second Edition

MARTIN KEENE

Focal Press
An imprint of Butterworth-Heinemann
Linacre House, Jordan Hill, Oxford OX2 8DP
A division of Reed Educational and Professional Publishing Ltd

℞ A member of the Reed Elsevier plc group

OXFORD BOSTON JOHANNESBURG
MELBOURNE NEW DELHI SINGAPORE

First published 1993
Reprinted 1993
Second edition 1995
Reprinted 1997

British Library Cataloguing in Publication Data
Keene, Martin
    Practical Photojournalism: A Professional
    Guide – 2 Rev. ed
    I. Title
    070.49

    ISBN 0 240 51432 7

Library of Congress Cataloging in Publication Data
Keene, Martin.
    Practical photojournalism: a professional guide/Martin Keene.
    p. cm.
    Includes bibliographical references and index.
    ISBN 0 240 51431 9
    1. Photojournalism.   2. Photography – Equipment and supplies.
    3. Photojournalism – Vocational guidance.   I. Title.
    TR820.K394   1995   95–22119
    778.9'907049–dc20   CIP

Printed and bound in Great Britain by The Bath Press, Bath

Contents

14 Careers   221
So you want to be a press photographer?   —   Finding a
job   —   Interview   —   Educational qualifications   —   Training
and the National Certificate   —   Pre-entry course   —   Other courses
—   Working for a news agency   —   Moving on   —   Freelancing
—   Commercial work   —   Working for a national newspaper
—   Agencies   —   Magazines

Preface

Press photography is not just a job. It is more than just a career. It is a way of life.

Nobody would urge a gardener, 'Always carry a fork'. But a press photographer would feel naked without a camera within easy reach. There is no knowing when or where the picture which will be flashed around the world within hours – or appear on the next day's front page – will be taken.

Some people maintain that there is a difference between a press photographer and a photojournalist: that the former provides 'snaps' or 'smudges' for newspapers, and the latter carefully researches and constructs images with an accompanying story for serious newspapers and magazines. Others, and this book, feel that there is no difference – one is just a posh name for the other – and use the terms interchangeably.

A press photographer is the eyes of the readers and takes them to see people, things and places which for reasons of cost, space or time, the readers cannot see for themselves. In the same way that a reporter tells readers what is going on in their world, a press photographer shows them.

As well as communicating with the readers, a photojournalist has to build a rapport with the people he or she is photographing. They may be royalty, showbiz stars, tramps, awkward officials or shy children, but a good photographer can talk as an equal with all of them and put them at their ease.

Sometimes a press photographer is warmly welcomed – and it may be a good idea to ask why. Is the welcome genuine? Or does the host wish to show off his best side and avoid the examination of other facets of his character or business? At other times the welcome is not so warm. Press photographers have been killed covering wars and civil disturbances; some by mistake or bad luck, others because combatants are aware of the adverse effects on their international image that one telling picture can have.

Sometimes press photographers receive the reception they deserve: dress decently, ask politely, behave with respect and people will welcome you. Turn up looking like a scruff, talk like a yob and demand co-operation – then do not be surprised if you leave empty-handed.

A photographer needs an inquiring mind, a wide range of general knowledge and an appreciation of the issues that interest readers today and the ability to guess the ones which will be of interest next week.

It is not a nine-to-five routine. News can happen at any time of the day or night and does not stop after a 40-hour week. Sometimes the job is distasteful. No right-thinking person enjoys calling on the relatives of people who have died in tragic circumstances to see if they have a picture that the paper can print the next day.

Sometimes there are disappointments. Not every picture makes it to the paper. Perhaps the story that accompanies it is not as strong as was originally thought or there is not enough space. A press photographer must not become disenchanted. Some newspapers consider the use and presentation of pictures just as carefully as they do the words. Others do not.

There can be enormous responsibilities. A newspaper may spend thousands of pounds for a photographer to travel to a particular event: editors want pictures, not excuses. Or where space is tight, there may be several newspapers, perhaps even scores, relying upon one person as the pool photographer to provide the pictures. A cool head is important.

The amount of equipment carried and the scrum encountered at some assignments requires a considerable level of stamina.

Technology has helped the photographer. Cameras have become lighter; film quality has improved; optical developments have produced zoom lenses whose convenience in use overcomes the very minimal loss of quality and aperture compared with lenses of fixed focal length; and there are telephoto lenses whose aperture (and cost) would astonish photographers of a generation ago. Sophisticated built-in exposure meters come close to guaranteeing perfect exposure; wire machines can use a negative to transmit a colour picture back to a photographer's office in seven minutes over a telephone line; portable telephones can be set up literally anywhere and bounce the signal off a satellite thousands of miles above the earth. By the year 2000, the use of electronic cameras will be widespread.

Printing methods have also advanced. Manual typewriters and compositors sitting in front of rows of typesetting machines have gone from newspaper offices to be replaced by computers; copy is handled electronically by journalists sitting at video screens; many papers regularly print colour pictures. Some newspapers never see pictures – either from their own staff or agencies and freelances – as paper prints, but only as electronic images on a computer screen after the negative has been scanned into an electronic picture desk.

But press photography faces challenges from the electronic media. Video cameras, improved international communications and the expansion of programming available from stations broadcasting via satellite all mean that the news from around the world, and around the country, can be beamed live into a viewer's home. Provided that the broadcaster is acknowledged, some lawyers consider that the current copyright laws allow these pictures to be used in a paper at no cost. The scale of British television news organizations means that they can send more people to an event than a newspaper can. Their material does not have to be processed. Two minutes of news footage from a war zone can easily provide six or seven images suitable for videograbbing from the screen.

After the photographer has processed the film it takes nearly an hour to send six or seven colour pictures. And the next edition of the paper might not reach the reader for 16 hours after the news bulletin. At the moment, those images transmitted by the photographer are of better technical quality than those 'grabbed' from the television. But high definition television is developing rapidly.

As well as having to wait until their next edition to provide their readers with the news, some newspapers also have a credibility problem. Proprietors may have a political axe to grind. Because the number of television outlets is comparatively few, statutory and self-imposed criteria about balance, fairness and impartiality are strictly observed. People trust and believe what they see on television more than what they read in many newspapers. This situation may change as more outlets develop or are permitted. And, of course, television news coverage can be highly selective.

That readers may not believe everything in their newspaper does not deter them from buying it. They may consider some of the content as 'entertainment' rather than 'news'. Television news is perceived as more serious than some newspapers.

Television, however, is ephemeral. Pictures from newspapers and magazines can be looked at again and again. They can be saved to be re-read later – maybe years later. The eye can linger over the detail. They have an element of permanence.

There is no formal career structure in press photography. Everybody starts at, or near, the bottom and claws their way upwards. Some fulfil their aspirations for a globe-trotting staff job on a national newspaper. Others receive just as much job satisfaction as a senior photographer on a provincial paper, or become picture editors, taking a pride in the organization and management of a team of press photographers. More move across to magazines either as staff or freelances, or start their own businesses.

A press photographer has a ringside seat on history. The camera may be at a revolution affecting a country – even the world – or recording the comings and goings of a local community. This book tries to explain how to make the most of that ringside seat.

Martin Keene

Acknowledgements

A visit to a jumble sale by my younger brother started my interest in photography. He wanted a bright red box, but did not want the contents – a developing tank – which he passed on to me. My first camera – one with a fold-down front and real leather bellows – followed at Christmas as a present from my parents.

I am grateful to many, many people who have helped me since in my career: David Williams and Eric Tall at the *Herald Express*; and elsewhere in South Devon, where I spent nine very happy years, Stuart and Leslie MacDowall, Chris and Judy Bryan, Arthur Kaye, Dawn Fricker, Paul Levie, Laura Joint, Richard Lappas, Tony Carney, Noel Wain, Keith Richmond and Lewis Blackwell; Cedric Tarrant at the *Cambridge Evening News*; my many friends and colleagues at the Press Association, especially Harry Aspey, Paddy Hicks, Colin Smith, Ron Bell, Rebecca Naden, Bridget Coaker, Mike Riches, Peter Smith and Tom Corby; Arthur Edwards (*The Sun*), Kent Gavin (*Daily Mirror*), Mike Forster (*Daily Mail*), Paul Edwards, (*Today*), Mike Dunlea (*Daily Express*), Terry and Jayne Fincher and Tim Graham, all of whom I have stood alongside on ladders in places I could never have envisaged five years ago, and who have kept me sane when total panic and insanity were just moments away.

My thanks also go to Freddie Hodgson for his skilful and tactful direction while I have been writing this book, and to the Editor of the *Press Association*, the Editor of the *Herald Express* in Torquay and Paul Levie of the Torbay News Agency for permission to use pictures I took while working for them and Photax UK, Nikon UK and Canon UK for supplying pictures and information about their products.

Lastly, but by no means least, thanks go to my friends and family, who may see more of me now that this is written (and Alison can have her word processor back).

The mistakes are all mine, even if the ideas are not.

1
Light and lenses

LIGHT – WHAT IS IT?

Light is the visible part of the electromagnetic spectrum of radiation. For years, physicists have pondered over the precise nature of light. Sometimes its properties can best be explained by considering it to be energy in wave form – at other times, as discrete packets, or quanta, of energy. Visible light has a wavelength from about 400 nm (violet–blue) to 760 nm (deep red): not surprisingly, the energy just beyond these boundaries is called ultraviolet and infra-red respectively. (1 nm = 1 nanometre = 1×10^{-9} metres.)

Any colour of light can be made by adding together a mixture of the three primary colours – red, green and blue. White light is an equal mixture of all three. Complementary colours are two colours which, when mixed together, produce white light.

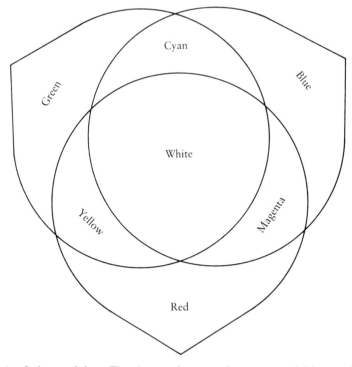

Figure 1.1   Colour mixing: The three primary colours are red, blue and green. If they are shone onto a screen, where they all overlap is white

Light is transmitted, emitted, reflected or absorbed by objects all around us. It may also chemically affect the material on which it falls.

If we process in an orderly manner the rays of light coming from an object, it is possible to form an image. The earliest and easiest way of doing this was with a pinhole.

In the simplest and theoretically ideal pinhole camera just one ray of light

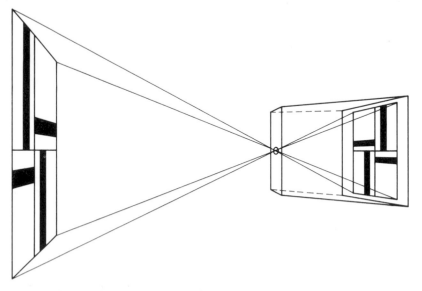

Figure 1.2 Pinhole camera: Rays of light passing through a simple pinhole camera show why the image on the film is back to front and upside down

from each part of the scene passes through the pinhole to the back of the camera. The image produced is upside down, and laterally reversed. As an exercise it is possible to take some quite interesting pictures with a pinhole camera, but there are drawbacks.

As the size of the pinhole is increased, letting in more rays from each point of the scene, so is the brightness of the image, but its sharpness is decreased as a point on the subject is now rendered as a small circle on the image. Making the pinhole too small will result in a loss of sharpness because of diffraction – a phenomenon occurring when waves of light diverge as they pass the edge of opaque material or through a small hole.

The speed of light varies according to the medium through which it is travelling. It is greatest in a vacuum. A ray of light crossing the junction between two media in which it travels at different speeds will be bent if it meets the interface at any direction other than at right angles. This phenomenon is known as refraction. The ratio of the speed of light in a vacuum to the speed in a material is known as the material's refractive index. The refractive index is a way of determining by how much light will be bent when it moves from one medium to another. However, the refractive index of a material varies with the colour and wavelength of the light, which is why white light falling on a prism is broken into its component parts, a phenomenon known as dispersion.

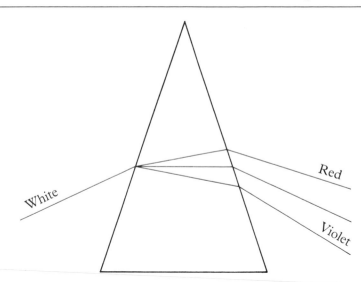

Figure 1.3   Refraction: White light passing through the interface of air and glass is refracted, breaking it up into its component colours. The amount of refraction is dependent upon the wavelength of the colour of the light

A simple lens, with two convex faces, can be likened to a series of prisms. When rays of light diverging from a point fall on the lens, they are focused to produce an image. Unlike the pinhole, which ideally handles just one ray, the simple lens can process rays emerging from a point in diverse directions. The distance from the lens to the plane in which parallel light is brought to a focus is known as the focal length of the lens. The greater the focal length, the larger is the size of objects in the image created.

In constructing optical diagrams for simple lenses, there are three rules.

1   A ray of light passing through the centre of the lens is transmitted without deviation.
2   A ray of light travelling parallel to the axis of the lens is refracted to pass through the axis of the lens at the same distance from the centre of the lens as its focal length.
3   Lenses with positive focal lengths produce real images which can be observed on a piece of paper, while lenses with negative focal lengths produce virtual images which cannot be focused on a sheet of paper.

It is possible to replace the pinhole in our camera with a simple lens which will let in much more light than a pinhole, but will have to be focused by moving it backwards and forwards relative to the image.

ABERRATIONS

The image produced by a simple lens is not perfect. It may be fuzzy at the edges, objects may have coloured edging, and straight lines in the object may not be rendered correctly.

These problems are known as aberrations – and there are six principal ones.

1   *Chromatic* aberration occurs because the refractive index of the

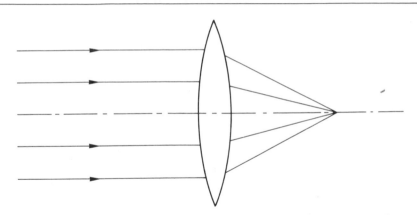

Figure 1.4 Ray diagram – positive lens: Parallel light converges as it passes through a simple positive lens

glass varies according to the wavelength of the light transmitted. Blue light, with a shorter wavelength, is bent more than red light with a longer wavelength. It means that light of differing colours is not focused in the same plane. It was overcome initially by cementing together two lenses, one positive and one negative, each with differing refractive indexes and powers of dispersion.

Chromatic aberration also leads to colour fringing of the image, a problem which gets worse as the focal length of the lens is increased. Special glasses have been developed to minimize this type of chromatic aberration. Lenses using these materials are often referred to as ED (extra-low-dispersion) lenses. It is these materials – for instance calcium fluorite – which have allowed the introduction of telephoto lenses with wide apertures and excellent colour correction.

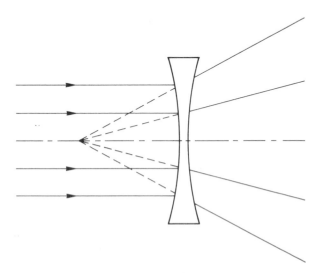

Figure 1.5 Ray diagram – negative lens: Parallel light diverges as it passes through a simple negative lens

Calcium fluorite is a naturally occurring mineral, but it can also be grown as large crystals. However, it is very delicate physically, and must be protected from the atmosphere and mechanical damage.

Mirror lenses do not refract light, but reflect it. Accordingly, they do not suffer from chromatic aberration.

2 *Spherical* aberration occurs because light hitting the outer parts of the lens is bent more sharply and comes to a focus sooner than that passing through the middle.

3 *Astigmatism* occurs at the edge of the image and is the inability to bring horizontal and vertical lines in the subject to the same plane of focus in the image.

4 *Coma* occurs when light falling obliquely on the lens and passing through different circular zones is brought to a focus at different distances from the film plane. A spot of light appears to have a tail, rather like a comet.

5 *Curvature of field* is the inability to focus a flat subject onto a plane. This occurs because those points at the edge of the flat subject are further away from the lens than those on its axis, and so are brought to a focus closer to the lens. It is an aberration which can be corrected, but can be useful when designing projector lenses, when the curvature of field of the lens can be designed to match the way that a transparency may buckle or bow slightly in the heat from the lamp.

6 *Pincushion and barrel* distortion is the inability to render a grid of parallel lines in the subject correctly in the image. They may bow inwards or outwards.

These aberrations can be overcome by using several elements of differing optical qualities to make up a lens. Using both positive and negative elements, with differing refractive indices, and perhaps cementing some together to form a group, the lens designer can play one element's shortcomings off against another, to produce a lens with the minimum of aberrations. Some modern lenses have as many as 20 different elements.

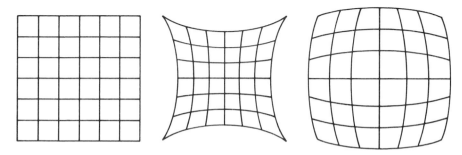

Figure 1.6 Pincushion and barrel distortion: Pincushion (centre) and barrel (right) distortions mean that parallel lines in the subject are bent in the image formed by the lens. It is particularly noticeable, and least desirable, when photographing buildings or documents

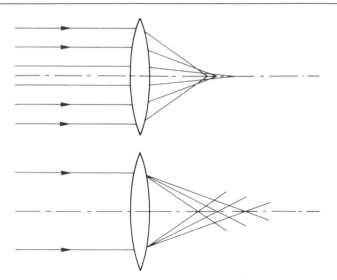

Figure 1.7 Spherical and chromatic aberrations: Spherical aberration (top) happens because light passing through the lens is bent more when it passes through the extremities of the lens than through the middle. Chromatic aberration (bottom) happens because light of differing colours is brought to a focus at different distances from the lens

Since some aberrations change with the distance of the lens from the object, designers may control them with 'floating elements', when the position of an element, or group of elements, is moved axially relative to the others as the lens is focused.

Because of the way it is manufactured, ground and polished, the surface of a lens element is part of a sphere. Certain aberrations can be controlled by using aspherical elements. These are expensive to produce from glass using conventional techniques, but there is some success in moulding them from plastic materials.

The calculations needed to predict the passage of a ray of light through a complex lens can be done on computers, greatly speeding up the design process.

FOCUSING

A lens needs to be moved relative to the image plane to compensate for changes in distance between it and the subject. The most common way is to move the entire lens backwards and forwards by means of a helical screw thread within the lens mount. Some large-format cameras place the lens on a board or plate parallel to the film plane which is moved backwards and forwards by a rack-and-pinion mechanism. A pair of bellows, normally made of a rubberized fabric, contract and expand between the camera body and the lens board to keep light out.

Alternatively it is possible just to move the front element of the lens. This method, called front cell focusing, is found mainly on inexpensive cameras and lenses.

Focusing is also possible by shifting an element or group of elements of the lens internally. This method of focusing is usually found on long telephoto lenses with a wide aperture. The benefits are:

- The lens does not change its overall physical dimension during focusing.
- The amount of movement required to change the focus at any given distance can be varied to allow greater sensitivity for distant objects.
- The physical amount of glass being moved is small and little mechanical force is needed to shift it.

Because of the final benefit, internal focusing is frequently used on lenses intended for autofocus cameras where the motors must be small and compact. Lenses using internal focusing are sometimes designated IF.

COATINGS

When light falls on the glass surface of a lens, the majority of it enters the lens, and the rest is reflected. Some of the light which is reflected eventually makes its way to the film where it may appear as flare, or ghosting. With the large numbers of elements found in modern lenses – especially zooms – the amount of light lost and turned into flare may be significant. It can be reduced by putting a thin anti-reflection coating on each surface. Because each coating only works for light of a specific wavelength, modern lenses can have several coatings, each designed to stop the reflection of light of a different colour. Each coating is a thin layer of material a quarter of the wavelength of the light whose reflection it is to stop. It is deposited upon the glass in a vacuum oven in which the coating material is vaporized by being either heated electrically or hit with a beam of electrons.

APERTURE

The aperture or 'stop' of a lens is important to the working photographer, and is controlled by the diaphragm within its optical system. Correctly described as the relative aperture, it is a measure of the amount of light that a lens will pass, and is the focal length of the lens divided by its effective diameter. A lens of the same relative aperture passes the same amount of light regardless of its focal length. The effective diameter is the diameter of the hole through which light can pass, as seen from the object. Although the effective diameter is controlled by the size of the diaphragm, their dimensions are not necessarily physically the same.

The diaphragm has a number of blades which can be moved to vary its diameter, and hence the amount of light passing through the lens. As shutter speeds vary by a factor of 2, it is desirable that aperture setting should alter by a similar factor. However, the amount of light that a lens passes depends upon its area, and hence the square of its diameter. To pass twice as much light, the diameter of the lens has to be increased, not by a factor of 2, but by a factor of the square root of 2 (= approx. 1.4). The settings of the aperture are conventionally numbers from the scale:

1, 1.4, 2, 2.8, 4, 5.6, 8, 11, 16, 22, 32

where the smaller the number, the greater amount of light passed by the lens. Each setting passes half the light of the next setting numerically smaller than it. It is possible that the maximum aperture of the lens may fall between two numbers of the scale, e.g. F3.5. To aid control of the diaphragm when the camera is at the eye and the scale cannot be seen, and to prevent accidental movement, lenses normally have indents at every stop, or, in some cases, every half stop.

A reduction in the physical size of the aperture when taking the picture, i.e. choosing a bigger number, or 'stopping down', will mean less light coming through the lens, which has to be compensated for either by a longer exposure which means an increased risk of camera shake, by using a more sensitive film with a consequent loss in quality, or by putting more light on the subject, which may not be possible. It also increases the depth of field of the picture – those parts of the picture in front and behind the plane of focus which are rendered acceptably sharp. Some aberrations are reduced by stopping down the lens. However, stopping down too far may increase others.

Simple cameras with fully automatic exposure may not permit the photographer to control the aperture. Some sophisticated electronic cameras do not have a conventional aperture scale, but control it electrically from the camera body, with the value in use displayed in the viewfinder or on a display panel on top of the camera.

The aperture of a lens matters to a photographer when actually taking a photograph, and, if using a reflex camera, when composing, focusing and viewing the picture.

A single lens reflex camera enables the photographer to view the subject at full aperture when the image is at its brightest, and only stops the lens down to the chosen taking aperture when the shutter button has been pressed. Once the exposure is complete, the lens is re-opened to its maximum aperture.

When composing, focusing and viewing the picture with a single lens reflex camera, the photographer needs a wide aperture to obtain the brightest possible image, and to minimize the depth of field, to help the image snap in and out of focus.

Lenses of most focal lengths are available in a variety of maximum apertures, with consequent variation in cost and weight. A wider maximum aperture helps with focusing and permits a higher shutter speed or the use of a slower, better quality film.

For example, look at the comparison for maximum aperture against cost and weight shown in Table 1.1.

Table 1.1

	35 mm lens			300 mm lens	
	Price (£s)	Weight (g)		Price (£s)	Weight (g)
F2.8	345.00	400	F4.5	700.00	1060
F2	475.00	280	F2.8	3500.00	2500
F1.4	800.00	240			

Any photographer buying a lens should carefully evaluate how much that extra stop of maximum aperture is worth, in terms of how often it will be used.

Until recently, interchangeable lenses were attached to cameras either by a screw thread or a bayonet mount which locked the lens to the camera body after turning it through less than 90 degrees; now almost all manufacturers use the latter, as they allow faster coupling and permit more links – both mechanical and electrical – between the camera and lens; screw threads were also prone to wear. While screw threads were standardized at 42 mm diameter, there is little standardization between bayonet mounts. Lenses made by Nikon, Canon, Minolta and Olympus will only fit their own cameras. Not only is the mount different, but so are the internal couplings, and, crucially, the thickness of the camera body, which determines the focusing range of the lens.

Modern cameras and lenses interchange information about:

- focal length;
- maximum aperture;
- the amount by which the lens is to be stopped down when the picture is taken;
- the distance at which the lens is focused;
- whether an exposure based on a shutter priority or program mode is planned.

This information may be exchanged mechanically through mating pins and levers on the lens mount and camera body or electronically via contacts on the circumference of the lens mount.

PERSPECTIVE

Perspective is the spatial arrangement of three-dimensional objects, as they are recorded in two dimensions from a particular place. From a viewpoint, the perspective of a scene does not alter regardless of how much or how little of the scene is viewed. Perspective only changes when the viewpoint moves.

Whether a print has a natural perspective depends upon the lens it is taken with, and, just as important, the distance from the eye at which it is viewed. We tend to view prints at distances between 30 cm and 100 cm from the eye.

Lenses with a narrow angle of view seem to flatten perspective, but this is because we are viewing them from too close. Look at a picture taken with a lens with a narrow angle of view from further away, and the perspective becomes more natural.

Similarly, pictures taken with wide angle lenses appear to have an unnatural steep perspective, but bring them closer to the eye, and the perspective becomes more natural.

FOCAL LENGTH AND COVERING POWER

The focal length of a lens was defined earlier as the distance from the lens to the plane where parallel light is brought to a focus. The covering power relates to the area of usable image that the lens produces. For example, a lens intended for use on a 35 mm camera will be capable of producing a circular image of usable quality of about 45 mm diameter. However, a 50 mm lens intended for use on 120 film, which uses a larger negative 60 mm square, needs to provide a usable image of about 85 mm diameter. Accordingly, a lens intended for use with one format will not cover a larger format. But it is possible to use the lens from a larger format, suitably adapted, for a smaller format.

The range of focal lengths available for the modern 35 mm system is vast, and

A

B

C

Figure 1.8 Perspective is independent of focal length: AA, BB and CC are enlargements of frames A, B and C – taken with 300, 200 and 80 mm lenses respectively – so that the final image size is the same. The perspective in each picture is the same – the only difference is a progressive loss of sharpness and increase in grain caused by the greater degree of enlargement of pictures BB and CC

AA

BB

CC

Figure 1.8 (*continued*)

Figure 1.9   Effects of changing focal length of lens: A series of nine pictures all taken from the same spot, but with the focal length of the lens varying from 15 mm through to 1000 mm

considerably greater than those available for even the most sophisticated 6 × 6 camera. For that reason the discussion about availability and use of interchangeable lenses will relate to those for 35 mm, but the principles are still relevant for other formats.

STANDARD LENSES

For a given film format, the standard or normal lens has a focal length roughly equivalent to the diagonal of the negative. It also gives an angle of view similar to the human eye.

For the 35 mm format, the standard lens is 50 mm, usually with an aperture between F2 and F1.4, but some are available as wide as F1. It has an angle of view of 46 degrees. The standard lens is the one most commonly sold with the camera, and is invariably of high optical quality. For the 6 × 6 format, which uses 120 film, the standard lens is 85 mm, normally F2.8.

WIDE ANGLE LENSES

Wide angle lenses are those whose focal length is less than that of the standard. For the same camera-to-subject distance they include more but the image size is smaller and the depth of field is increased. Their increased depth of field makes them particularly useful when there is little time to focus accurately. As well as simply 'getting more in', they have the ability to stretch the planes within a picture, accentuating those things close to the lens. It is possible to move the camera closer to a person or object, and include them and their surroundings. Although wide angle lenses are sometimes accused of distortion – and they may be guilty of optical shortcomings – they are only recording the perspective of the scene from where they view it.

Some wide angle lenses may use floating elements to reduce aberrations, especially at reduced focusing distances.

Wide angle lenses create problems for optical designers. In the model of the simple lens, the focal length is the distance from the lens to the film, and the shorter the focal length, the nearer to the film is the lens. This presents no problems for non-reflex cameras, but the single lens reflex needs to have space between the film and the rear of the lens to raise the mirror. The technique used by lens designers is the inverse telephoto design, where the front group of the lens is divergent or negative, and the rear group convergent or positive. This gives a lens which has a large distance from the rear element to the film, compared with its focal length.

It is for these reasons that wide angle lenses for non-reflex cameras – where the lens can be as close as necessary to the film – are smaller and often perform better.

35 mm

Some photographers prefer to use a 35 mm lens rather than a 50 mm lens as their standard. It is eminently suitable for many types of photography, without introducing too much distortion into a picture.

It has a view of 62 degrees, and is available from most manufacturers as an F2.8, or F2, and some even offer an F1.4.

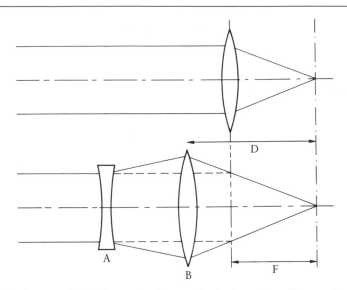

Figure 1.10   Inverted telephoto: An inverted telephoto lens (bottom) is a special construction used for wide angle lenses for reflex cameras which places a negative element (A) in front of a positive element (B). It means that the distance (D) from the film to the rear of the lens is greater than the actual focal length of the lens (F)

28 mm

This is the next wider option, is usually available as F2.8, or F2, and was once widely popular, but has recently yielded to the 24 mm.

24 mm

This lens includes some four times the area of the standard 50 mm lens, and is probably the most popular wide angle lens for news photography. It is usually available as F2.8 although some manufacturers make an F2, and one makes an expensive F1.4. It is very handy for 'grab' pictures taken in a hurry when precise focusing is not always possible. Because of the exaggerated perspective from its viewpoint it can produce dramatic images of objects placed close to the lens.

20 mm through to 14 mm

At these short focal lengths, lens manufacturers are struggling to keep the optical distortions in the picture to a minimum, and the illumination in the corners from falling off. These lenses can be recognized by the large front element which gets increasingly bulbous as the focal length is reduced. The exaggerated perspective that these lenses are capable of certainly makes for unusual pictures, but if used too often, the effect can become tiresome. Because of the difficulty of fitting filters to the front of the lenses, some have them built in, the choice being made by rotating a wheel on the outside of the lens. Some permit the filter to be screwed to the back of the lens.

TELEPHOTO LENSES

Telephoto lenses enable the photographer to obtain a larger image of things – for instance sportsmen or wild animals – which would normally be out of reach with a standard lens. However, because their angle of view is reduced, the effects of camera shake are magnified. They have less depth of field than a standard lens and appear to compress the planes in a picture, making objects seem closer together.

Although the word telephoto is used to cover all lenses longer than a standard, is specifically relates to an optical arrangement whereby the physical size of a lens is less than its focal length. This is achieved by placing a negative element behind the front, positive element.

85 mm

This is the first lens up from the standard, and is usually available as an F2 or F1.4, with one manufacturer offering an F1.2.

This is a good lens for portraits, with a limited depth of field. It is a very popular general news lens.

105 mm

This was popular when it was suggested that each lens that a photographer owned should be twice that of the next shortest one – 105 is twice the standard 50 mm – but is not used a lot now.

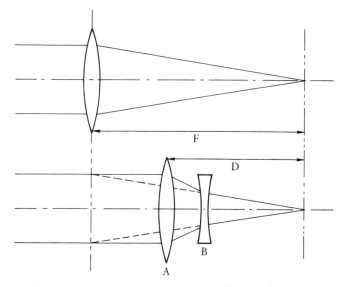

Figure 1.11 Telephoto lens: A telephoto lens (bottom) places a negative element (B) behind a positive element (A), so that its effective focal length (F) is longer than its physical size (D), making it more compact than a comparable long-focus lens

135 mm

A once popular focal length, but not used a lot now, although still in favour with some sports photographers. It can have a maximum aperture of F2, making it very useful in low light. It is significantly longer than, and not really interchangeable with, the 85 mm. It was very popular with amateur photographers before the availability of telephoto zoom lenses that were reasonably priced and of acceptable optical quality.

180 mm

A favourite lens amongst professional photographers. It normally has a maximum aperture of F2.8, and is popular for sport, news and photocalls because of its ability to focus on only one plane, and render cluttered backgrounds out of focus.

200 mm

An alternative to the 180 mm – but the longer lens is often a stop slower. Some manufacturers do make an F2 version which may use internal focusing and extra-low-dispersion glass, but the size and weight does not always make it a lens suitable for carrying around all the time for general photography.

300 mm

As we have seen earlier in this chapter, there are several options available. Those with an F2.8 aperture can be used for a wide range of photography with slow film in poor light, and can be used with a teleconverter to produce a lens of greater focal length. It can be hand-held, or mounted on a monopod or tripod. Hand-holding the F2 version is an acquired art.

400 mm

Available as F2.8, F3.5 or F5.6, it is popular for sport, but possibly a little too long for general news photography. Before the introduction of the superfast telephoto lenses using internal focusing and extra-low-dispersion glass, the 400 mm lens made by Novoflex was almost standard throughout the industry. It was a long-focus lens with a single group at the front end of a tube, and was focused by the photographer squeezing a pistol grip which reduced the distance between the lens and the film. It was possible to change the focal length from 400 mm to 640 mm merely by unscrewing the end of the tube, and replacing it with another, containing a lens of longer focal length. The pistol grip made for a well-balanced combination, which was easy to handle. Recently Tamron, an independent manufacturer of lenses, teamed up with Novoflex to produce a 300 mm F2.8 lens with squeeze focusing, but it does not appear to have caught on.

500 to 2000 mm

These really are specialized lenses for news, sports and nature photography and, depending upon their aperture can cost several thousand pounds. Some may only be available by special order. Although it may be possible to use the shorter ones hand-held, they should be used on a monopod, or, for best results, be mounted on a rigid tripod.

Specialist lenses

Zoom lenses

Zoom lenses cover a range of focal lengths. Prime lenses have a fixed focal length. The variation in focal length is achieved by moving groups of elements axially within the barrel of the lens either by turning a second ring on the barrel of the lens or by moving the focusing ring backwards or forwards relative to the camera body. The ratio of a zoom lens is its maximum focal length divided by its minimum. Although lenses for television and cinematography may have ratios as high as 20 : 1, those intended for 35 mm cameras seldom exceed 4 or 5 : 1.

Typical zoom lenses cover 20–35 mm, 28–85 mm, 35–70 mm, 35–200 mm, 80–200 mm and 180–600 mm. Canon have recently launched a 35–350 mm F3.5–5.6 autofocus zoom.

As important as the range is the maximum aperture. Until very recently, most zoom lenses had an aperture at the long end which was comparable with that of the same fixed focal length lens, but the aperture at the short end was smaller than that available on a prime lens. For instance, an 80–200 mm F4 zoom has an aperture which is acceptable at the long end, but most 85 mm lenses are F2 or wider – two stops better than the zoom. Some manufacturers produced lenses where the maximum aperture was increased at the short end of its range.

A zoom lens has more elements than a prime lens, and their separation has to be precisely controlled. For a long time some professional photographers were wary of zoom lenses, feeling that their results were optically inferior to prime lenses, and that they were more delicate.

Some of these problems have been overcome. Several manufacturers offer an 80–200 mm lens with a maximum aperture of F2.8 throughout the range. Using this with a 35–70 mm F2.8 lens means that the vast majority of a news photographer's work can be done on just two lenses. The optical quality may not be quite as high as with a prime lens, but this is a small price to pay for the convenience of carrying just two lenses and the ability to frame a subject precisely, thereby reducing the amount of enlargement needed.

Ten years ago, few professional photographers used zoom lenses on a regular basis. That many do so today is a tribute to the optical designers' abilities.

Mirror lenses

Instead of refracting the light through a lens, it is possible to form an image by reflecting it from a concave mirror. By 'folding up' the light path the lens can be made much shorter than its actual focal length. For instance, the Nikkor 500 mm lens is just 142 mm long, and is eminently hand-holdable.

Figure 1.12   Balcony scene: Members of the Royal family were on the balcony at Buckingham Palace to watch a fly-past to mark the anniversary of the Battle of Britain, when Prince Harry put his hand over the mouth of Princess Beatrice. Despite using a 600 mm F4 lens and a 2× teleconverter, the image on the negative is still small. This picture was a runner-up in the Royalty Section of the British Telecom Press Photographer of the Year Awards (© Press Association)

A mirror lens does need some glass elements in it to correct spherical aberrations, but it is much lighter than the comparable all-glass lens, and does not suffer from chromatic aberration. Filters are screwed into the rear of the lens.

Mirror lenses have two drawbacks. They have no iris diaphragm, so there is no control over the depth of field, and the amount of light transmitted has to be controlled by placing neutral density filters, which darkens the image for focusing. Mirror lenses also produce out-of-focus highlights in the picture which are rings rather than discs. Sometimes – for instance, when the highlights are caused by sunlight falling on water – this is a desirable effect, while at other times it can be irritating.

Mirror lenses are available from 500 mm to 2000 mm.

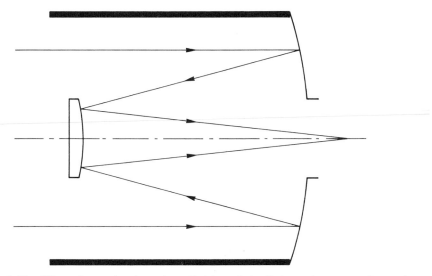
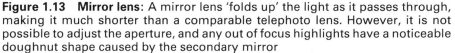

Figure 1.13   Mirror lens: A mirror lens 'folds up' the light as it passes through, making it much shorter than a comparable telephoto lens. However, it is not possible to adjust the aperture, and any out of focus highlights have a noticeable doughnut shape caused by the secondary mirror

Fish-eye lenses

These are lenses of extremely short focal length with an angle of view which can be in excess of 180 degrees. They produce characteristic images in which lines not passing through the centre of the picture suffer from barrel distortion. The traditional fish-eye lens produces a circular image. Other fish-eye lenses produce an image which fills the entire frame, but which has a 180 degree angle of view across the diagonal of the negative. Some early ones had elements which were so close to the film that it was necessary to lock the mirror in reflex cameras in the raised position and use a separate viewfinder. Modern ones use a retrofocus design to permit through-the-lens viewing and metering and have built-in filters. Particular care should be taken, as the bulbous front element of the lens is highly exposed to physical damage.

It is very hard to justify the purchase of one of these lenses, given the frequency with which they are used. However, they can be easily hired when the need arises.

Figure 1.14 Fish-eye lens: A fish-eye lens takes distortion to the limit – only those straight lines which pass through the centre of the lens are rendered correctly. All others are bent – and the degree of bending increases with their distance from the centre

Macro lenses

These are specially computed to minimize aberrations at close distances. They usually have a focusing range which permits objects to be reproduced on the negative at half life size. They have a focal length of about 50 mm, but some are available with a focal length of about 105 mm to permit a greater camera-to-subject distance. If a photographer expects to do a lot of copying, it may be worth buying a 50 mm macro instead of a conventional standard lens.

Teleconverters

These will not form an image by themselves as they are negative lenses but they are placed between the lens and the camera and multiply the focal length of the lens in use. They are available as 1.4×, 2× and occasionally 3×. Because the effective diameter of the lens remains unchanged but the focal length has been increased there is also a corresponding reduction in the aperture and consequent light loss. A 1.4× converter loses one stop, a 2× loses two stops and a 3× just over three stops. For cameras with through-the-lens metering, this is taken care of automatically. Otherwise it must be appreciated that the aperture scale on the lens no longer reflects the correct values and must be adjusted accordingly.

Teleconverters work with lenses of all focal lengths, but there may be a loss of quality, which can be minimized by closing down the lens by a couple of stops, and restricting their use to lenses with a focal length of 135 mm or greater. There is little point in using a 2× teleconverter with a 28 mm lens to make a 50 mm lens, when a good one is probably to hand, but it is worthwhile to convert a 300 mm lens to a rarely used 600 mm.

Some manufacturers make specialist converters for extra-long, wide aperture telephoto lenses. These extend a short distance into the throat of the lens, and eliminate the vignetting which may occur with ordinary teleconverters.

A 2× teleconverter is not expensive, and is a useful item which can get a photographer out of trouble when the lenses available are not long enough for the job in hand.

Perspective control lenses

When photographing a building, it is not always possible to get it all in without tilting the camera upwards. In the finished photograph, the building seems to be toppling over backwards, and the edges of the building appear to converge. This is a natural effect of tilting the camera, but appears strange when viewed on a print. It is exactly the same effect which makes railway lines appear to converge in the distance.

It can be overcome to some extent in the darkroom by tilting either or both the enlarger baseboard and the negative carrier – but this is not an option for those people using transparencies or commercial photofinishers, or scanning their negatives electronically.

Perspective control lenses allow the optics to be moved off centre, up or down, left or right, parallel to the film. This means that in the case of tall buildings, the back of the camera can be kept vertical, and the lens shifted upwards to accommodate the top of the building.

The lenses are usually available with a focal length of 35 mm or 24 mm, and because they are being shifted off centre, have a wider than normal covering power. Because the optics and iris leaves are not fixed relative to the camera body, automatic diaphragm operation is not always possible.

Unless a photographer has a particular need for this specialist lens, they are best hired when needed.

Guide number lenses

Before the introduction of computerized electronic flashguns, the exposure for flash photography was dependent upon the distance between the camera and the flashgun. Nikon introduced a lens which had a direct link between the aperture and the focusing distance. It is no longer available.

(a)

(b)

Figure 1.15   Converging verticals: When a camera is pointed upwards, vertical parallel lines appear to converge. Although this effect is optically accurate, it can give the impression that a building is toppling backwards (a). The ideal solution is a perspective control lens which shifts the lens off the axis of the camera and eliminates the effect when the picture is taken. However, few press photographers have access to such a specialized lens. It is possible to correct the convergence by tilting the enlarger easel when the print is made in the darkroom. Alternatively it may be possible to use a wider angle lens, keeping it vertical, and cropping the desired part of the image from the complete negative

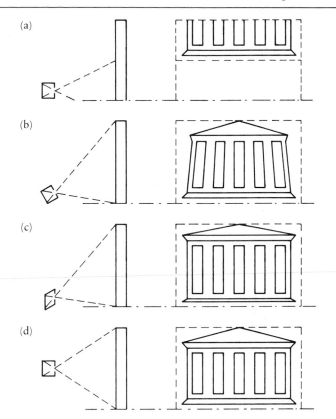

Figure 1.16 Converging verticals: Photographing tall buildings from ground level can present problems: (a) Keeping the camera level results in the top of the building going out of frame; (b) Tilting the camera keeps all the building in the frame, but means that the verticals converge; (c) One solution is a perspective control lens, which can be shifted off the axis of the camera, enabling the planes of the lens, film and building to be kept parallel. A similar effect can be achieved in the darkroom by tilting the enlarger baseboard; (d) Take the picture from a high point nearby so that there is no need to tilt the camera

WHAT TO BUY

No two photographers' needs and preferences are the same, but when facing the bewildering array of optics available from camera manufacturers and independents, here are some pointers.

If one is happy to use zooms, then the choice is fairly straightforward: a 35–70 mm F2.8 and 80–200 F2.8, with either a 24 mm or a 20 mm as a useful wide angle, and a 300 mm, hopefully F2.8, with a 2 × converter. Some manufacturers make a very useful 20–35 mm F2.8 zoom, which with a standard lens could replace the short zoom and the prime wide angle lens. The only drawback with using zoom lenses is that if one fails, then one has a large hole in one's coverage. A photographer who is travelling away from the office or from a convenient repair workshop would be well advised to take either a spare zoom, or some prime lenses.

If one prefers to use fixed focal length lenses, then the tried and tested combination could include 24 mm F2.8/20 mm F2.8, 35 mm F2, 85 mm F2, 180 mm F2.8 and the 300 mm.

Camera manufacturers naturally manufacture a range of lenses designed for their own cameras. There are also independent manufacturers who make lenses for a range of different cameras. Some of them use an interchangeable mount between the camera and the rear of the lens to make them compatible – and these have the advantage that if the photographer changes camera system, only a new set of mounts needs to be purchased. Others can only be fitted to a specific camera. The costs of lenses from independents vary. Normally they are significantly cheaper than those from the camera manufacturer. Some independent lenses have focus rings that turn towards infinity in the opposite direction to those from camera manufacturers, which can be confusing.

It really is worth buying lenses from the camera manufacturer if funds permit. The optical and mechanical quality control standards will probably be higher, and they will match the camera in every way intended, and have consistency of colour balance throughout the range. However, any lens from an independent whose price starts to approach that of the equivalent from the camera manufacturer is worthy of consideration.

Possible exceptions to this advice are those lenses which will be used less frequently – and the saving made is greater than the possible loss of optical quality. For instance the Tamron 17 mm lens costs about £200 – the Nikkor equivalent 18 mm costs nearly £700.

It is possible to buy good lenses secondhand. Check the optical surfaces carefully, and see that the focus ring turns freely without any grating or roughness. Shake the lens gently and listen to see if any of the elements are loose. Ensure that the leaves of the aperture open and close easily, and make a uniformly circular hole. Examine the barrel for any sign of physical damage. Finally ask the dealer if you can put the lens on your camera and put a test film through. It is important to put the camera and lens on a firm tripod and use the slowest possible film. Choosing a suitable subject (an evenly lit sheet of newsprint square on to the camera is a good subject), take a series of pictures at different apertures (record them in a notebook!) and either have enlargements made, or study the negatives under a magnifier to assess the quality of the lens. Not all the small type may be visible at the edges at the widest aperture, but with the aperture closed down by two or three stops, all the writing should be clear.

LENS CARE

A lens is a precision optical instrument, which, if cared for, will last almost indefinitely. Its front element should always be protected by a filter, and when not in use the rear opening should be covered by a back cap. They should never be put on a table in such a way that they can roll off. Dirt on the elements can be removed first by blowing compressed air across the surface, and only then by using a piece of lint-free cloth or chamois leather lightly moistened with lens-cleaning fluid.

2
Cameras

What we see with our eyes is transient – we may remember it, but we cannot record it accurately or show it to other people. To do that we need a camera and some light-sensitive material.

All cameras are light-tight boxes of differing sizes, with five vital elements:

- lens, or pinhole, to focus rays of light diverging from the subject onto the film;
- aperture or diaphragm to control how much light reaches the film;
- shutter to control when, and for how long, that light falls on the film;
- viewfinder to determine what will be included in the picture;
- film holder and transport mechanism to hold the light-sensitive material in the correct plane and move new, unexposed film into position for the next picture.

The design of lenses, their aberrations and the choices available have been covered, along with the diaphragm, in the previous chapter.

Shutters

A shutter may appear in two positions in a camera; either between the elements in the lens, when it is called a leaf shutter, or adjacent to the film, when it is described as a focal plane shutter.

In the same way that adjacent aperture settings let in half or twice as much light as their neighbours, shutter speeds alter by a factor of two: 1, 1/2, 1/4, 1/8, 1/15, 1/30, 1/60, 1/125, 1/250, 1/500, 1/1000, 1/2000, 1/4000, 1/8000.

Longer speeds are difficult to make available mechanically; when they are provided on a camera, it is usually evidence that the shutter has electronic timing. If the slower speeds are not used often and are mechanically timed, it is a good idea to use them periodically to exercise the mechanism.

Some shutters have B and T marked on them – these are settings for exposures longer than one second. When a shutter is on B, it will remain open all the time that the shutter button is depressed. On T it will remain open, even once pressure on the button has been released, only closing when, according to the particular camera, either the button is pressed again, or the shutter dial is rotated to another setting.

Leaf shutters

A leaf shutter consists of several metal leaves between the elements of the lens which overlap when closed. Before the picture can be taken, the shutter must be tensioned. At the moment of exposure the leaves spring open almost instantaneously and close again after the selected time. The speeds offered usually range from one second to 1/500th of a second.

Because it exposes all the film simultaneously, the shutter can synchronize at all speeds with electronic flash, which has an extremely short duration.

Leaf shutters are found in lenses which are permanently attached to a camera body, in lenses for cameras using sheet film, and in some interchangeable lenses for 6 × 6 format cameras.

The speed of a leaf shutter is usually selected by moving a pointer round the lens to align with the different speeds engraved on the barrel.

Focal plane shutters

A focal plane shutter is a pair of blinds or curtains made of opaque material which move across the film with an adjustable slit between them. The length of the exposure is governed by the size and speed of the slit as it sweeps across the film. The film is exposed sequentially, other than at low speeds when the size of the slit is the same as the dimension of the film.

It is usually found in 35 mm cameras using interchangeable lenses, thus eliminating the need for a shutter in each lens and reducing cost. Because the blinds cover the film between exposure the lenses may be swapped at will.

Problems of uneven exposure may arise with focal plane shutters if the two blinds do not move at identical speeds, and synchronization with electronic flash is only possible at those speeds when the entire film is uncovered simultaneously.

Early focal plane shutters used rubberized fabric which was wound around rollers and the slit travelled along the length of the film. The top speed available was 1/1000th, or occasionally 1/2000th, of a second, and flash synchronization was possible at speeds at or below 1/90th of a second.

Modern focal plane shutters have a slit which moves vertically, rather than horizontally, and the blinds have been replaced with a series of blades made from aluminium alloys or titanium, which have low inertia, meaning that they can accelerate and decelerate faster. Speeds of up to 1/8000th of a second and flash synchronization at 1/250th of a second are now typical.

While the speed at which the slit crosses the film is fixed, the gap between the first and second blind can be controlled electronically to provide an almost infinite variation in shutter speeds.

The speed of a focal plane shutter is usually chosen by rotating a dial with the possible exposure lengths engraved upon it. Some cameras select the shutter speed by rotating a ring around the lens mount – the idea being that the same hand can control both the aperture and the shutter speed. Cameras with complex electronics may have no shutter speed dial; the speed is instead selected by rotating a thumbwheel, which changes a display both inside the viewfinder and on a panel on top of the camera.

At fast shutter speeds the film is not all exposed simultaneously. This can lead to the apparent distortion of fast-moving objects if their position in the frame moves during the time of exposure. This effect is reduced by the shorter duration of the overall exposure of a vertically as opposed to a horizontally running shutter. The effect is of very little practical importance.

Viewfinders

In its simplest form, a viewfinder consists of a wire frame on the camera which, when held up to the eye, defines the area to appear in the picture.

More sophisticated ones replace the wire frame with simple optics, and may define the picture area with a white outline box which appears to 'hang' beyond the camera. Called direct vision viewfinders, they may change the size of the outline as the focal length of the lens is changed, and incorporate a rangefinder to assist with focusing the lens.

Cameras with a rangefinder project another image of the central part of the picture, obtained from a second window via a mirror, into the viewfinder. The images will only coincide for a specific angle of the mirror. The rotation of the mirror is linked via cams and gears to the focusing of the lens.

Direct vision viewfinders do not see the subject from exactly the same point as the camera lens. This shortcoming is known as parallax error and is particularly noticeable at close distances. Some cameras may make allowance for it by altering the position of the box as the focusing distance is reduced.

Some cameras permit the scene to be viewed through the actual lens taking the picture. Cameras using sheet film are focused and the image examined on a sheet

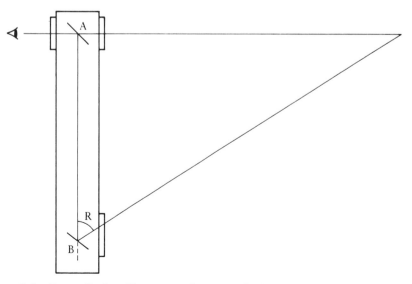

Figure 2.1 Rangefinder: The user of a rangefinder views the subject directly through a semi-silvered mirror (A) and via a totally silvered mirror (B), whose angle of rotation (R) can be varied until the two images are coincident. The rotation of the mirror is coupled to the focusing mechanism of the lens

of ground glass, which is replaced by a dark slide holding the film before the picture is taken. The image is not bright – and the photographer and the viewing screen must be under a dark cloth.

Single lens reflex cameras reflect the image from the lens which will take the picture, via a mirror in the light path, onto a focusing screen. Viewing the picture through the lens which will take it means that the photographer's vision is interrupted at the precise moment of exposure.

Twin lens reflex cameras focus and view the image through an identical lens positioned above the taking lens.

Film transport

Early cameras, like modern sheet film cameras, permitted just one exposure before the dark slide carrying the film had to be covered and removed before a fresh slide was inserted.

When film was first made in rolls, it was advanced by turning a knob while watching through a red window on the back of the camera for the next frame number on the backing paper to appear. Sprocketed 35 mm film could be easily and accurately advanced by a thumb lever on the top of the camera.

The first motor drives were accessories screwed onto the bottom of the camera. Now they may be miniature electric motors built in to the camera, capable of advancing the film through the camera at up to five frames a second.

Camera types

35 mm Single lens reflex

The 35 mm single lens reflex (SLR) is the commonest working tool of most press photographers.

Its benefits are:

- Viewing and focusing of the picture is done through the lens which takes it – eliminating parallax errors and enabling the depth of field to be checked. It is normally used at eye level.
- The camera has been highly developed and a wide variety of models are available at differing cost, reflecting the level of sophistication.
- A wide range of interchangeable lenses are available to provide for every assignment. Because viewing of the subject is done through the lens, there is no need for additional viewfinders.
- The 35 mm film that it uses is relatively inexpensive and universally available, with a choice of emulsions.

Its drawbacks are:

- Because the mirror is raised while the picture is taken, the photographer cannot see the subject at the precise moment of exposure.
- The mirror, shutter and other mechanism make the camera noisy.

(a)

(b)

(c)

(d)

(e)

Figure 2.2   State of the art photographic equipment from Canon: (a) 20–35 F2.8 zoom; (b) 28–80 mm F2.8–F4.0 zoom; (c) 80–200 mm F2.8 zoom; (d) top of the range EOSI camera providing sophisticated auto-focus and auto-exposure; (e) 300 mm F2.8 fixed focal length lens

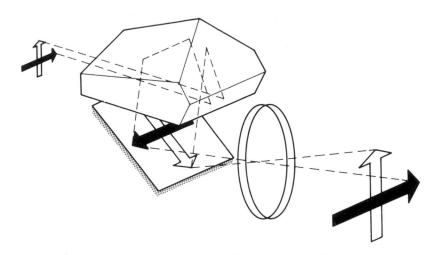

Figure 2.3   Pentaprism: A pentaprism enables the user of a camera to see an image through the lens which is the right way up and laterally corrected. The photographer's view is interrupted during the exposure when the mirror is raised

- The 35 mm film requires careful handling to produce results of the highest quality.

Viewfinder

The image produced on the focusing screen is back to front. This can be corrected and the camera used at eye level if it is viewed through a pentaprism.

Such prisms are made from solid glass, and, as the name suggests, have five sides.

Most 35 mm SLRs have fixed pentaprisms, with only a few top of the range models giving the user the opportunity to replace it with different viewfinders. Typical alternative viewfinders available include:

- Waist-level finder – for use low down when the photographer cannot get his or her eye to the camera, or on a copying stand. It usually has a flip-up hood with a magnifier to help observe the image on the focusing screen which is the wrong way round. For complicated multiple exposures, it can be useful to draw on the focusing screen with a grease pencil.
- Action finder – enables the full image to be seen even though the photographer's eye is not next to the camera, because of a helmet or a mask.

In practice there are occasions when it is useful to be able to remove the prism from the top of the camera, especially to compose low angle shots – for instance, when the camera is placed on the ground behind a horse racing fence – but it can be done quite successfully without a waist-level finder.

The drawback of removable prisms is that the join between the viewfinder and the camera body is a means by which dust and moisture can enter unless it is well sealed.

Spectacle wearers may have difficulties in seeing the entire viewfinder if the frames keep the eye too far away from the eyepiece. It is possible to purchase correction lenses of varying strengths to screw into the eyepiece so that photographers can use the camera without wearing spectacles. Some cameras provide an internal adjustment within the viewfinder to minimize the need to purchase a correction lens.

Focusing screens

Modern focusing screens have a variety of aids to help the photographer decide whether or not the picture is in focus and have developed greatly from the early ground glass ones. They may not even be made from glass at all, but from plastic, and laser etched to improve their brightness. Most have a Fresnel lens built in to provide even illumination over the entire screen.

The most popular aid is the split-image rangefinder. This consists of two thin adjacent semicircular prisms aligned in opposite directions in the centre of the screen. To focus the image the photographer places a straight line – for instance, a flagpole, a car door, the edge of a pair of spectacles – across the edge of the screen. Moving the image in and out of focus will cause the line to split. The image is in focus when the line passes through both prisms without deviation. It is a particularly simple way of focusing the lens as the eye can easily detect whether a line is straight or broken.

Derivatives of the split-image rangefinder are microprisms – tiny prisms or pyramids on the focusing screen. When the image falling on them is in focus,

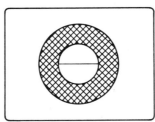

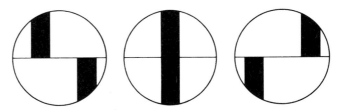

Figure 2.4 Focusing screens: A typical focusing screen has a ground glass screen with a split-image rangefinder at the centre, surrounded by a ring of microprisms. The split-image rangefinder uses two semicircular glass wedges. When the image is in focus, a parallel line passes across the join unbroken. When the image is out of focus, the line is broken and moves apart. Microprisms break up and out-of-focus image and cause it to shimmer

it is clear and sharp; when it is out of focus, it breaks up and appears to shimmer.

Cameras are usually supplied with a screen which has a central split-image rangefinder, surrounded by a collar or ring of microprisms, with the rest finely etched to enable focusing anywhere.

Professional cameras usually offer the user a choice of focusing screens. Some photographers prefer a totally plain ground glass screen; others specializing in copying or architectural work may find a screen with a ruled grid useful.

Both the split-image rangefinder and microprisms have the drawback that the angle of the prisms for maximum efficiency varies with the maximum aperture and focal length of the lens in use. With long lenses or small maximum apertures, one or other of the prisms will darken, or the microprisms take on a grainy aspect. A camera manufacturer may offer a range of screens with microprisms and split-image rangefinders set at differing angles suitable for lenses of varying focal length.

If the camera has a removable viewfinder, the screen is replaced from the top of the camera; otherwise it has to be replaced through the lens throat on the front of the camera.

As well as composing and focusing the picture, the viewfinder can convey information about the settings of the camera to the photographer. The chosen shutter speed and aperture may be displayed either electronically, or through a small window which shows the F-stop set on the lens and a disc whose segments with the different values are introduced into the viewfinder as the shutter speed dial is rotated. The viewfinder may also show if the exposure selected is correct, and display the status of the flashgun and the number of frames of film used.

Shutter

35 mm SLRs invariably have a focal plane shutter. As explained earlier, they now run vertically rather than horizontally, and offer a top speed of up to 1/8000th of a second, and a flash synchronization speed of 1/250th of a second.

Sequence of operations

The sequence of operation for an SLR with a focal plane shutter is as follows. The picture is viewed and focused and the exposure assessed through the lens, via the reflex mirror; at the moment of exposure, the mirror is raised, the lens is stopped down to the chosen aperture and the focal plane shutter exposes the film; once the shutter is closed, the mirror is replaced in the light path and the lens is re-opened to its maximum aperture, whereupon the film can be advanced to the next frame. The interruption to the photographer's vision through the lens is like the blinking of an eye.

Exposure determination

Correct exposure of sensitized material requires an appropriate choice of shutter speed and aperture. While some photographers use a separate meter, all 35 mm SLRs currently made include some form of exposure metering. Almost without exception, exposure measurement is carried out through the lens (TTL), using cells within the camera to measure the light reflected from those parts of the scene which will appear in the picture. The benefits of TTL metering are that it only measures light from the scene that will appear in the picture, and takes into account the use of any filters, teleconverters or extension tubes on the lens.

There are several ways to indicate in the viewfinder that the correct exposure has been chosen. A needle may have to overlap another one, or align with a fixed cursor. Sometimes + or − signs lit by red light-emitting diodes (LEDs) indicating over- or underexposure have to be extinguished, leaving just one central one, perhaps coloured green, to indicate the achievement of correct exposure. A liquid crystal display (LCD) may be used instead of LEDs. While LEDs are self-illuminating, an LCD needs to be illuminated in the dark.

Most exposure meters include a timing circuit to turn them off to prevent battery drain.

Modern cameras use full aperture TTL metering, in which the lens stays at its maximum aperture during the metering process, and a mechanical or electrical linkage with the camera body 'tells' the exposure meter by how many stops it will be shut down during the exposure. The older and slower alternative to full aperture metering was stop-down metering, when the exposure was assessed with the lens stopped down to the aperture at which the picture was to be taken.

Early cameras with TTL metering used cadmium sulphide (CdS) – a material whose resistance varies with the amount of light falling upon it. It has the drawback of being unable to respond to rapid changes of light and having a 'memory' which affects readings after the cell has been exposed to bright light.

Modern TTL meters use either a silicon photodiode or a gallium arsenide phosphide photodiode. These generate a minute amount of electricity which varies with the intensity of the light falling upon them. They both need amplifiers to produce a useful output.

The cells may be placed in the pentaprism, and measure the brightness of the focusing screen. Alternatively the reflex mirror may allow some light to pass through it, which is then reflected by a second mirror to a cell on the floor of the camera's mirror box. This method has the benefit that the cell can also measure the light reflected from the film itself during the exposure, and take account of any changes. This position is appropriate when flash exposures are determined by TTL metering.

TTL metering is not foolproof. In its simplest form, it averages the entire scene to grey, and assesses its brightness to determine the correct exposure.

It is not desirable that all parts of the picture should be given equal importance when assessing the exposure – for instance, many pictures have bright sky at the top which, when the scene is averaged out, would lead to underexposure. Instead, meter systems are biased, or weighted, to a particular part of the picture.

Centre weighting is the most common, when the brightness of the central part of the picture may take account of 60% of the reading, and the rest 40%.

Spot metering is possible, when the meter measures the brightness of just the centre of the screen – the area may be as small as 3.5 mm in diameter. It may be possible to take spot meter readings from different parts of the subject and store them electronically, before averaging them out to obtain a reading.

Matrix metering divides the picture into segments – sometimes as many as six – and takes an exposure reading from each. Through a built-in mercury tilt switch the camera may know if it is being held horizontally or vertically. Using these readings, and by comparing them with known distribution of bright and dark areas in many pictures analysed by particular camera manufacturers, it advises the user of the 'correct' exposure.

Entering film speed

The camera must know the speed of the film to assess the exposure correctly. Film speed is measured numerically. It is often input on a scale on the shutter speed dial, which is adjusted by lifting the dial's collar and rotating it until the appropriate speed appears in a small cutout. Some cameras keep one dial specifically for the film speed.

The most recent method of inputting the film speed – DX coding – is by electrical contacts inside the camera which align with a painted pattern on the metal of the cassette. The contacts detect where there is paint and where there is metal, and determine both the film speed and the number of exposures in the cassette.

Some cameras have a small window in their back through which the photographer can read the small print on the cassette detailing the film type, its speed and the number of exposures.

Automatic exposure

A photographer planning on taking a photograph may have some idea of the constraints which apply to the picture or situation. For instance, at a football match, it may be felt that the shutter speed should not drop below 1/500th of a second but the aperture chosen is of secondary importance; when using a long lens without any support, camera shake is a problem, so the photographer may need to use it at maximum aperture in order to obtain the shortest possible exposure; when taking a picture outdoors with a wide angle lens, maximizing the depth of field may be important with the shutter speed being of secondary interest.

So on many occasions, the photographer selects one variable, either aperture or shutter speed, and then adjusts the other until the correct exposure is obtained.

The exposure systems in some cameras can do this for the photographer. If the photographer picks the shutter speed and the camera chooses the aperture, then it is described as 'shutter priority'; if it is the reverse, then it is 'aperture priority'. Aperture priority is simpler to engineer, as with electronic timing of the shutter it is easy to vary the length of exposure. Shutter priority usually requires that the lens is set at its minimum aperture, and the camera determines how far it is actually stopped down.

One step further is programmed exposure, when the camera chooses both the shutter speed and the aperture. Clearly there will be many times when the camera's choice will not be the same as the photographer's. The camera has no way of knowing whether it is taking a still life picture of a bunch of flowers or a picture of a racing car. Some cameras have several different programs from which the photographer can choose. They may take into account the focal length of the lens fitted, and the increased risk of camera shake with longer lenses. One may always favour a high shutter speed while another accentuates depth of field. When using programmed exposure, the camera should indicate within the viewfinder the exposure and aperture it has selected.

For both shutter and aperture priority and programmed exposure, it is usually possible to store the reading in the exposure meter, normally by pressing a button, while the picture is recomposed. This might occur when a subject is on a light background. The correct exposure could be obtained by going close to the subject, and filling the frame, before 'locking' the exposure and returning to where the picture was to be taken from.

For fine tuning of exposure control, most cameras have an exposure compensation dial which allows the exposure to be altered by as much as + or − 3 stops in 1/3 intervals. Altering the film speed will have the same effect as using the dial.

It is one of the ironies of modern photography that while film makers are striving to produce materials which have greater tolerance to exposure inaccuracies, camera manufacturers are producing cameras with ever more sophisticated exposure systems.

Film transport

Most SLRs entering the market have replaced the thumb lever used to advance the film with a built-in motor drive. Some have also replaced the rewind crank with an electric motor.

The thumb lever was the conventional way of advancing the film, but its speed was limited to about one frame a second. Professional cameras had motor drives as accessories, and these reached speeds of up to $5\frac{1}{2}$ frames per second, and rewound the film in about five seconds. Some were bulky, using ten AA batteries; others were temperamental, especially in the wet when they would either refuse to work when wanted, or run off an entire roll of film as the photographer desperately tried to turn them off. They were also quite noisy. At some events, for instance funerals or state occasions, it may be specified that no motor drives may be used.

The motor drives built in to many modern cameras are quiet, and can advance the film at speeds similar to or better than those of the previous noisier generation. A motor drive may have several settings:

- *Continuous*, enabling the camera to take a series of pictures for as long as the shutter release is depressed. It may be possible to control the rate at which the film is exposed.
- *Single* takes just one picture each time the shutter release is depressed.
- *Quiet* mode in which operations of tensioning the shutter and winding on the film may occur sequentially rather than simultaneously to minimize noise.

Although many cameras can rewind the film automatically after the last frame, it is important to be able to rewind the film manually. Otherwise, if the batteries fail, the film cannot be removed from the camera. Power rewind also contributes to battery consumption. Some cameras which rewind the film leave the leader out, some do not, and some offer a choice. Leaving the leader out means that the cassette does not have to be broken into to retrieve the film before it is processed. Winding it in means that the film cannot be inadvertently used again. Many photographers leave the leader sticking out, but tear the tongue off, so the film cannot be used again. The rewind crank serves as a useful indication to the photographer that the film is progressing satisfactorily through the camera.

That modern cameras have no thumb lever film advance is an indication of the total changeover from mechanical to electronic operation. Electronic cameras are not inherently less reliable than mechanical cameras. Indeed they have brought a level of sophistication to exposure control that was not possible with cameras of a generation ago. But there are two areas of concern with electronics – wet and batteries.

Professionals work in all conditions, and modern cameras are supposed to be well protected from the ingress of moisture, but everybody should carry both a few plastic bags which can be used to protect equipment and a chamois leather to dry the exterior of camera bodies. It is important when a camera has been exposed to rain that it is dried out thoroughly but gently before being put away.

Although all cameras have some kind of battery test built into them, a spare set of batteries for a camera should be no further away than the photographer's pocket. Many cameras use AA batteries which are obtainable virtually anywhere in the Western world, but anybody venturing far off the beaten track should ensure that they take a more than adequate supply with them. Those obtained locally may be of indeterminate age and quality.

Double exposure

Some cameras allow for double exposures, when the shutter is retensioned without advancing the film. It is a facility little used by press photographers.

Frame counter

All cameras have a frame counter. Recently some have added a frame counter inside the viewfinder – a particularly handy innovation. Some frame counters count back to zero as the film is rewound back into the cassette – useful to stop the leader disappearing back into the cassette.

Electronic controls and displays

Many of the controls found on a conventional camera as dials or switches that have to be rotated or turned by the user can be replaced by an alphanumeric LCD panel on top of the camera and a thumbwheel. The display shows the photographer the various settings that the camera is using – and they are changed by rotating the adjacent thumbwheel. The display will indicate the shutter speed and aperture selected either by the photographer, or by the camera's exposure system if aperture priority, shutter priority or program exposure control is in use, as well as the speed of the film, the number of frames exposed and other functions of the camera.

Whether electronic displays and a thumbwheel are better than conventional dials and knobs is a matter of opinion. Most people find the displays confusing until they have got accustomed to them, after which they would never go back to conventional controls.

Fixed mirror

A variant of the SLR uses a semi-silvered mirror which is fixed in position, rather than one which moves out of the light path during the exposure. Because the mirror is stationary the camera is quieter in operation and less susceptible to shake, and there is a reduction in the delay between the shutter release being pressed and the film being exposed. This in turn can increase the rate at which the motor drive can advance film through the camera. The drawback is that because the light coming through the lens is split between the viewfinder and exposing the film, the finder image appears darker, and the aperture/shutter speed combination is not a true measure of the exposure that the film is receiving.

Autofocus

It is a logical progression that camera manufacturers, who have introduced a high level of sophistication into exposure control, film transport and flash systems, should endeavour to automate focusing the lens.

For some years, compact cameras have been equipped with autofocus systems of varying designs. Professionals have been slower to accept the new technology.

Now most major manufacturers offer professional 35 mm cameras with an autofocus capability. In basic terms they pass some of the light through the reflex mirror and onto a CCD array. The output from this CCD is processed to detect if the image is out of focus, and to establish which way the lens must be turned to bring it into focus.

In very much the same way that a conventional focusing screen has a split-image rangefinder in the middle, a camera with autofocus has a central 'target' which must be placed over the part of the subject on which the photographer wishes the camera to focus. This can cause difficulties if the subject matter is off-centre. If there is one person standing in the middle of the frame, there is no problem. But if there are two, there is the risk that the target will not be on one of the people, but on the background, resulting in a back-focused picture. Most cameras have an autofocus lock which allows the picture to be recomposed once the focus has been confirmed. One has three autofocus sensors, one in the middle and two off-centre, and allows the photographer to make a rapid choice between them.

Autofocus sensors can fail in low light or on subjects lacking in contrast – but so can conventional manual systems. When an autofocus system loses the point of focus it can start 'hunting' – moving throughout its entire range looking for the point of focus.

The sophistication and performance of some autofocus systems is most impressive – they can track sprinting athletes or racing cars every bit as well as a competent photographer. As the technology is further developed, their failure rate will come down and autofocus will be grudgingly accepted by professional photographer, in much the same way that 35 mm film, automatic exposure control and zoom lenses have been.

120 Single lens reflex

These are the big brothers of the 35 mm SLR. Probably the best known manufacturer is Hasselblad, but others are Pentax, Rollei, Mamiya, Fuji and Bronica.

Their attraction is the large size of the negative produced from the 120 or 220 size film that they use, which means that prints of the same size can be made negatives with less enlargement than from 35 mm negatives – with a consequent reduction in grain and blemishes. Some have interchangeable magazines, permitting the film to be changed in mid-roll.

Their drawbacks are their size and weight, the potentially high cost – both of

Table 2.1

Manufacturer	*Negative size**	*Frames on roll of 120*
Hasselblad	6 × 6 cm	12
Pentax	6 × 7 cm	10
Mamiya	6 × 7 cm	10
	6 × 4.5 cm	15

* Some permit masking, or the use of alternative magazines to produce negatives of a smaller size.

the camera and the interchangeable lenses – and their slow speed of operation; even those with motor drives are limited to one or two frames per second. Some of these cameras are more at home in the studio than outside.

Few press photographers will use a 120 SLR from one year to the next. Their use tends to be restricted to the studio, commercial photography or for taking a picture which the photographer knows will be used particularly large. However, it is worth knowing the facilities of some of those available, if only for when a friend or colleague asks you to take his or her wedding pictures!

The Hasselblad produces square negatives, so there is no need to turn it sideways to obtain an upright picture. Accordingly, a simple magnifying viewfinder for the large focusing screen is sufficient for many purposes. The image, of course, is back to front. This is a problem, especially with moving subjects, but is quickly overcome with experience. A pentaprism, which presents the image the correct way around, is available for when the camera is used at eye level. The interchangeable film magazines make swapping films a matter of moments.

The Pentax 6 × 7 looks and operates just like a big 35 mm SLR – with an interchangeable pentaprism, instant return mirror and thumb lever film advance. It has a focal plane shutter, but the flash synchronization speed is slow. For those photographers who need flash synchronization speeds of up to 1/500th of a second, Pentax manufactures an interchangeable lens with a built-in leaf shutter. Lenses are available from 35 mm to 1000 mm, as well as teleconverters. There is no facility for interchangeable magazines.

Mamiya produces the 645 range with a focal plane shutter; as with the Pentax, a lens with a leaf shutter is available for sophisticated fill-in flash photography, and again the film cannot be removed from the camera in mid-roll without wastage. Because of the shape of the format, a pentaprism is needed for vertical pictures. The range of lenses is fairly comprehensive, from a 24 mm fish-eye through to a 500 mm telephoto. The Mamiya 645 is probably the least expensive entry into 120 SLR photography. Mamiya also makes a range of cameras which produce a 6 × 7 cm negative on 120 film; however, they are much more at home in the studio than out on assignment.

Twin lens reflex

The twin lens reflex camera has two lenses, one above the other (see Figure 2.5). The bottom one – with a leaf shutter – takes the picture; the image from the top one is projected, via a reflex mirror, onto a focusing screen. The viewfinder is usually a simple magnifying hood, but can be a pentaprism.

The camera's benefits are that it is quiet – there is no mirror to be raised and lowered, and the photographer's vision is not interrupted at the moment of exposure. Its drawbacks are its bulk, parallax error, and the inability to preview the picture's depth of field.

At one time, the twin lens Rolleiflex was the most common press camera in use, but it was replaced by the SLR, and went out of production for some time. It has recently been upgraded and reintroduced. Before the advent of the SLR, Rolleiflexes were made with fixed telephoto or wide angle lenses.

Considerably cheaper than the Rolleiflex are Mamiya's TLRs, whose main features are their interchangeable lenses which range from a 55 mm wide angle through to a 250 mm telephoto. Mamiya also makes an ingenious device which raises the camera before the exposure, putting the taking lens in the same position as the viewing lens, and thus eliminating parallax errors. They also supply one lens pair in which the viewing lens also has an adjustable aperture, so that the depth of field can be assessed.

Compact cameras

These are the simple 'point and shoot' type used by many members of the public, which is why they can be useful to the press photographer on those occasions when they would prefer not to be identified as a journalist.

These cameras, made by most manufacturers, use 35 mm film and have a lens between 35 and 45 mm, with an aperture of F2.8; some even have either a zoom lens or a lens offering a choice of two different focal lengths. They usually have a high level of automation – automatic exposure control, automatic focusing, built-in flashgun and motorized film advance and rewind. Some will not operate in low light unless the flashgun is turned on first; others turn the flashgun on for the photographer.

In some of these cameras the shutter and aperture have been combined. Between the elements of the lens are two overlapping blades with V-shaped

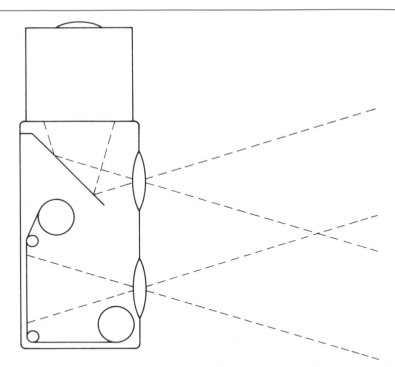

Figure 2.5   Twin lens reflex: A twin lens reflex uses two similar lenses – the top one for viewing and focusing, the bottom one for taking the picture. A serious disadvantage is that when the subject is close to the camera the views seen by the top and bottom lenses are not identical. This problem is known as parallax error

notches on them. For the exposure, these blades move apart and then come together again. Depending upon the length of the exposure, they may have formed a small aperture for a short length of time, or a larger aperture for a longer period.

As these cameras are totally battery dependent, it is important to ensure that the batteries they use are readily available and can be easily changed.

The results from these cameras are, for many subjects, indistinguishable from their more expensive counterparts. It is an excellent idea to carry one in the car at all times. Sometimes a picture which can be missed in the time it takes to put the lens on an SLR packed in the boot of the car can be taken with a compact.

At other times, a photographer may not be able to get to whatever or whoever has to be photographed, but can lend a camera to a relative or other person to take the picture. A compact camera, with its simple point-and-shoot operation, is ideal.

Rangefinder cameras

More sophisticated than the compact camera is the rangefinder camera with interchangeable lenses. These have a direct vision viewfinder, use a coincident-type rangefinder and have a focal plane shutter. Leica is the best known manu-

Figure 2.6 Vietnamese pot-bellied pigs: All press photographers should keep in regular touch with their local zoo, wildlife sanctuary or rare breeds centre. They are an invaluable source of exclusive pictures for a slow news day. I took this picture of a baby pot-bellied Vietnamese pig and her mother with a telephoto lens on a Mamiya camera which uses 120 film because I wanted the extra quality that the larger negative provides. The picture appeared in the *Sunday Express*, which at that time used several pictures every weekend of animals, models frolicking on the beach or starlets arriving at Heathrow Airport (© Torbay News Agency)

facturer of this type of camera. The Zorki was a Russian-made camera with features similar to early Leicas.

The benefits of the cameras are their small size, quietness of operation – unlike a reflex camera, there is no mirror being raised and lowered – and the accuracy of the focusing system in low light, especially with wide angle lenses. They are ideal for unobtrusive photography.

Lenses are available from 21 mm through to at least 560 mm. Depending upon the model, the integral viewfinder can adjust for lenses between 24 and 85 mm. For shorter lenses, specific viewfinders have to be clipped into the camera's accessory shoe; for longer ones, a special reflex housing is added between the lens and the camera body to aid focusing and viewing.

These cameras are mechanical, and depending upon the model, may have TTL metering. It may be possible to add a motor drive unit to the bottom of the camera.

Leicas are expensive – a new Leica M6 with a 50 mm F2 lens costs over £1800 – but they will last a lifetime, and are capable of results of the highest quality.

WHAT TO BUY

Most professional photographers using 35 mm SLRs will normally be working with two cameras, and sometimes three. Accordingly, if there is access to a 'pool' spare, for use while a body is being repaired, a photographer should have three bodies. If access to a spare is not possible, then it is probably wise to have four bodies. They do not all have to be the top of the range model; one, or perhaps two, could be a less expensive version. Depending upon the system chosen, it would be useful to have one which was purely mechanical.

Purchasing camera bodies secondhand is riskier than buying lenses. Lenses can be inspected and tested, and the amount of use that they have had can be assessed; they will, if looked after carefully, last almost indefinitely. Without professional examination it is much harder to see if a camera body has been dropped, or if it is suffering from more than cosmetic damage.

The vast majority of professional photographers use either Nikon or Canon equipment, with a few favouring Leica, Minolta or Olympus.

It is a lucky photographer who is able to look around and decide which camera system to purchase purely on its individual merits. For most of us the choice may be limited by price, or the need for new equipment to be compatible with that which we or our employers own already.

Leica equipment is undoubtedly expensive but is beautifully made and the lenses are excellent. Whether the cost can be justified is a personal decision. Olympus cameras found favour when they were first introduced for their small size and weight, and the brightness of their viewfinder.

But the big battle for the professional 35 mm market is between Canon and Nikon. Each offers both autofocus and manual cameras and lenses.

Canon's autofocus system uses a separate range of cameras and lenses from their manual focus system. Their autofocus lenses have no aperture rings, and a different bayonet mount to their manual ones.

Nikon have maintained the same bayonet mount found on the earliest Nikon F, introduced in 1959. Any of their lenses, regardless of age or autofocus status, can be used on any of their cameras. In 1977 they changed the diaphragm link between the camera and the lens, but some earlier lenses can be converted for use on later cameras. Autofocus is only possible with an autofocus lens on an autofocus camera.

The most obvious difference between the two autofocus systems is that Nikon has the motor which focuses the lens in the camera body, while Canon has it in the lens. It is suggested that this enables the motor to be specifically designed to take account of the particular requirements for each lens.

Initially it may be possible – or necessary – to purchase some equipment secondhand, and there is far greater choice in the market from Canon and Nikon than from other manufacturers. Another area to consider is servicing and repair. Although modern equipment is reliable, it does go wrong. Some camera manufacturers offer professional photographers preferential service for repairs, or may organize special facilities at large sports event for photographers to have their equipment checked or mended on the spot.

Many hire shops cater for Nikon or Canon users, but those with other makes of cameras may find it harder to hire specialist telephoto or wide angle lenses.

Which system to buy is a personal decision, and anybody contemplating a purchase of equipment which will cost several thousand pounds and have to last many years should have a 'hands-on' trial for as long as possible before making a decision.

Every photographer should own a small compact camera to carry in the car, or on those other occasions when it is not appropriate to carry the full SLR equipment. The specifications of these cameras are improving all the time, and as a glance in any High Street photo store will show, the choice available is very large.

The rangefinder camera will appeal to those whose photography is discreet and unobtrusive. There is no real choice – it is Leica or nothing.

Many photographers will have no regular need for a large-format SLR, and will be able to hire one when needed. But for anyone interested in taking pictures of the highest technical quality, and who enjoys the slightly more leisurely pace that their use affords, a Hasselblad can almost be justified on aesthetic grounds alone. If funds do not run to a Hasselblad – even though, like Leicas, they keep their prices so well that they can almost be regarded as an investment – then consider a Mamiya or a Pentax.

3
Other equipment

Early flashguns were little more than a tray filled with magnesium powder ignited by a spark from a flint wheel. After the blinding flash, the photographer and those around were surrounded by a cloud of white smoke.

The next major development was the disposable flashbulb. These use fine metal wire enclosed in a glass bulb filled with oxygen and are ignited by the current from a battery, which allows them to be synchronized to the opening of the camera shutter. The metal in small bulbs is zirconium or hafnium, while larger ones use an alloy of magnesium and aluminium. Flashbulbs are clean and provide a great deal of illumination, but are expensive as they can be used only once.

The modern electronic flashgun can be a sophisticated device, costing as much as a good camera, and accompanied by a thick instruction book. After the initial capital outlay, operating costs are virtually negligible, limited to the price of replacement batteries.

Electronic flash guns appear in all shapes and sizes, from the small unit in compact cameras to large studio outfits. This chapter discusses the principles of operation of the portable electronic flashguns used by press photographers working 'on the road'. The use of electronic flashguns in studios is examined in Chapter 9.

Most flashguns slide into a camera's 'hot shoe', which is usually found on top of the pentaprism – early Nikon cameras are among the exceptions; theirs is an accessory slipped over the film rewind knob. The flashgun in synchronized with the camera shutter through an integral contact in the middle of the hot shoe. Other flashguns are too large and bulky to go in the hot shoe, and are mounted on a bracket fastened to the bottom of the camera. They are fired by a cable which plugs into a socket on the camera. Flashgun cables have a habit of failing at inconvenient moments, and a wise photographer always carries at least one spare.

An electronic flashgun uses batteries to charge a device for storing electricity called a capacitor. Once the capacitor is full, or nearly full, a neon light illuminates to show the user that the equipment is ready for use. When the flashgun is fired, the electricity stored in the capacitor is discharged through a tube containing an inert gas at low pressure. The gas in the tube, normally argon, krypton, xenon or a mixture of any of them, only becomes conductive when a triggering voltage of about 10 kV is applied to an external electrode wrapped around the tube.

Although the triggering voltage is only present at the moment of firing, voltages of about 400 V can be present across the terminals of the capacitor for some time after use, so any repairs of the DIY nature to electronic flashguns should be approached with extreme caution.

The time taken by a flashgun to recharge the capacitor from empty so that it is ready for the next flash is called the recycling time. Typically, it is from four to ten seconds. Clearly a short recycling time is desirable.

Most flashguns, except certain very heavy duty professional ones, are powered by either four or six 1.5 V AA size batteries obtainable virtually anywhere. The alkaline manganese type give better performance in terms of a shorter recycling time and more flashes per set of batteries than the cheaper zinc carbon ones.

Anyone using an electronic flashgun on a regular basis should consider buying rechargeable nickel cadmium batteries. Although they cost several times more than alkaline manganese batteries, they can be recharged virtually indefinitely, and reduce the recycling time. They will pay for themselves very quickly. Their associated charger costs a few pounds, and will recharge the batteries overnight. Some flashguns, for instance the Metz 45 range, have an optional nickel cadmium battery pack, which can be inserted in place of the cluster of conventional batteries. If nickel cadmium batteries are frequently recharged before they are completely flat, they may develop a 'memory', which may limit their capacity. It is a good idea occasionally to discharge them completely before they are recharged. Some flashguns with a separate power pack use wet lead acid cells, similar to those found in cars. These can be recognized by the coloured balls visible on the side which rise and fall in the acid to give an indication of the state of charge. However, they do need to be topped up occasionally with distilled water.

The physical dimensions of the flashgun determine the size of the batteries that can be used. At least one manufacturer now supplies an external rechargeable battery pack containing larger and heavier cells which can be attached to the photographer's belt or worn over the shoulder. It is connected by a cable to a module which fits inside the flashgun's battery compartment. These alternative battery packs provide considerably more flashes per charge than a normal set of nickel cadmium batteries. They have a series of lights which extinguish as the charge held in the batteries is reduced, advising the user when they should be recharged.

Some flashguns allow their capacitor to be charged directly from a high-voltage battery (typically 400 V). The Quantum Turbo battery goes one stage further and derives the necessary high voltage from built-in rechargeable cells. The recycling time for a full power flash is reduced to about a second. An accessory allows two flashguns to be run from the same pack.

The duration of the light produced by an electronic flashgun is very short – typically less than 1/1000th of a second – and can be synchronized with leaf shutters at all speeds. However, the brief duration of the flash means that the speeds at which focal plane shutters can synchronize with electronic flashguns are limited to those when the whole frame of film is uncovered at the same time. The fastest speed usable with electronic flash is often marked on the shutter speed dial, and is normally 1/125th or 1/250th of a second. Using a shutter speed faster than allowed will result in only a part of the frame being exposed.

Some combinations of camera and electronic flashgun will warn the photographer if the shutter speed set is too fast for correct synchronization. Others will override the photographer's choice and select the correct one.

Olympus and Nikon have developed an electronic flashgun with a longer-lasting flash, enabling synchronization with a focal plane shutter at higher speeds than normal. The length of illumination is extended by firing a rapid series of pulses of light.

Some cameras may have two sockets for synchronizing cables, marked X and M. Electronic flashguns should be plugged into the one marked X. M is for flashbulbs, which take a brief but significant time to reach peak output, and therefore have to be fired a fraction of a second before the shutter opens. An electronic flashgun connected to the M synchronization will have fired and finished before the shutter opens – and the picture will be unexposed.

Exposure

The amount of light reaching the subject from a flashgun depends upon the distance between them, and is governed by the 'inverse square law' which states that the intensity of the light falling on an object is inversely proportional to the square of its distance from the source of illumination. For instance, if the distance between the subject and the flashgun is doubled, it will receive only a quarter of the amount of light.

Somewhere in the instruction book will be details of the flashgun's 'Guide Number'. This is a measure of the power of the flashgun, and can be used to calculate the exposure. Suppose that with 100 ISO film, the guide number is given as being 32, working in metres.

The aperture that must be set on the lens is determined by dividing the guide number by the distance. So if the subject is 4 metres away, then the aperture required is 32/4 = F8. Most flashguns have a table or calculator to help with guide number calculations.

Guide numbers are helpful, but they are not perfect. They require that the photographer is a good judge of distance, and assume that the subject is of average tone and that the picture is taken in an average room.

All but the very cheapest flashguns have an integral sensor which measures the amount of light reflected from the subject and when it considers that the picture has been correctly exposed, turns off the flash tube by means of an electronic switch called a thyristor. Any energy in the capacitor not used for the flash is either discharged through an internal 'quench' tube which does not illuminate the subject, or is retained for the next exposure, contributing to a reduction in recycling time. A flashgun may offer the user a choice of several different apertures and have a light which illuminates briefly after taking a picture to let the photographer know that the auto-exposure control has worked successfully.

A table or calculator on the flashgun shows the photographer what apertures are available at any given film speed, and over what distances they will provide correct exposure; the selected aperture is set on the lens, and provided the subject stays within range, the sensor will do the rest. Wider apertures will provide automatic exposure over a greater distance and use less power than smaller ones, but at the price of a reduction in the depth of field.

Automated flash exposure has been developed one stage further. Instead of placing the sensor on the flashgun, it is built into the camera where it can measure the light coming back from the subject through the lens and reflected off the film. This allows the exposure to relate precisely to the subject included in the picture irrespective of the focal length of the lens in use, and permits a greater choice of lens apertures for a particular situation.

TTL flash metering requires additional electronic links between camera and flashgun. Flashguns with these links are described as dedicated, and are designed to work with a specific camera or range of cameras. They communicate with the camera through extra contact on the hot shoe. The Nikon's top of the range SB25 Speedlight has four contacts on its foot. The camera and flashgun exchange information about:

- the speed of the film;
- the aperture set on the lens;
- the focal length of the lens;
- whether the flash is to be fired at the start or the end of the exposure;
- any desire for deliberate over- or underexposure;

and ensure that the shutter speed set is appropriate for the use of flash. A light in the viewfinder is illuminated prior to the exposure to inform the photographer that the flashgun is ready, and afterwards to confirm that the automatic exposure was successful. If working in an autofocus mode, the camera also turns on the autofocus illuminator built in to the flashgun.

The flashgun should cover the entire angle of view of the lens in use; most cover the angle of a 35 mm lens, and may be supplied with a diffuser for use with wider angle lenses. Some may allow the angle of coverage to be adjusted by internal movements of the flash tube relative to a lens at the front of the flash-head. Typically, they can be 'zoomed' to cover lenses from 24 mm to 85 mm. Dedicated flashguns may zoom automatically to match the focal length of the lens in use. This is particularly useful with telephoto lenses, where the subject is some way away, and ensures that the output from the flashgun is not wasted by illuminating too wide an area.

What to buy

The first choice for anybody with a sophisticated 35 mm SLR camera is the manufacturer's dedicated flashgun. This will enable the photographer to make full use of the camera's facilities. Other flashguns, which are not dedicated, but which are well worth considering, include:

- Vivitar 283 – a powerful, well-built unit with a hot shoe offering four different aperture settings. The flash-head can be tilted, but not rotated.

- Metz 45CT series – a range of flashguns attached to the camera by a bracket and especially suitable for bounce flash. Some models also link to the camera's TTL and autofocus system. There is an optional nickel cadmium battery pack that can be recharged in the gun.
- Starblitz 200TQS – relatively inexpensive, simple, with just one choice of aperture, it recycles especially fast when using nickel cadmium batteries and can be fired remotely by another flashgun. However, it is easily damaged if dropped.

Taking pictures with flash

It is convenient and easy to mount a flashgun on or next to the camera, but the lighting produced is very flat and featureless, with harsh black shadows behind the subject. Flash on the camera is best kept for hard news situations when getting a picture is more important than sophisticated lighting techniques.

The quality of the lighting will be improved if the flashgun is held above the camera and to one side. To this end it is worth buying an extension cable to fit between the flash and the camera. Although extension cables are usually plugged into the flash synchronization socket, it is possible to buy cables which link the hot shoe of the camera and flash gun and retain full TTL exposure capability. These are particularly useful if the flash is to be bounced off an umbrella, or several flashes are being used to light the picture.

Holding the flashgun away from the camera lens will reduce an effect known as red-eye. This occurs when a person is looking at the camera, and the flash is reflected off the red retina at the rear of the eyeball back into the lens. The effect is more pronounced in colour, when the red dots in people's eyeballs give them a ghoulish appearance. There is a greater chance of its occurring when using telephoto lenses because the angle between the camera and the flash is reduced, and in low levels of ambient light, when the iris of the eye is wide open. Some flashguns, especially those built-in to compact cameras, offer the user the chance to fire a small pre-flash to close the iris of the eye a moment before the picture is taken.

Bounce flash

While keeping the flash on or next to the camera, it is possible to improve the quality of the illumination by reflecting or 'bouncing' the light off the ceiling or a nearby wall. This softens the light and produces a more natural effect. Some flashguns have heads which can be tilted or rotated while keeping the sensor pointing at the subject. Ideally, the head should be pointed up at about 45 degrees.

Drawbacks to this technique are that the ceiling or other reflector scatters the light in all directions, reducing the proportion of the output from the flashgun which reaches the subject, and that the light has to travel further. Both of these factors mean that a bounced flash uses more power to achieve the same level of illumination than a direct flash. It is a great help when using this technique to have a flashgun which lets the user know if the automatic exposure facility has worked correctly. If the ceiling is too high, or the subject too close to the camera, causing the flash to be pointed up at an angle greater than 45 degrees, then the subject's eye sockets may appear dark, with the eyes themselves lacking sparkle. Some flashguns have a secondary tube which uses a small proportion of the output to illuminate the subject directly, but the problem with these is that the ratio of the output from each tube is fixed by the manufacturer, when it should be adjusted for each picture to take account of the individual circumstances.

When using colour film it is important to ensure that the ceiling or reflector chosen is white to avoid a colour cast appearing on the finished picture.

Fill-in flash

A flashgun can be used to illuminate or 'fill-in' the harsh shadows which may appear on photographs taken in bright sunlight, when the contrast range between the darkest and lightest parts of the picture is greater than the film can handle.

Sometimes called 'synchro-sunlight', the technique balances the light from a flashgun with the existing illumination to reduce the overall contrast range of the picture. Care must be taken to ensure that the picture still looks natural, and does not have too much 'fill-in'. The exposure provided by the flash should be about a half or a quarter of the intensity of the main light falling on the subject. If the exposure was, for example, 1/250th of a second at F11 on 200 ISO film, then a photographer wishing to 'fill-in' the hard shadows on a person or object should set the sensor on the flashgun, not to F11, but to F8, or F5.6, as this will provide a contrast range which is both natural to the eye, and acceptable to the film.

Sophisticated electronic cameras and their dedicated flashguns can assess the brightness and contrast levels present in a scene and perform automatically the calculations necessary to ensure just the right amount of 'fill-in'.

Most modern cameras will synchronize their focal plane shutters at speeds up to, and including, 1/250th of a second, so reducing the risk of moving subjects appearing as two images on the film – one recorded by the daylight, and one recorded by the flash. The higher shutter speeds mean that 'synchro sunlight' pictures can be taken at wider apertures and filled in using smaller flashguns than were necessary when the typical synchronization speed was 1/60th of a second. That leaf shutters can synchronize with electronic flashguns at all speeds up to their normal maximum of 1/500th of a second is one of the reasons that Hasselblad and other similar cameras are so popular with wedding photographers who have to record details in the enormous contrast range contained in the bride's white dress and the groom's dark suit.

'Fill-in' can be used to light up a backlit picture, where the main source of illumination is behind the subject. And on dull days outdoors a portrait can be given a lift with a very small amount of flashlight, which brings a sparkle to the eyes.

Multi-flash techniques

More advanced techniques involve the use of two or more flashes. Sometimes it is as simple as adding a light behind a model to backlight her hair, or perhaps a scene outdoors at dusk requiring several flashes to highlight different areas. If using them on automatic, care must be taken to ensure that the light from one flash is not fired into the sensor of another. The flashes will have to be positioned without the aid of modelling light, found only on studio flashes. The exposure for multi-flash set-ups is best assessed using a purpose-designed flashmeter.

It is possible to plug the synch cables from several flashguns into the same camera through an adaptor. If they are all of the same make, then they will probably work; if they are different, the chances of them working are reduced, and there is a risk of damage to either the flashguns or the camera. There are also the problems caused by the trailing cables.

Far better is to plug the synch cable from each flashgun into a slave unit, which will fire the flash when it receives a pulse of light from another one. These contain a small photoelectric cell, and are no bigger than a box of matches.

Figure 3.1   Flooded Torquay: All photographers should carry a tripod in the boot of the car, either to support a telephoto lens, or to allow a time exposure at night. This picture was taken with a short time exposure of about ¼ of a second, and a little bit of flash to 'lift' the shadows in the parts of the picture nearest the camera. Freak weather always makes for good pictures – and an experienced photographer will know the most likely places in the area to be affected. If it rained very heavily in Torquay and there was a high tide, then the storm water could not run away fast enough and the town centre flooded. The flooding didn't last long: ten minutes after this picture was taken the water had disappeared. I have also photographed the same street flooded in daylight, but the night-time picture has far more drama (© Torbay News Agency)

TRIPODS AND MONOPODS

Thankfully, a tripod is a piece of equipment which will not be improved or replaced by electronic wizardry, so unless it is lost or stolen, it is a one-off purchase. It therefore makes sense to buy the best that one can afford.

A flimsy tripod is worse than useless, so when selecting one, make sure that it really is rigid. Generally, the heavier a tripod is, the more rigid and stronger it is. It is worth considering one in which the legs are braced onto a central column. With the centre column extended, a good tripod should be at least six feet high. Check in the shop before buying a tripod that it is easy to erect so that the centre column is vertical: some have a spirit level built in. The legs are usually constructed from concentric telescopic sections, and particular attention should be paid to how the legs lock together. Cheap screw-up collars can strip their threads if tightened over-enthusiastically. Extra stability may be added to a tripod by hanging a large stone, or a sandbag, from the bottom of the centre column.

There are many ways of linking the camera to a tripod. Long, heavy and very expensive telephoto lenses are often used on tripods, so be sure that they will be supported safely. Some people prefer a ball and socket head, which gives almost unlimited freedom of movement; others prefer a pan and tilt head. When selecting a tripod, ensure that it is possible to turn quickly from the horizontal to the vertical format. I have kept a Slik 67 tripod in the boot of my car for many years, and found it strong and easy to use.

A useful accessory to accompany a tripod is a cable release. This screws into a thread in the shutter button and enables the picture to be taken without touching or shaking the camera. Many cameras can also be fired using an electronic cable which plugs into the motor drive. The only limit then to the distance from which the camera can be fired is the length and resistance of the wire.

A monopod is a one-legged support for a camera and lens. It does not hold the camera steady by itself, but helps the photographer reduce camera shake by taking the weight of the equipment, and can be particularly useful at sports events like football or golf, where the photographer needs to be mobile, but also has to keep the camera to the eye for a long period. It is important to check that a monopod is long enough to be used when the photographer is standing up. Again, the quality of the locking mechanism for the legs, and the ability to shoot both horizontal and vertical formats, should be assessed before purchase.

Another useful gadget is a clamp which can be used to attach a camera to scaffolding, a tree branch, the wing of a small plane or any other place where a photographer cannot stand. It is not always possible to fire cameras mounted on these by a cable, so some photographers use a two-piece radio release. The receiver is connected to the socket on the camera's motor drive and the transmitter is held by the photographer or someone else who can decide when to take the picture. Pressing a button on the transmitter sends a pulse to the receiver, which trips the shutter. Most radio releases offer a choice of at least two channels, so that more than one photographer can work in the same vicinity. All radio transmitting equipment has to conform to government regulations, and anyone purchasing such equipment should satisfy themselves that use of their particular equipment is legal.

EXPOSURE METERS

Modern cameras have TTL meters, which are very accurate, but some photographers still favour separate hand-held exposure meters. Both are capable of assessing the exposure by measuring the light reflected back from the subject, but only the hand-held meter can conveniently measure incident light.

Incident light measurement is a particularly effective way of assessing the exposure when using colour transparency film as it assesses only the intensity of the light falling on the subject, pegging the exposure to the highlights of the picture. Reflected light exposure readings depend upon the brightness of the objects being photographed.

To take an incident light reading, the meter is held as close to the subject as possible with a small diffuser placed over its sensor and pointed back towards the camera position.

The light-sensitive cells in an exposure meter vary. Early ones used an element called selenium which generates electricity when light falls on it. The current produced is measured on a meter by a pointer on a calibrated scale and the value transferred to a calculator dial to work out the exposure. The benefit of this kind of meter is that it requires no batteries; the disadvantages are a reduced sensitivity at low levels of illumination and the fact that the moving coil meter which measures the current is susceptible to shock. The Weston series of meters use a selenium cell.

Other exposure meters use a cell made of cadmium sulphide (CdS) whose resistance varies with the intensity of the light falling on it. A battery is connected across the cell and the resulting current displayed on a meter. Although the cell needed is smaller than those for a selenium meter, CdS meters can be slow to respond, especially in low light, and have a 'memory' which can affect a reading if the cell has previously been exposed to a high level of light. CdS meters were the first ones to be found in cameras with TTL metering.

The most sophisticated exposure meters use either a silicon photodiode (SPD), or gallium arsenide phosphide photodiode (GaAsP). Like the selenium cell, these generate electricity when light falls on them, but in much smaller amounts which must be amplified before they can be measured. These cells have no memory, a wide range of sensitivity and a fast response to a change in light levels. Hand-held meters with such cells may display exposure information digitally, to within 1/10th of a stop, rather than on a scale. Because of their excellent speed of response, some can also calculate the exposure when using flash, and although the extra cost for the facility may be hard to justify at the time, it is well worth paying. Minolta makes a good range of exposure meters with digital display. As they have very few moving parts, they are robust.

Flashmeters must measure both the strength and duration of the light to assess the exposure correctly. Some have a calculator which derives the correct exposure from the value given by the deflection on a meter; others replace the meter with a row of LEDs, and the value entered into the calculator is the number of LEDs illuminated. It is also possible to have the F-stop displayed digitally. Flashmeters use the incident light method.

Some meters must be physically connected to the flashgun. The user presses a button on the meter, the flash fires, and the appropriate F-stop is evaluated. Other meters are cordless and react only when the flash is fired, either by tripping the shutter, or using the open flash button. Both types should be capable of measuring the total exposure when ambient and flash light are combined.

FILTERS

Filters allow the transmission of light of certain wavelengths, and absorb light of all other wavelengths. They are normally circular discs of glass mounted in metal, and attached to the front of the lens, either by a screw thread or a bayonet mount. Camera manufacturers try to make as many lenses as possible use the same filter diameter. Some lenses which have such large front elements that it would be prohibitively expensive to purchase a range of filters allow the user to fit one in a slot at the rear of the lens. Other filters can be purchased as squares of an optically correct plastic material, and these are placed in special holders in front of the lens. Some very wide angle lenses – like fish-eyes – have filters built in between the elements. These can be rotated, and a choice made from the four or five provided.

A filter provides valuable protection to the front of a lens from dirt, moisture, fingerprints and physical damage. Lenses should always have a filter in place. If a filter is damaged or scratched it can be replaced far more cheaply than the front element of a lens. Lenses – for instance mirror lenses or wide aperture telephoto lenses – which provide for a filter at the rear should always have one in place as it is part of the optical design of the lens. This can be demonstrated by focusing the lens and removing the filter, when it will be seen that the point of focus has shifted.

Putting more than one filter in front of a lens, especially a wide angle one, may lead to vignetting – a darkening or cut-off effect at the corners of the image. It may be possible to see any vignetting by stopping the lens down to its minimum aperture and looking through it at its closest focusing distance. Although most manufacturers try to ensure that the majority of their lenses use the same-size filters, stepping rings make it possible to use large filters on lenses of a smaller diameter.

Filter for black and white

In black and white photography, where colours are rendered as different shades of grey, filters are used to help change the contrast between two colours which would otherwise be recorded as similar tones. The most frequent use of filters in black and white photography is to bring out the clouds in a blue sky.

The contrast between sky and cloud will be enhanced by a yellow filter, which allows the yellow component of the white light from the clouds to pass through, but stops the blue light from the sky passing through. Orange and red filters will further increase the contrast. It is not necessary to carry all three filters. I have found that a yellow one is suitable for a modest increase in contrast, and use a red one when going for the 'big effect'.

Graduated filters are not uniform all over. For instance, the top half may be orange, and the bottom half clear. The benefit is that it is possible to both darken and alter the tones of the sky by using the orange part of the filter, without affecting the bottom half of the picture. The obvious drawback is that the horizon is rarely a straight line.

(a)

(b)

Figure 3.2 Filters for contrast in black and white: In black and white photography it is possible to artificially increase the contrast between two areas of differing colour, but similar tone. Yellow, orange and red filters absorb progressively larger amounts of blue light, and will thus increase the contrast between white clouds and blue light. (a) was taken without a filter, (b) with an orange one

Filters for colour

Filters for colour photography are mainly concerned with adjustments to the overall colour balance of a picture. For instance, ordinary transparency film is balanced for use in daylight. Using it indoors with tungsten light will give the pictures a warm cast, which may or may not be acceptable. Placing a blue filter in front of the lens will absorb some of the excess of red and yellow light present in the illumination from tungsten bulbs and allow the colours to be reproduced correctly. Graduated filters do have a use in colour photography, for instance to put colour into what would otherwise be a featureless white sky.

Filters for black and white and colour

Skylight and ultraviolet filters can be thought of as being virtually interchangeable, and remove a little of the haze in distance scenes and take out some of the bluish cast in pictures taken in the shade or on overcast days. One should be left on a lens when no other filter is being used, serving as a kind of transparent lens cap.

Polarizing filters

Light travels in waves, vibrating up and down, from side to side, and all ways in between at right angles to its direction of travel. A polarizing filter will transmit light vibrating in a particular plane and absorb light vibrating at right angles to that plane. Light vibrating in intermediate planes is partially transmitted. They are supplied in a rotating mount so that the effect can be observed as the plane of polarization is altered. The light passing through these filters is said to be 'linearly polarized'.

Polarizing filters can have two effects. Firstly, they reduce some of the reflections from shiny objects, and secondly, they can darken a blue sky. Both effects depend upon the orientation of the filter, and can be seen when viewed through the filter.

Reflections off some surfaces can be more polarized than those of others. The degree of polarization depends upon the surface and the angle at which the light strikes it. Polarizing filters have no effect on reflections from metallic surfaces but will almost completely remove the reflections from glass, water and painted surfaces if the camera position is chosen carefully. Reflections from glass and foliage are partially polarized, and can be reduced by a filter giving a corresponding increase in colour saturation. In all cases the photographer should rotate the filter while looking through the lens to achieve the desired effect.

A polarizing filter darkens a sky best in those areas at 90 degrees from the sun. The effect is quite dramatic, and works well in colour and in black and white. When shooting in black and white a red and a polarizing filter combined together can produce an almost jet-black sky.

The operation of exposure and autofocus sensors on modern cameras can be affected adversely by linearly polarized light, and manufacturers may recom-

Figure 3.3   Polarizing filter: A polarizing filter can be used to remove or minimize unwanted reflections, as, for example, in this shop window. The angle between the photographer and the window is critical if all the reflection is to be totally eliminated

mend the use of a filter which circularly polarizes the light. These have two elements. The front one polarizes the light, and the second then imparts a spin to the plane of polarization.

Special effect filters

Filters which produce rainbows, starbursts, multiple images, soft focus and other effects should be used sparingly. However, they can enhance what would otherwise be a rather mundane picture.

Neutral density filters

Neutral density filters cut down the amount of light passing through regardless of wavelength. They are used on occasions in very bright conditions when even a slow film will not permit slow shutter speeds and wide apertures to be used. They are also used to control the amount of light passing through mirror lenses which have a fixed aperture.

Filter factors

As filters, other than special effects and ultraviolet ones, absorb some light, an adjustment must be made to the exposure. Most TTL meters take this into account. Some metering systems are not equally sensitive to all colours, and it may be worth taking pictures at exposures a stop greater and a stop less than that suggested by the meter. For cameras without TTL meters, all filters have 'filter factors' stamped on their mount or in their accompanying instructions which indicate by how much the exposure must be increased. For a light-yellow filter, it might be ×2, an increase of one stop, and for a deep red, ×8, an increase of three stops. The factor for polarizing filters varies between ×2 and ×5, depending upon the angle of rotation; if it is being used on a camera without a TTL meter, then again it is worth taking several pictures at slightly different exposures.

EXTENSION TUBES AND CLOSE-UP LENSES

There will be occasions when a photographer has to photograph a small object, perhaps a rare postage stamp being auctioned, or a picture of somebody in the news. Invariably, the greater the news value, the smaller the item to be photographed.

Purpose-made macro lenses have an extended focusing range, which enables them to focus to about half life-size. However, one of these is seldom to hand when needed.

A typical 50 mm lens will focus to about 60 cm, when objects on the negative appear about a tenth life-size. To focus any closer, it is necessary to move the lens further away from the film.

This can be done by extension tubes which fit in between the lens and the camera body. They are usually sold in sets of three, which can be used alone or together to provide a range of different lengths of extension. To obtain a life-size image on a negative when using a 50 mm lens, a tube length of about 10 cm is needed. Extension tubes can be used with lenses of any focal length, and their effect is increased as the focal length of the lens is shortened. Because they are moving the lens further away from the film the exposure has to be increased. This will be taken care of by the camera's TTL metering system. For cameras without TTL meters, the tubes are usually accompanied by a table showing by how much the exposure must be increased, depending upon the extension and the focal length of the lens in use. Good extension tubes maintain the links between the lens and camera body which enable focusing and viewing to be carried out at full aperture. A good set of tubes could cost £50 from an independent manufacturer, and well over twice that from the specific camera manufacturer. Similar in principle to extension tubes are a set of close-up bellows. These permit a greater flexibility in camera-to-lens distance and a greater extension than tubes, but because there is a considerable distance between the lens and the camera even when they are fully closed, they are not suitable for modest close-ups. Their use is restricted to specialist close-up workers.

An alternative to using extension tubes is the *close-up lens*, which screws into the filter thread of the existing lens, and moves the maximum and minimum focusing distances of the lens closer to the camera. They do for the camera what reading glasses do for people with poor eyesight.

Their strength is measured in dioptres – and the greater the number, the more powerful the lens. A one dioptre lens attached to the front of any lens moves its maximum focusing distance from infinity to one metre. A two dioptre lens moves the focusing distance to half a meter, and so on. The maximum focusing distance is independent of the focal length of the lens in use. Close-up lenses are sold either individually or in sets and can be screwed together, when their strength is the sum of the individuals. The benefits of close-up lenses are that they are small and easy to carry in a bag at all times, require no extra exposure and can be used on different lenses with the same filter size. The drawback is that there is a loss of sharpness. This can be minimized by stopping down to F5.6 or F8 when using them. Close-up lenses cost about the same as an ordinary filter – about £5.

Anyone expecting to copy pictures or photograph small items regularly should consider purchasing a purpose-made macro lens. However, most people will find a limited range of close-up lenses sufficient for their day-to-day needs. I carry a four dioptre lens which I have found adequate.

LENS HOODS

Lens hoods shield the lens from light which is not making up the image, and protect it from rain and physical damage. Non-image-forming light can add to flare, reducing contrast and colour saturation. Hoods are built in to some telephoto lenses and merely extended for use. Others are screwed in the filter thread, or attached by a bayonet mount on the front of the lens. They may be rigid, or made from rubber, folding back over the lens when not in use. Zoom lenses create a particular problem as the hood must be designed to ensure that vignetting does not occur at the wide angle range. Sometimes it is best to improvise a lens hood – for instance, holding a hand to block a light source flaring on the lens or attaching a piece of cardboard with a rubber band round a telephoto lens to reduce the glare from a low sun.

CAMERA BAGS

There is a vast array of bags, cases and holdalls on the market. Ideally, a photographer should have two; one which will hold all the equipment and can be used when travelling or be left in the office or boot of the car, and a smaller one into which you can put the gear needed for a particular assignment.

Aluminium cases provide the greatest level of protection, but have to be put down to be opened and attract the attention of thieves. However, they can be used to sit or stand on.

Soft cases, like those made by Billingham, should have internal dividers so that cameras and lenses do not rub together, a strap whose length can be adjusted so that the bag is slung over the shoulder at a convenient height, strong zips and a number of pockets for accessories. Check to make sure that you can get easy access to all the contents while it is on your shoulder. Camera bags appear expensive, but when the value of the equipment being protected is taken into consideration, it is worth purchasing a good one.

A photographer's jacket is a useful alternative to a small camera bag when working on assignment; spare lenses, exposure meters, notebooks, film and flashgun can be stored in the numerous pockets. They are derived from the multi-pocketed jackets worn by anglers and help distribute the weight of equipment evenly around the body. A 'bum bag' of the type favoured by skiers, which is slung around the waist, is another alternative to carrying a small camera bag.

FILM

It goes without saying that a photographer should always carry a good stock of film. Keeping it in its original cartons takes up space. Four film cassettes will usefully fit into one of the plastic boxes in which processed and mounted slides are returned. Twelve cassettes will fit in the tin used by manufacturers to supply bulk 35 mm film in 30 metre lengths.

The spiral – metal or plastic – is loaded either in the dark or in a light-tight changing bag, so that the film is in an open coil. Once the spiral has been placed in the tank and the lid attached, all further operations can be carried out in daylight. The lid of the tank has a light trap through which the processing chemicals can be poured.

Tanks come in a variety of sizes to accommodate different quantities of film, and while metal spirals will only accept one size of film, plastic spirals can be adjusted to take a range of sizes. However, metal spirals are more robust than plastic ones, and are easier to load when damp. Plastic spirals are loaded from the outside inwards by pushing the film in along the circumference. Metal ones are loaded by attaching the film to the centre, and filling the spirals from the middle. For many years I used plastic spirals, but tried metal ones once, and have been hooked on them ever since.

A frequently overlooked benefit for those photographers who may have to carry their processing chemicals with them is that metal spirals use a significantly smaller volume of processing chemicals than plastic ones. The lid of commonly used plastic tanks allow a thermometer to be inserted into the processing chemicals – something not possible with metal tanks.

Many newspapers and photographers use a system half-way between the deep tank and the hand tank. It is possible to purchase a rectangular tank intended for the processing of 10 × 8 inch sheet film, which uses about 15 litres of chemicals. Films are then loaded on to a spiral – metal or plastic – and developed in one of these tanks before being transferred to another adjacent tank for fixing.

Thermometers

Provided that it is within the range of 14°C to 24°C, the temperature of the processing chemicals is not critical. What is important is to know what the precise temperature is. Conventional thermometers use a glass bulb filled with spirit or mercury, which expands along a calibrated rod as the temperature increases. For black and white processing, where accuracy of ± 1°C is sufficient, spirit thermometers are adequate. Glass thermometers are fragile and expensive, and because of the risk of damage, mercury-filled ones should not be carried on aircraft. Should they break, the mercury vapour released is very poisonous and the metal reacts violently with the aluminium from which aircraft are built.

Dial thermometers use two metals with different coefficients of thermal expansion to turn a pointer around a dial. They are less fragile than glass thermometers, but less accurate.

Electronic thermometers have a probe which is dipped into the liquid, and the temperature is displayed on a digital readout. They are as accurate, if not more so, than mercury thermometers, and much more robust. They need a battery – and a wise photographer will carry a spare. If it is not going to be used for some time, it may be a good idea to slip a small piece of paper over one of the battery terminals to prevent current drain. Some thermometers use a LED display, and others use a LCD. The former uses more current, so the thermometer needs a bigger battery, but has the advantage that the display can be seen in the dark.

Clock

Although it is possible to time the development of a film with a watch, it is better to use a clock or timer which will sound an alarm at the end of the preset time.

Measuring cylinders

The deep tanks themselves can be used for making up the large volumes of chemicals that they require – although some method of stirring the contents may be needed. For more modest requirements it is possible to buy special photographic measuring cylinders. Alternatively, take a money-saving trip to the local hardware store, and buy measures made from unbreakable plastic which are meant for use in the kitchen. If using some of the highly concentrated liquid developers, it is essential to have a cylinder which will accurately measure the small quantities involved.

Squeegee

A squeegee is used for removing the water from the film before it is hung up to dry. It is a pair of tongs with two soft rubber blades through which the film is drawn to wipe off surface water. Because the wet emulsion is soft and delicate, the rubber blades of the squeegee must be kept scrupulously clean. If the blades become worn, or catch a piece of grit, the result will be parallel scratches running the length of the film.

Changing bag

A changing bag is a lined light-tight black bag with two elasticated armholes and a large hole which can be sealed with a zip. It is used to load films into spirals in the absence of a darkroom.

Negative filing sheets

As soon as the negatives are dry they should be cut up and filed. Some people like to put the negatives initially into continuous plastic sleeving. I prefer to cut the film up into strips of six frames and place them in clear plastic negative filing sheets, through which it is possible to view the film and make contact prints. Cotton gloves may be used to prevent fingerprints on the negatives.

Constituents of a developer

Developers are rarely solutions of just one chemical, but a carefully researched mixture of several. Typically a developer will contain:

1 *Developing agent* to convert the latent image into metallic silver. There are several alternatives, and depending upon the properties required, a developer may contain more than one agent.

Metol and hydroquinone are often used together, when the developer is labelled as an MQ developer, and are found, for instance, in Kodak's D76 and Ilford's ID11. To some extent MQ developers are a benchmark for the performance of others.

Phenidone can be used as a replacement for Metol, when the developer is labelled PQ.

Other developing agents include amidol and para-phenylenediamine.

2 *Preservative* – usually sodium sulphite – to prevent the developer from premature oxidation by oxygen in the air dissolved in the solution, or in the bottle in which the developer is stored. The preservative may also stabilize the by-products of the developing process to prevent them staining the negative.

3 *Accelerator* or *alkali* to ensure the correct level of alkalinity within the solution for the developing agents to function properly. Sodium or potassium carbonate are common accelerators.

4 *Restrainer* to minimize fog on the film caused by the development of silver halides unaffected by light. Potassium bromide is often used.

DEVELOPER TYPES

There are many different developers available on the market with a variety of benefits to the press photographer. In deciding which to use, there are several factors to take into account.

Powder versus liquid

Some developers, like D76, are supplied as a powder in sachets to be dissolved in the correct order in warm water. The sachet supplied makes up a fixed volume of solution – for instance 2.5 litres – and it is not practicable to use a proportion of the powder to make up a smaller amount. The developer produced is described as a 'stock solution'. Depending upon the manufacturer's instructions, it may be used neat, or diluted further before use.

Liquid developers, like Ilfotech, are merely diluted for use with a specific amount of water – for instance 1 part developer to 30 parts water.

Because of their ease of use, the speed with which a working strength solution can be prepared and the facility to make up small quantities, liquid developers are more useful to the working press photographer than powder ones. However, they are more expensive.

One shot versus reusable

Instead of using the developer once and throwing it away – one shot – it is possible to keep it and use it again, with an appropriate increase in development time to take account of its reduced activity.

One shot processing is particularly suitable for the amateur as it removes one variable from the processing equation by ensuring that the developer always has the same activity.

Reusable developers are most practical when the volume of developer available is large compared with the amount needed to develop a particular film. This ensures that the changes in the developer's chemical properties will be gradual.

The developer's manufacturer will supply information as to how many films may be processed in a given volume of chemicals before the development time has to be increased.

As the developer is used, its volume will decrease as some is carried over into the next stage of the process. This lost volume can be replaced and the developer's activity maintained by replacing the volume lost with replenisher.

REPLENISHER

Replenisher has ingredients similar to those of developer. The manufacturer's instructions should be observed as to the rate of replenishment – they may specify how much replenisher must be added for each film which passes through the developer. It may be necessary to add the replenisher manually to deep tanks although machine processors may use automatic replenishment systems.

SPEED-INCREASING DEVELOPERS

Developers like ID11, D76 and Ilfotech offer a balanced choice to the photographer. They provide full emulsion speed and fine grain. Others may offer an increase in nominal film speed of up to three stops, but the price may be an increase in grain and contrast – examples are Ilford's Microphen and May and Baker's Promicrol. There are many claims made for how much extra speed some film and developer combinations can produce. A good test is to see if there is shadow detail in the negative.

SPECIFIC DEVELOPERS

Some film manufacturers recommend that to get the best results from their films, they should be processed in a developer intended for that particular film – Kodak's TMax films and their TMax developer are an example.

PUSH-PROCESSING

If a film has been deliberately underexposed or 'pushed' and a speed-increasing developer is not available, it is possible to compensate with some loss of quality by extending the development. For one stop, extend the development by 50%. For two stops double it, but expect an increase in grain size and contrast. For anything more than a one stop push, better results will probably come from a speed-increasing developer.

CHOOSING A FILM AND DEVELOPER COMBINATION

With the many different films and developers on the market, and the competing claims made for them, the temptation to chop and change from one combination to another can be great. It can also be disastrous. It is important to get to know a particular film and developer combination, so that you can predict how it will react to different lighting conditions, and how exposure and development can be altered to take account of changing circumstances.

The majority of prints appearing in newspapers are smaller than 8 × 6 inch and magazines very rarely use prints at larger than 10 × 12 inch. It is perfectly possible to produce prints with acceptable grain for this size of reproduction from 400 ASA film using standard developer, like ID11 or Ilfotech. There are some occasions when 400 ASA film is not fast enough. The photographer then has the choice of either using a faster film, or 'pushing' the 400 ASA film, either by extending the developer or by using a speed-increasing developer.

My preference when working in black and white is to use Ilford's HP5 Plus and Ilfotech. The film can easily be pushed to 800 ASA, merely by extending the development. For a faster film, I use Fuji Neopan 1600, again processed in Ilfotech. It too can be pushed one stop merely by extending the development.

Photographers who on occasions have to carry all the processing chemicals to an assignment will appreciate the economy of Ilfotech, and Kodak's similar product HC110, as they can be diluted at 1 : 30 to make working strength developer.

TIME AND TEMPERATURE

When pictures were taken on individual glass plates and emulsions were not sensitive to all colours of light, they were developed in a dish. Under a dark safelight it was possible to watch the image building up, and when it was judged satisfactory, the plate was transferred to the fixing bath.

Clearly this is not practical with modern panchromatic emulsions – and 36 different pictures on a roll. Development, however, is a chemical reaction, and the rate of the reaction depends upon the temperature.

Developers come with a chart showing how the processing time varies with temperature. The optimum temperature is 20°C (68°F), but it is possible to work as low as 14°C, beyond which the processing reaction is slowed down so much that development times are inconveniently long, or at temperatures up to 24°C, above which there is a risk of fog and the development times become so short that small errors in timing represent large percentage variations.

There should not be a difference in temperature of more than ±5°C between the developer and the fixer and then the fixer and the wash water. If the difference is any greater, the emulsion may suffer from reticulation, a crazed or mottled effect caused by the sudden expansion or shrinking of the gelatine. When printed the picture appears very grainy. The effect is irreversible.

If a one-shot liquid concentrate developer is used, there is little problem in mixing hot and cold tap water together to reach the desired temperature before adding the concentrate. Volumes of working strength chemicals of the order of a litre can easily be warmed up using a small immersion heater.

Cooling developer can represent a greater problem. It may be possible to immerse ice cubes in a plastic bag in the developer, or put it in a measuring cylinder surrounded by cold water. A steel measuring vessel will conduct the heat away much quicker than one made from plastic.

The temperature of developer in deep tanks may be maintained by keeping them in a thermostatically controlled room, or by an immersion heater. For small deep tanks using 15 litres of chemicals a fish-tank heater bought from a pet shop will suffice, but be sure to cover the neon indicator light with black tape to prevent fogging.

One golden rule when using deep tanks is to check the temperature before processing. It may have been 20°C every day for the last six months, but the day that you do not check will be the day that the heater failed overnight, and the temperature has dropped to 12°C.

AGITATION

Agitation of the film brings fresh developer to the emulsion. It is of critical importance in obtaining good quality negatives of even development and correct contrast. A developer manufacturer will specify the frequency and duration of agitation as it is important in determining processing time. Agitation also dislodges any air bubbles clinging to the film. It is important, too, during the fixing and washing of the negative.

Too little agitation means that stale developer stays in contact with the film; this may manifest itself on films processed in spirals as light bands joining the sprocket holes on opposite sides of the negative. Too much agitation will lead to excessive contrast and density.

Metal spirals and tanks are usually agitated by inversion. Those made from plastic allow for inversion, but also for the spiral to be rotated within the developer.

Agitation in deep tanks is either done manually by lifting the film a few inches out of the developer and then returning it or automatically by bursts of nitrogen fired through valves at the bottom of the tank.

STOP BATH

Stop bath – a weak solution of acetic acid – arrests development immediately and extends the life of the fixer. It is not used much nowadays; photographers either use a rinse of water between developers and the fixer or more commonly just pour the fixer straight in.

FIXING

Fixing stabilizes the image by removing the unprocessed silver halides. At the start of the fixing process, the silver image is visible but the film appears milky; at the end the film is clear.

Fixers are either ammonium thiosulphate or sodium thiosulphate. The former is faster but more expensive, and only available in liquid form. Fixing is done to completion; it is impossible under normal circumstances to overfix an image. The manufacturer will provide details of the fixing time required; alternatively it can be estimated as being twice the time it takes to clear the milkiness from the film. This can be assessed by immersing a piece of scrap film in a measuring beaker of fixer. It is usually safe to expose the processed film to daylight as soon as it has cleared – but some fast films should not be exposed to daylight until the fixing process is complete.

The temperature of the fixer should be within a few degrees of that of the developer to avoid reticulation.

Fixer removes the unexposed silver halides from the emulsion, and it is possible to recover this silver. The small amount involved makes the recovery only worthwhile for organizations with a large turnover of sensitized materials, but in this environmentally conscious age it makes sense to try to recycle the silver, rather than pour it down the drain.

WASHING

The purpose of washing the film is to remove the surplus chemicals left in the emulsion. Failure to remove these will eventually result in the silver image being attacked and degraded. This may not happen for some time, so an inadequate washing technique may not be noticed until it is too late.

There was a time when it was suggested that washing was only complete after 30 minutes in running water – a procedure which wastes both water and time. However, five minutes in continuously changing running water will probably suffice for most purposes. It is vital that fresh water reaches all parts of the film. The worst way to wash a film is merely to trickle a tap into the top of the tank, as there will be very little flow of water past the emulsion at the bottom of the spiral.

In winter months the temperature of running water can drop quite low, and there is a risk of reticulation. If running water is not available, then it is acceptable to fill the tank with water, agitate for a minute or two, and throw the water away. The film should be adequately washed after five or six changes.

In areas where the water is known to be hard, chemical residues similar to those found in an electric kettle may appear on the dried film. In these circumstances, it may be worth rinsing the film in distilled water as the last stage in the washing process.

DRYING

Once the film has been washed, it must be dried. A little wetting agent should be added to the water in the tank, and then agitated. If wetting agent is not available, a couple of drops of household detergent are an acceptable standby. The wetting agent prevents droplets of water forming on the film. If the film has been processed in a deep tank, it will be impractical to add the wetting agent to the deep tank – instead pass the film through a container of water with wetting agent added.

The film should then be carefully removed from the spiral and the surplus water removed from it with a clean rubber squeegee before hanging it up in a drying cabinet. A weighted clip at the bottom will prevent the film from curling as it dries.

Drying cabinets are commercially available – or it is quite possible to make one's own from a metal cupboard and a fan heater. It is while a film is drying that it is at its most delicate and susceptible to attract dust, so a home-made version should be easy to keep clean; if possible, incorporate some kind of air filter.

If a drying cabinet is not available, the film can be removed from the spiral, squeegeed, and dried with a hair drier. This is labour-intensive and can take some time if there are several films to dry.

An alternative home-made arrangement using a hair drier is to keep the films on the spirals and place them at the bottom of a 50 cm length of drainpipe; two cross-wires will stop them from falling out. At the other end of the pipe should be a screw cap, with a hole cut for the nozzle of the hair drier. Attach a length of string to the cap so that the pipe can be hung vertically from a hook or door handle. Turn the hair drier on and after a few minutes the film in the top spiral will be dry. That spiral is removed, and by the time the film has been cut into strips of six and sleeved, the next one will be dry. Such an arrangement is ideal for a mobile darkroom.

It is also possible to buy chemicals into which the film is immersed after it has been squeegeed which will promote rapid drying.

Once the film has been processed it should be cut up and placed in protective sleeving or negative filing sheets.

COLOUR FILM

Modern colour films are extremely complicated, both physically and chemically, but it is easy to understand the principles on which they work. The major difference is that the final image is not made of silver but of coloured dyes – as such they are described as 'chromogenic'.

In their simplest form, negative and transparency films both have three layers of emulsion. The top one is sensitive to blue light, the next one records green light and the bottom one red light. In practice emulsions which are sensitive to green light and red light are also sensitive to blue light. This problem is resolved by putting a yellow filter layer below the first emulsion to prevent blue light reaching the second and third layers. The filter is removed during processing. To increase exposure latitude, many colour films replace the one layer of emulsion sensitive to a particular colour with two, each of differing speed.

Photographers use both negative and transparency film. Negative film is obviously intended as the intermediate stage in the production of a print, has a wider exposure latitude and is easier and faster to process. However, without experience it is hard to 'read' the colours of a negative. While transparencies are the accepted medium for many glossy magazines, the majority of colour newspaper pictures are shot on colour negative film. It is possible to produce prints from transparencies and transparencies from colour negatives.

Colour film needs more careful storage than black and white. 'Professional' films should be stored in a refrigerator until required for use as they leave the factory with their emulsion in its optimum condition. Lengthy storage at room temperature will 'age' the emulsion, causing its properties to change. However, film taken from the refrigerator should be allowed to warm up before it is opened and placed in the camera. Failure to do this can lead to condensation forming on the emulsion. Film intended for amateur purchase from retail outlets is sent from the factory slightly before the emulsion reaches its optimum to allow for it to age while on a shelf at room temperature before it is sold.

As it is only a means to a photographic end and because corrections to the colour balance of the picture can be made when it is printed, negative film can be used in a variety of lights with different colour temperatures – daylight, electronic flash or tungsten light. However, transparency film is intended for use with light of a certain colour temperature, and while most film is balanced for daylight or electronic flash, it is possible to buy film balanced for tungsten light. Alternatively it is possible to place a filter on the lens to make the correction for daylight film exposure under tungsten light, or vice versa.

Colour negative film

There are five basic steps to producing a colour negative:

1 The colour developer reacts with the silver halides in each layer of the emulsion to produce silver and oxidized developer. The oxidized developer combines with chemicals within the emulsion of the film called couplers to release a dye. The dye produced is the complementary colour of the layer. Yellow dye is released in the blue-sensitive layer, magenta in the green layer and cyan in the red layer.
2 The unwanted silver image is bleached out chemically.
3 Unexposed silver halides are removed by a fixer in much the same way as in black and white.
4 Wash.
5 Dry.

Steps 2 and 3 may be done sequentially or simultaneously, when the combined process is called 'blixing'.

All readily available colour emulsions are processed in similar chemicals, described as C41. Because there are three different emulsions being processed simultaneously, the controls on processing are much tighter than with black and white film. Processing is normally done at 38°C (100°F) with a $3\frac{1}{4}$ minute development. If done consecutively, bleaching and fixing take a total of 13 minutes – if a combined blixing bath is used instead, that takes just six or seven minutes. After washing, the film may be passed through a stabilizer bath. This contains a hardener, a wetting agent to promote trouble-free drying and other chemicals to stabilize the dyes in the emulsion.

Processed colour negatives exhibit an overall orange cast. This is quite normal, and is a mask to compensate for shortcomings in the dyes used in both the negative and the print.

Because of the difficulties in maintaining precise time and temperature control in hand processing, most colour films are machine processed. They are available at differing levels of sophistication, reflecting their hourly throughput rate, but generally they take 15 minutes from dry to dry. Some of these machines do not even need running water – the film is washed by passing it through three consecutive baths of stabilizer.

It is possible to compensate for deliberate underexposure by increasing the development time. This works when the film is being developed by hand but is not usually practical with a machine processor. However, there is a risk of upsetting the colour balance of the completed negative.

Several manufacturers offer C41 compatible systems. The choice for machine processing may be determined by the support offered by the manufacturers of the machine and the chemicals. Some provide test strips to be developed daily and returned to them so that a quality control check can be maintained.

For use away from the office, Photocolor II is ideal. It is a two-bath process, develop and blix, and is easy to make up in small quantities to develop just one or two films. It comes with comprehensive instructions, and an additive to make the developer suitable for colour prints.

Both Nova Darkroom Equipment, of Warwick, England, and the German firm, Tetenal, market powder chemistry suitable for processing C41 films. They both make a litre of solution, enough to process ten to twelve films. A complete kit takes up the size of a paperback book. They are of particular interest to photographers who travel overseas as they offer a reduction in weight over liquid chemistry and eliminate the risk of liquids leaking in transit.

Even on a mobile assignment, a photographer would be well advised to find a nearby one hour photo centre and ask them to process the films. When it is explained that they are urgent news films and that no prints are needed, the staff will usually put them through straight away and they will be ready in 20 minutes or so. Even if all the chemicals are diluted and at the correct temperature back where the photographer is wiring from, it is just about possible to do it oneself in the same time, but the one hour photo centre should have good quality control, and the time can be usefully spent preparing the wire machine or having a well-earned cup of tea.

However, there will be occasions when the film has to be processed by the photographer. Once the film has been successfully loaded it is important to warm the tank before processing starts. Developer at 38°C will drop several degrees in temperature if it is poured into a cold stainless steel tank. The tank, whether it is metal or plastic, should be pre-heated by pouring in water two or three degrees hotter than the developer. Do not worry when emptying the tank that the water is coloured – it is dyes coming out of the film. During development and blixing a drop in temperature can be prevented by placing the tank in a water bath at the desired processing temperature.

It is possible to buy or make thermostatically controlled water baths which will hold the developing tank and containers of developer and blix. They can be prepared at the start of the day and be ready for use at the correct temperature the moment the photographer returns. DevTec, a firm based in Pasadena, California, makes a suitable heater with a built-in thermostat, and it is worth adding a small pump similar to those found in tropical fish tanks to circulate the water within the bath to prevent local hot spots from forming.

I would recommend stainless steel tanks for processing colour films. They are easier to keep clean – cross-contamination is one of the greatest problems with colour processing – and heat flows through their walls better than through plastic ones. They also use less solution per film, which is particularly important as colour developers are not as concentrated as those used for black and white processing. Typically, one part of developer is diluted with two parts of water.

Colour transparency film

Transparency films are very similar in construction to negative films – it is the processing that is different. Like negative films, most transparency films contain the couplers within the emulsion which react with the oxidized colour developer to form dyes. They are described as substantive. The only non-substantive film, where the couplers are in the developer, is Kodachrome and its complex processing will be discussed latter.

Modern transparency films are processed in E6 chemicals. There are seven basic stages:

1 The first developer produces a black and white image in each of the three emulsions; however, the developer by-products are such that they do not react with the couplers, and no dyes are produced. Temperature control during this stage in the process is vital as it determines the density of the finished transparency. The recommended temperature is $38 \pm 0.3°C$. There is now a negative image in each emulsion layer.
2 The film is then fogged. This was once done by exposing the film to light, but is now done chemically, either by a separate solution or in the next step in the process, the colour developer. When the film has been fogged, there is a latent positive image in each layer of emulsion.
3 The colour developer, as with negative film, reacts with silver halides which have been fogged to form silver and oxidized developer, which in turn combines with the couplers to release dyes. The dyes released in each layer are the complement to the colour to which it is sensitive.
4 Bleach.
5 Fix.
6 Wash.
7 Dry.

Including intermediate washes, the wet stages of the process last more than half an hour. However, once the film has been fogged, the remaining processing steps may be carried out in daylight.

To understand how the colours are formed, let us examine what happens in an area where, say, red light has hit the film. After the black and white development there is an image in the red-sensitive layer, but none in the other two. Fogging the film produces a latent image in the blue and green layers. The colour developer releases yellow dye in the blue layer and magenta dye in the green layer. When light is shone through the transparency, the yellow and magenta dyes allow only red light to pass through.

It is possible to compensate for the deliberate under- or overexposure of colour transparency films by extending the initial black and white development.

Because of the length of the process and the need for very accurate control over time and temperature, nearly all professionally exposed transparency films are machine processed.

NON-SUBSTANTIVE PROCESSING

As mentioned earlier in the chapter, Kodachrome film contains no dye couplers within the emulsion; instead they are in the developer.

In outline the processing stages are as follows:

1 Black and white development to form a silver image in all three layers.
2 The film is exposed to red light through the base to create a latent image in the red-sensitive layer while the other two layers remain unaffected. The latent image is now developed with a developer containing dye couplers which will create a cyan dye.
3 Step 2 is repeated, using blue light from on top of the film to release the image in the blue-sensitive layer.
4 Step 2 is repeated using white light to release the image in the green-sensitive layer.
5 Bleach.
6 Fix.
7 Wash.

The process is so complex that the film is usually returned to Kodak for developing, except in America where a few independent processors offer a facility.

The benefit of Kodachrome are its intense colour saturation, excellent contrast and fine grain. Its disadvantages are its slow speed, its exposure latitude and the fact that it cannot be user-processed.

CHROMOGENIC BLACK AND WHITE FILMS

Ilford's XP2 and its predecessor XP1 are chromogenic black and white films. They can be processed in standard C41 chemicals or their own very similar chemicals to yield almost grain-free negatives over quite a wide range of film speeds. It is possible to push the film by extending development.

5
Making the print

THE PRINT

Much of the effort spent taking a good picture can be wasted if it is not printed well. A skilled darkroom printer can transform a technical disaster into a page one picture and turn a run of the mill photograph into one to catch the reader's eye.

Recent developments in newspaper printing methods and the better use of pictures have led readers to cast a more critical eye over the technical quality of news photographs. Some of the organizations which sponsor annual awards to photographers have recognized the importance of the darkroom staff in the production process with a special category just for printers, while others present a prize to the person who printed the picture as well as the photographer who took it.

Some photographers may dislike printing, but everyone should be competent. Although newspapers employ darkroom staff and modern wire machines only need negatives, there may well come a time when the printer is sick, or the only wire machine available has a drum and needs a print.

This chapter, like the previous one on film and processing, will look initially at the equipment, skills and techniques needed to print black and white photographs and then extend them to colour.

PHOTOGRAPHIC PAPER

Traditional photographic papers consist of a layer of light-sensitive emulsion containing silver bromide and silver chloride coated on a paper base. Above the emulsion is a thin clear supercoat to minimize damage to the emulsion layer.

Resin-coated paper

Virtually all press pictures are now printed on resin-coated paper which uses a thin layer of polythene on the front and back of the base to render it virtually waterproof. The consequent advantages are a reduced carry-over of chemicals from one processing solution to the next, faster washing time and a print which dries faster and flatter than conventional papers.

Paper is available in a variety of surface finishes. For press pictures, which need to show the fullest range of tones and maximum detail, the only choice is glossy. For photo sales prints for customers and others used for display purposes a pearl finish, which does not have as much surface shine as glossy, is very acceptable.

Paper contrast

Photographic paper is usually developed to completion – a process which means that extending the development time will not significantly increase the maximum density of the print. There is not the same opportunity to control the contrast of the finished print by altering the exposure and development time as there is with negative camera films.

For this reason paper is available with different grades of contrast to take account of variation in negative contrast and the type of enlarger light source used. Manufacturers make paper graded from 0 (the softest) to 5 (the hardest), although it may not be available or routinely stocked in all sizes and quantities.

Soft paper is used for printing negatives with a high contrast, while hard paper is used for printing negatives with little contrast.

Most negatives can be printed on grades 2 or 3, with 1 and 4 being kept for extremes. Grades 0 and 5 are useful in emergencies, usually after a technical disaster. If you are using either on a regular basis, then you should reassess your exposure or processing techniques.

The speed or sensitivity of a family of papers is usually the same, regardless of the grade in use, except for grade 5, which is half the speed of the others. This is because it is frequently used with thin, underdeveloped or underexposed negatives which require very little exposure.

Soft papers have a greater exposure latitude than hard ones.

Variable-contrast papers

The problems of keeping in stock a range of different grades in each size of paper can be overcome with paper that has a variable contrast.

These materials have two emulsions, one soft and one hard, which are each sensitive to light of a different colour, for instance blue and purple respectively. By varying the proportion of blue and purple light it is possible to alter the contrast of the finished print. In addition to the convenience of requiring just one box of paper, it is possible to adjust the contrast in steps of half a grade.

The light colour, and hence the contrast, can be varied by placing filters manually between the light source and the negative. Purpose-built lamphouses can be purchased which contain two bulbs and the appropriate coloured filters. A control box, which may also include a timer, is then used to vary the output of the bulbs and hence the colour of the light. The lamphouses, which are available for a range of popular enlargers, and the control box, cost several hundred pounds. This may seem expensive, but as one manufacturer's variable-contrast paper is about 10% less expensive than their comparable fixed grade paper it is possible to estimate how quickly the savings made will cover the cost of the equipment.

THE ENLARGER

The most important pieces of equipment in a darkroom are the enlarger and its lens. There is little point in spending thousands of pounds on good cameras and a range of lenses and then saving a few pounds by buying a poor enlarger.

All enlargers work on a similar principle. A lamphouse contains a source of

5

4

3

2

1

0

Figure 5.1   Effect of varying printing contrast: This picture on Ilford Multigrade paper shows the effect of differing grades of paper contrast from 0 (very soft) at the bottom – where the image looks muddy and contains neither true black nor a true white – through to 5 (very hard), where the picture is virtually only black and white with no shades of grey. The best rendering of the image lies between grades 2 and 3. Multicontrast papers allow for the contrast to be adjusted in ½ grades – something not possible with paper made in fixed grades

light which illuminates a negative held in a carrier. Light passes through the negative and is focused by a lens onto a sheet of light-sensitive paper on the enlarger's baseboard. The enlarger head, which contains the lamphouse, negative carrier and lens, is raised and lowered on a vertical column attached to the baseboard to vary the degree of enlargement. After the exposure, which is usually between five and thirty seconds, the paper is processed to render the image visible and stable.

It is crucially important that the enlarger is rigid. Any movement of the enlarger head relative to the baseboard during exposure will result in a lack of sharpness on the finished print. Similarly, the negative carrier, lens and baseboard must all be parallel, otherwise the projected image will not be sharp all over.

Some enlargers will only print 35 mm film, while others will also accept larger 6 × 6 cm or 6 × 7 cm negatives from cameras which use 120 roll film. Although most press work is done on 35 mm, it is worth buying an enlarger that can also print negatives from 120 film. Readers may bring in newsworthy pictures shot on 120 film and negatives from the library may have been shot on a Rolleiflex, the standard press camera of two decades ago, which produced 6 × 6 cm negatives.

Only news organizations which regularly supply pictures from their library which were originally taken on 5 × 4 inch sheet film or glass plates will find it worthwhile to have the large and expensive enlargers required for that format.

Illumination

It is important that the negative is evenly illuminated. The most common manifestation of uneven illumination is a processed print with light corners.

Early enlargers used a small electric filament or carbon arc as a point source of light which was directed through the negative by two condensers and brought to a focus at the enlarger lens. Such a method of illumination is optically very efficient and yields a high-contrast image with great detail, but with the drawback of showing every blemish on the negative. In addition, changing the size of the enlargement meant moving the position of the light relative to the lens.

In a diffuser enlarger, the light from a bulb reaches the negative only after passing through a sheet of opal glass or a mixing box. The light produced by this method of illumination is very soft and negatives which are printed on diffuser enlargers may need to be developed to a slightly higher contrast than those intended for a condenser enlarger. However, diffuser enlargers do reduce the appearance of grain or blemishes on the negative. Diffuser enlargers are not very efficient optically and may give rise to longer exposure times than with a condenser enlarger.

Some enlargers for the 5 × 4 inch format use a cold cathode light, which is similar to a row of small fluorescent tubes. This does not require a condenser but is separated from the negative by a diffuser. It provides a very soft light.

Most black and white enlargers compromise by using a condenser and an opal bulb. The opal bulb does not have to be moved every time the enlarger head is raised or lowered and gives some of the benefits of diffuse lighting while the condenser improves the optical efficiency of the system and provides for reasonable exposure times.

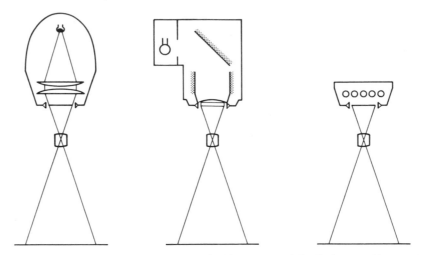

Figure 5.2   Enlargers: Some enlargers (left) use a small bulb, focused by a pair of condensers to illuminate the negative. This arrangement provides excellent contrast and maximum optical efficiency, but highlights any dirt, dust or scratches on the negative. A diffuser enlarger (centre) uses a low-voltage halogen bulb and scrambles the light before it reaches the negative. It is particularly suitable for colour printing when filters are introduced into the light path and the light mixed thoroughly. Cold cathode enlargers (right) use an array of discharge tubes, similar to domestic fluorescent lights, as a source of illumination

Filter drawer

This holds manually inserted filters used with variable-contrast papers. It may also contain a sheet of infra-red-absorbing glass which reduces the heat reaching the negative. It is usually above the condenser.

Negative carrier

The function of the negative carrier is to hold the negative totally flat. This can be done by sandwiching the negative between two pieces of glass. However, this introduces four additional surfaces which can collect dust that will appear as white spots on the print. For 35 mm and 120 film the metal carrier frequently dispenses with the glass and grips the film by its edges. However, the heat from the lamp may cause the film to buckle slightly in glassless carriers. In extreme cases it may not be possible to render the negative sharp over the entire picture. A frequently used compromise is to sandwich the film between a glassless lower mask and the flat bottom of the condenser.

It is useful to be able to read the number in the rebate of the film while the negative is in the carrier, and to be able to release the pressure on the film when moving it through the enlarger to select another frame for printing.

Lens

Buy the best lens you can afford. There is no point in using expensive camera manufacturer's lenses and skimping on the enlarger lens.

The enlarger is focused by moving the lens relative to the negative. This is usually done manually, either by rotating the lens in a helical screw mount, or by racking backwards or forwards a pair of bellows which has the lens on the front.

Some enlargers have automatic focusing where the movement of the lens is linked to the movement of the enlarger head.

The ideal focal length for the enlarger lens is the same as for the standard lens for the format in use; a 50 mm lens for 35 mm film and an 85 mm lens for 6 × 6 cm. A good 50 mm enlarger lens typically has a maximum aperture of F2.8.

Some manufacturers produce lenses with a focal length shorter than the ideal. These produce a bigger image for any given lens to paper distance than when using the standard lens.

When changing formats it is necessary to change lenses. A 50 mm lens will not cover the 6 × 6 cm format, while a 85 mm lens used with 35 mm film will mean an inconveniently large distance between lens and paper for any reasonably sized enlargement.

Unlike a camera lens an enlarger lens is closed down manually before the paper is exposed, and has indents or 'click stops' at every aperture setting to aid control in the dark. Some have illuminated aperture scales.

How much an enlarger lens should be stopped down is a matter of experience. Although most modern lenses produce excellent results at their widest aperture, their performance may be improved by closing them down a couple of stops. Stopping down increases depth of field, which reduces the effects of the negative 'popping' in the heat, and overcomes any slight misalignment of the enlarger baseboard, lens panel and negative carrier. How far the lens is stopped down is directly related to exposure time. Exposures of less than five seconds cannot be done repeatedly with accuracy unless they are electronically timed and leave little opportunity for burning-in and dodging.

Minolta and Nikon both produce excellent enlarger lenses called El Rokkors and El Nikkors; another good name to look for is Schneider. Lenses intended for 35 mm and 120 formats all have the 39 mm screw thread mount.

Most enlargers have a red filter which swings across the path of light from the lens to permit the photographic paper, which is not sensitive to red light, to be accurately positioned on the baseboard.

Ease of use

Check how easy it is to move the enlarger head up and down. Some of the best enlargers have a counterbalanced parallelogram arm between the lamphouse and the column which enables the size of enlargement to be altered very quickly and efficiently. Others use a friction drive to wind the enlarger head up and down the column.

What to buy

There is not a vast range of enlargers on the market. Probably the most comprehensive range is made by Durst. If one was only going to buy a 35 mm enlarger then the FOCOMAT made by Leitz, admittedly expensive, would be well worth considering.

Masking frame

The masking frame or enlarging easel aids composition of the picture and prevents the paper from curling at the corners during the exposure. It has two flat arms which are adjusted to suit the paper size in use. Some only allow a fixed ¼ inch border. Other more sophisticated ones allow the borders to be varied.

Alternatives include magnetic clips which hold the corners of the paper and allow for borderless prints, or vacuum easels which hold the paper in place by suction.

Timer

The length of the exposure can be controlled either by a stopwatch or by guesswork, but it is more precise to use a timer. As we will see later, it is possible to compensate a little for incorrect exposure when processing manually, but it is not possible if the processing is carried out by a machine. Using a timer means that the exposure can be adjusted accurately and that it is repeatable, which is important if many identical prints are required from the same negative.

A good timer will be adjustable from 0 to 99 seconds in steps of 0.1 and have a switch to turn the enlarger on for focusing. Some extinguish the safelight in the darkroom when the enlarger is on. Others incorporate an exposure meter to assess the length of exposure required. These may measure the light reflected from the baseboard prior to the exposure and set the required time automatically, or assess the light reflected from the paper during the exposure and turn the enlarger off when the exposure is complete. Others are placed on the baseboard before the exposure, a diffuser is placed between the meter and the lens and the required time is displayed.

However, exposure meters have to be calibrated with the paper speed, which has to be determined initially by the user, and like the meters found in cameras, they can be fooled by subjects which are not 'average'.

Most experienced printers find that they can assess the exposure for a print as well as any exposure meter, and that a straightforward timer, which allows for accurate control, is more useful.

Focus finder

This stands on the masking frame and reflects a small part of the enlarged image onto a crosswire, where it can be examined through a magnifier. When the enlarger is correctly focused it is possible to see the grain structure of the image.

Some are about four or five inches tall, which is fine for small prints, but because one has to have an eye on the focus finder and a hand on the enlarger's focus control, which can be tricky for big enlargements, there are others available which are about 18 inches tall.

Safelighting

Photographic paper used for black and white printing is not panchromatic, i.e. sensitive to light of all colours. It is most sensitive to blue light, making handling possible under a red or orange-brown coloured safelight.

Safelights come in many shapes and sizes, usually with interchangeable filters. Some stand on the bench while others can be hung on the walls or from the ceiling. Provided that the paper manufacturer's advice is followed it is possible to have a surprisingly high level of illumination in the darkroom.

To see if the level of safelighting in the darkroom is too high, place a coin on a piece of photographic paper and leave it on the bench near the enlarger for at least three times as long as a typical exposure. If, after developing and fixing the paper, the image of the coin is at all visible then the safelighting is too bright.

PROCESSING PHOTOGRAPHIC PAPER

The steps in processing black and white paper are very similar to those for black and white film. When done by hand, the paper is developed and fixed by chemicals contained in shallow dishes. The temperature of the developer should be about 20°C; if this is not close to the ambient temperature of the darkroom, it can be maintained by standing the dish on a purpose-built thermostatically controlled heater. The temperature of the fixer is less important, but it should not be allowed to fall below 15°C. The paper should be agitated during processing to ensure that fresh chemicals are constantly reaching the emulsion. This can be done by rocking the dish, or lifting up a corner of the paper with a pair of tongs.

Dishes, thermometers etc.

Use dishes which are at least a couple of inches larger than the size of the print being made, and do not skimp on chemicals. A dial-type thermometer is ideal for measuring the temperature of the developer as it is more robust than those made of glass, which use spirit or mercury. Two pairs of tongs are needed. One is used in the developer and to drop the print in either the fixer or an intermediate wash stage. The other is used to collect the print from the intermediate wash and agitate the print while it is in the fixer. The two pairs should be colour-coded to prevent them from becoming mixed up and contaminating the developer. Print tongs can leave marks on prints – I have found those with rubber-tipped bamboo arms to be better than those made of plastic. Measuring jugs can be purchased inexpensively at a hardware store; as print developer is made up at one part developer to ten parts, or less, of water, and processing is carried out by inspection, there is not the same need for the precise accuracy required when diluting developers for films.

Development

The developer turns the latent image into a visible silver image. As the grains of silver which make up the finished image are so minute that their final size is of no importance, there is no need for fine-grain or speed-increasing developers.

Most developers in press darkrooms are liquid concentrates for ease of handling although it is possible to purchase powder developers which are mixed with water to form a stock solution which is further diluted for use. There are universal developers which can be used for processing both film and paper, but the best results come from developers intended for paper processing. Some variable-contrast papers should be processed in their own specific developer.

Unlike film, which is processed out of sight for a specific time at a particular temperature, it is possible to watch the image on a piece of paper build up as development proceeds. Paper developer manufacturers recommend a time and temperature but there is a limited opportunity to curtail or extend the process without affecting the print quality. Removing the paper prematurely to correct for overexposure will reduce the maximum density of the blacks and increase the chance of uneven development across the print, while extending development may lead to staining and the highlights becoming fogged.

A correctly developed and exposed print may look a little darker than normal under the safelight, but this is quickly learnt by experience.

Manufacturers provide guidelines as to how much paper a given volume of developer will process; an indication that the developer is nearing the end of its useful life is when it turns dark. If at any stage the developer starts to smell of ammonia, that means it has been contaminated with fixer, and must be changed straightaway. Diluted developer has a dish life of only a few hours.

Although it may be tempting to use hands and fingers to develop prints, it should be avoided. It increases the risk of cross-contamination between developer and fixer, and can cause marks on prints. Furthermore, some people are affected by skin problems after exposure to some of the chemicals found in developers.

Fixing

After development the print can be briefly washed or immersed in a stop bath to terminate development immediately. The print can be put straight into the fixer, but this may lead to staining and reduce the life of the fixer. Again, there are powdered fixers, but liquid fixers are more convenient and faster working. Unlike films, papers do not require a fixer with a hardener. It is important to agitate the print once it is in the fix for the first 15 or 20 seconds to prevent the possibility of staining. The print can then be examined under white light, and checked for density and contrast. Fixing for resin-coated papers is complete within a couple of minutes. Fixing for significantly longer than recommended by the manufacturer should be avoided as the chemicals start to attack the silver in the image.

Fresh fix has a distinctive 'bite' to it when you put your hand in it, and while manufacturers have guidelines as to the amount of material that can pass through a given volume of chemical, it is sometimes possible to 'feel' if the fix needs replacing. Alternatively, take a piece of paper into white light where it will darken slightly and then immerse it in the fix, and see how long it takes to clear, compared with the manufacturer's recommendations. Unlike developer, fixer does not oxidize and go 'off' when diluted and used in a dish.

When using the same volume of fixer and developer, the fixer will need replacing first.

Washing

The purpose of washing the print is to remove the chemicals which otherwise would attack and degrade the silver image. Because of their waterproof base, resin-coated papers can be completely washed in running water in two or three minutes, whereas ordinary paper needs as long as 30 minutes to remove all the chemicals.

There are various devices available which aid efficient washing. They all aim to keep prints moving through a constantly changing stream of fresh water. One of the best is a large free-standing sink into which water is supplied at each corner through nozzles which agitate the prints. The sink fills and overflows through a syphon which drains it completely, and the process starts again.

It is sometimes tempting to skimp with washing. News pictures may be going into a library and it might not be until some years later that it is noticed that the image has faded or become stained, by which time it is too late to save the print. Similarly, readers who buy photographs will be cross if they fade prematurely.

Drying

Resin-coated prints can be dried by hand with a hair dryer after the surface water has been removed with a large rubber print squeegee. There are several machines available to dry larger quantities of prints. Simple ones blow hot air across prints placed on wire shelves. More complicated ones have a pair of motorized rollers into which the print is fed; they remove the water from the surface of the print before passing it through a current of hot air and out the other side through a pair of foam rollers. I would highly recommend the one made by Ilford which uses infra-red elements rather than hot air and is capable of taking a 20-inch-wide print. Like much good photographic equipment, it is expensive, but it will last a very long time.

Hot-bed driers can be used for conventional paper. These are thermostatically controlled, and the print is placed face upwards and covered with a tensioned cloth. Drying takes about five minutes.

Machine processing

Dish processing requires no expensive equipment and has the advantage of speed; a print can be very quickly assessed for density and contrast while it is still in the developer, and alterations made either to the exposure or chosen paper grade. Minor exposure errors can be corrected by extending or curtailing the development time. However, it is messy and labour intensive and maintaining print quality with a high throughput can be hard.

Machine processors accept an exposed sheet of paper and develop, fix, wash and dry it in about 90 seconds. They are capable of a high throughput and automatically replenish the processing chemicals. Of course it is not possible to alter the development time to take account of exposure errors. They are best suited for darkrooms which have a high throughput, especially if many prints are frequently made from individual negatives.

Exposing the print

With the negative in the carrier, the enlarger head at the correct height and the lens carefully focused and closed down one or two stops, the first step is to make a test strip. This is a piece of photographic paper which is placed across a representative section of the print and given a range of exposures. After development, the best exposure can be selected. Typically, for a 10 × 8 inch print from the entire negative, one might try 5, 10, 15 and 20 seconds. Grade 2 or grade 3 paper is a good starting point. It is important that the strip is developed for the manufacturer's recommended time.

After processing it should be possible to determine either that one of the strips received the correct exposure, or that the correct exposure lies between two adjacent sections. If all the print is either too light or too dark then the enlarger lens should be opened up or closed down a stop or the exposure time given adjusted accordingly.

When the correct exposure has been determined, expose and process an entire sheet of paper. It may then be that the mid-tones of the print appear correctly, but that the highlights are burnt out with no detail and the shadows are jet black. Try again using a softer grade of paper. If the highlights appear muddy and there is no black in the shadows, then use a harder paper.

A good print has a full range of tones, with only the darkest shadow appearing totally black and only the brightest highlight appearing true white. If there is a person wearing a black suit and a white shirt, then it should be possible to see detail in the shirt – for instance, the buttons, or the collar – and also to see the lapels and the flaps of the jacket pockets.

Print presentation

After the print has been dried, it may need to be trimmed if the picture has not filled the standard paper shape. Do not necessarily remove all the white borders. They may be needed by the sub-editors when the print is sized for making a block. A wire print will certainly need borders for the clips which hold it on the drum and a space left for a typed caption.

Occasionally a print will have marks from dust, hairs or fingerprints on the negative. The first course of action is to try to remove them from the negative, either with a compressed air blower, or, if the marks are not on the emulsion, by polishing the film gently with a clean soft cloth.

Marks on the emulsion side of the film are harder to treat as there is a risk of causing further damage. Having made the best print possible in case of an accident, soak the negative in some warm water to which has been added a few drops of wetting agent. The emulsion of the negative is delicate at this stage, but

Figure 5.3   Effect of varying printing exposure: This picture shows the effect of varying the exposure in steps from 5 to 25 seconds. The ideal exposure step falls between the strips exposed for 10 and 15 seconds

it may be possible to rub it very gently to loosen the particles. Drying marks – deposits left when the water evaporated from the film – can be removed if a little vinegar is added to the water. The film must be carefully redried. Sometimes a short strip of 35 mm negatives is best hung from a partially unbent paperclip passing through a sprocket hole.

Dust and hairs on the negative appear as white marks on the print, while scratches tend to appear as black marks. Parallel scratches running the entire length of the film can be caused by dirt in the film cassette mouth, a dirty squeegee or drawing the film carelessly through the enlarger's negative carrier.

Scratches on the non-emulsion side of the negative can be reduced by cleaning it meticulously and then dripping it in scratch remover. This is a fast-drying solution of material which fills the scratch and has the same refractive index as the base of the film.

Scratches on the emulsion are more difficult to remove. It is possible to soak the negative in warm water, and hope that the emulsion will swell sufficiently that it knits together and does not part when it is dried.

The message is very clear: keep the darkroom clean and free from dust and handle negatives with great care.

Spotting and retouching

Should it not be possible to remove the cause of the marks, then they may have to be 'spotted out.' This is a useful skill which is not as hard as it appears. You will need a very fine brush and tubes of black and white water-based paint of the kind used by artists.

Squeeze a little of each paint onto a piece of white paper and mix it with a matchstick or something similar until it is the same tone as the area around the mark which has to be filled in.

Slightly moisten the brush with your mouth, and draw the brush across the paint, before wiping it gently across the adhesive found on the flap of an envelope (this helps the paint 'stick' to the print), and then very gently just touch the area to be spotted. Larger areas may need several touches. If the process goes wrong, or the tone does not match, the water-based paint can be wiped away with a damp cloth.

Retouching starts where spotting ends. Whereas spotting involves minimizing or removing technical imperfections, retouching is done on a larger scale and can involve toning down distracting highlights, suppressing the background of a picture, painting out an unwanted face or drawing round a batsman's pads which have blended into his white trousers. It is mainly the work of a newspaper artist who may use an airbrush. Retouching pictures can improve them for publication, or make them look unnatural. A news agency should not retouch pictures without making it very clear to its customers that the process has happened.

Some sports pictures are retouched by adding or moving the ball. Before doing this, it is vital to check that the ball really is not in the original picture. It is very difficult to explain to readers how a football game came to be played with two balls. Care must be taken that the ball is of the correct proportion.

Most newspapers now handle pictures electronically and the retouching and removal of blemishes is done on screen using Adobe Photoshop – or a simialr computer program.

SPECIAL TECHNIQUES

Dodging and burning

Sometimes, because of the lighting conditions under which the picture was taken or the subjects involved, it is not possible to get sufficient details in the shadows and the highlights while maintaining a good mid-tone range.

Examples of this might be when a person's face is in shadow under a hat or a picture taken by flash has one person closer to the camera, and therefore more brightly lit, than another. Such areas require local exposure control, which is called dodging or burning-in.

In the first case, the area to be dodged can be shielded by a piece of stout card on a length of thin wire. The dodger is held a few inches above the baseboard to soften its outline on the print, and moved gently so that it does not cast an obvious shadow. The skill is in matching the shape of the dodger to the area requiring less exposure, and deciding how much dodging is required to reveal the shadow detail and still allow the print to appear natural. For areas adjoining the edge of the print it may be possible to dodge the shadows using one's own hands.

Dodging reduces the light falling on part of the print and obviously takes place during the main exposure of the print.

Burning-in happens after the main exposure and increases the amount of light falling on part of the picture. Hands make the best implements for burning-in as they can be manipulated to match the area requiring additional exposure. Again they must be kept moving and held above the baseboard to soften the edges of the treated area.

Many photographers burn in the sky and the corners of their prints as a matter of course.

When using paper with a variable contrast, it may help to make a dodger cut from the filter used to obtain the highest contrast. This not only reduces the exposure to the area being held back, but increases its contrast, which helps to maintain the shadow detail.

Burning-in and dodging turn printing from a semi-mechanical process to a skilled occupation.

Big enlargements

There will be occasions, either because a large print is needed, or because the subject on the negative is too small, that the enlarger column is not long enough to produce the required degree of enlargement.

It may be possible to swing the enlarger head through 180 degrees, and project the image onto the floor. It will be necessary to counterweight the enlarger baseboard to prevent it from toppling over; the five litre containers in which developer or fixer are supplied are ideal for this purpose. This method has the benefit that the paper is held in the masking frame on the floor.

Alternatively, some enlarger heads can be rotated through 90 degrees to project the image onto a wall. Care must be taken to ensure that the enlarger is pointing squarely at the wall. The printing paper can be held to the wall with double-sided adhesive tape.

Some enlargers are built on special frames which permit the baseboard to be lowered for big enlargements.

When making big enlargements special care should be taken that the safelight does not fog the paper or the negative pop during the long exposure.

Figure 5.4 Waving goodbye to HMS Torquay: HMS Torquay was the Royal Navy's oldest ship and when she left her twin town for the last time I was looking for a picture which would publish both in the national and local press. There were a few relatives and well-wishers on the harbourside, and I moved them together so that I could include them waving goodbye and the ship in the same frame. I underexposed the negative slightly to accentuate the silhouette of the ship, and back in the darkroom printed in the top of the sky. The picture published well locally, and in two national newspapers, and we had many requests for the picture from men who had served aboard her and who had seen the picture printed (© Torbay News Agency)

Correcting converging verticals

Whenever the camera is pointed upwards, vertical parallel lines will appear to converge. This is most noticeable on tall buildings which appear to be falling backwards; the effect can be avoided at the time by using a perspective control lens. It can also be reduced in the darkroom by tilting the enlarger easel. The end where the parallel lines are widest has to be lifted closer to the enlarger lens. The amount by which it must be raised is determined by observation.

Because the paper is no longer parallel to the baseboard it is necessary to focus the enlarger lens on an area a third of the way down the print and then stop it down as far as possible to gain the maximum depth of field and hope that the entire print is rendered sharp. As the higher end of the print is closer to the enlarger lens it will be darker on the finished print unless it is progressively shaded. The height of the building is exaggerated and the finished print is not rectangular, with the end closest to the lens narrower than the end resting on the baseboard.

Some expensive enlargers permit the lens to be tilted to overcome the focusing problem. For the plane containing the paper to be in focus it must pass through the imaginary intersection of the planes of the negative and the lens.

Printing to size

Some newspapers print their pictures to the same size that they will appear in the paper. This helps in preparing them for the page by 'screening' since the operator can screen several pictures at the same time.

It means that the masking frame must be calibrated in column widths, rather than inches, and that the photographers or printers have a sensible and realistic attitude to the size that their pictures will appear in the newspaper if reprinting is to be minimized.

Contact prints

As its name implies, a contact print is when the negative is printed touching the paper, usually under a sheet of glass. They are used for the first stage of editing a photographer's work and for library purposes as it is easier to inspect a sheet of positive prints than hold a page of negatives up against a light box.

Contact prints are normally made on a soft grade of paper which has a greater latitude to the possible variations in negative density on a roll of pictures. For the image to be the right way round on the finished print the film emulsion (matt side) must be in contact with that of the paper.

Commercial models contact print an entire 36 exposure film on a sheet of 10 × 8 inch paper once the negatives have been cut up into strips of six. For speed and convenience some newspapers use paper from a roll to produce a contact print of an entire film as a long narrow strip. This method provides a useful record of the uncut film to compare with the captions that the photographer returned to the office.

Black and white prints from colour negatives

There are three problems with printing black and white prints from colour negatives onto conventional paper, which is sensitive mainly to blue light. Firstly, the negatives have an orange cast which is similar to the colour of a safelight. This can lead to longer than normal exposure times, even with the enlarger lens open as wide as possible. Secondly, because the paper is not sensitive to light of all colours, the tones in the picture will not be rendered accurately. Thirdly, colour negatives are softer than black and white ones. To get a satisfactory print it may be necessary to use a harder grade of paper than normal. This accentuates the grain of the negative on the finished print.

Some brands of colour negative film print on to ordinary black and white paper more successfully than others, and it is worth making a few tests to discover which one gives the best quality. All these problems can be overcome by using a Kodak's PANALURE paper, which is manufactured specifically for this task. It handles just like ordinary photographic paper, but because it is sensitive to light of all colours, it must be exposed and processed in total darkness. It is only available in one grade.

COLOUR PRINTING

Introduction

Colour pictures in newspapers used to be reserved for special events like royal visits or for special displays and effects, and the principles and practice of colour photography were unknown to many photographers only a few years ago. Nowadays the majority of national newspapers and an increasing number of provincial newspapers routinely use colour pictures.

A colour picture is printed in a newspaper or magazine from three separations, which represent the yellow, magenta and cyan content of the photograph; sometimes, especially for high-quality reproduction, an additional black separation is used.

Initially, colour photographs intended for use in a newspaper were shot on reversal film as transparencies were considered easier to scan to make the separations than prints. The balance has changed and now it is just as easy to make the separations from a print as from a transparency. The majority of colour pictures which appear in newspapers are shot on negative film.

Whereas the printing and processing of black and white photographs is mainly a manual process, the colour darkroom is usually highly automated.

The principles behind colour printing are not difficult to understand; it may require more practice than black and white, but the results can be just as rewarding.

Theory

The previous chapter explained how colour films have, in their simplest ideal form, three layers of emulsion. One, sensitive to blue light, records an image in yellow dye, another is sensitive to green light, and records an image in magenta dye, and a third, sensitive to red light, records an image in cyan dye. Whether the images are positive or negative depends upon the method of processing.

The same principles hold true for the most straightforward colour printing papers.

One subtle difference of colour printing paper compared with film is the order in which light reaches the separate emulsions. Films have the blue-sensitive emulsion at the top, a yellow filter, then the green, and finally the red emulsion adjacent to the base.

Paper is constructed slightly differently. When the human eye assesses the sharpness of the print, the most critical image is the cyan, and if possible this image should be at the top, where it will be both formed and seen without the light being scattered as it passes through the other two. The next most important image is the magenta, and then the yellow. By carefully minimizing the sensitivity of the red and green emulsions to blue light, the yellow filter can be dispensed with and the red-sensitive layer promoted to the top of the film, the green retaining the middle position and the blue layer being placed next to the base.

Additive printing

Colour prints can be made with three separate exposures of varying duration through red, green and blue filters. Each exposure affects just one layer of emulsion. This is called additive printing. It has the benefit of requiring just three filters, but there must clearly be no relative movement between the lens, negative and paper between exposures, and it is impractical to burn in or dodge the print. In order to keep the enlarger as still as possible between exposures, the filters are placed below the lens, and therefore need to be of optical quality.

Additive printing is used in some commercial machine printers.

Subtractive printing

Subtractive printing exposes the three layers of emulsion simultaneously. If the enlarger light source used is initially white – which is a mixture of the three primary colours – then the amount of blue light reaching the blue-sensitive layer can be controlled with a filter which will absorb blue light, i.e. a yellow filter; the green light can be controlled with a magenta filter and red light with a cyan filter. As there is only one exposure, the filters can be between the negative and the light source where they do not have to be optically perfect and there are similar opportunities to burn in and dodge as there are in black and white printing.

The colour balance of the print is varied by altering the intensity of the filters used. Manufacturers supply filters in a range of marked strengths; a typical range is 025, 05, 10, 20, 30, 40, 50. Individual filters are made from squares of acetate or gelatine and are inserted in a filter drawer, usually directly above the negative. It may be necessary to have several filters of the same colour, but of different strengths, to make the appropriate 'filter pack'.

The filtration required will depend primarily upon the film, the paper and the enlarger's illumination source. It will also be affected by the light source by which the picture was taken, any inaccuracies in processing the negative, and the variations from batch to batch of the film and paper.

A filter pack should only ever contain two colours. An equal amount of magenta, cyan and yellow filtration represents neutral density, which only lengthens the exposure.

Combining individual filters into a filter pack is time-consuming and not very practical when using a colour analyser to assess the filtration required. In addition, gelatine filters exposed to a bright light may fade over a period of time.

Colour heads

Enlargers intended for colour printing are fitted with special lamphouses with built-in filters which can be continuously adjusted by external dials.

The modern colour head in an enlarger focuses the illumination from a low-voltage quartz halogen bulb into a small beam of light into which three filters, yellow, magenta and cyan, can be inserted. The strength of filtration of any particular colour depends upon how far the individual filter is moved into the beam. The light is then thoroughly mixed in a white-sided box or similar diffusing arrangement before it passes through a condenser to the negative.

Although a colour head may use gelatine filters, it is better to use dichroic filters, made by depositing several very thin layers of material on glass or quartz, and which use optical interference to transmit light of a specific colour, and to reflect, rather than absorb, all other colours. The principle is similar to the way lenses are coated to minimize reflections at glass–air surfaces to improve transmission. As they do not contain dyes, dichroic filters do not fade.

Enlargers used to print colour require both ultraviolet and infra-red filters within the light path.

As well as conventional enlargers with a baseboard and a head which slides up and down a column which produce prints on individual sheets of paper, there are totally light-tight enlargers which can be operated in daylight and print onto a roll of paper which is cut up after processing.

Simple examples of these are the printing machines used to produce en-prints in High Street one hour photo centres; most of these process the paper as well. At the other end of the scale are machines used by commercial photofinishers which can print negative formats from 110 to 120 to a variety of sizes. For example, a machine using 10-inch-wide paper in a cassette can print two 5×5 inch prints next to one another, an 8×6 inch print with one inch of wasted paper either side, a 10×8 inch print and a 10×12 inch print. The paper from these is processed by another machine.

The most recent photofinishing equipment to arrive in High Street shops enables the customers to insert their own negatives, view the picture on a television screen and control the cropping, colour balance and size of enlargement, which the machine then prints and processes for them while they wait. The equipment can be operated with the minimum of skill, and requires no intervention from the shopkeeper apart from routine maintenance. Machines similar to these are proving very popular within the newspaper industry.

Analysers

Finding the filter pack required for a print can be done by trial and error but it is a costly and time-consuming process; fortunately there are a variety of electronic analysers which can estimate the correct filtration needed to produce a first-time print of an acceptable standard.

They assume that when all the colours in the picture are mixed together, they come out a neutral grey. The analysers are used in conjunction with a diffuser swung into the light path. Some require the filtration to be altered until the analyser considers it correct. Others are used with white light shining through the negative, and instruct the operator what filtration must be inserted.

All analysers need an initial calibration which takes into account the enlarger in use and the particular film/paper combination. Depending upon its sophistication, an analyser may be able to remember several film/paper combinations which the operator can recall at will.

Analysers which integrate to grey will fail when the picture has one predominant colour. This problem can be overcome with video analysers which scan the negative with a television camera and use a colour monitor screen to show the printer how the picture will appear with a particular filtration. They need not be in the darkroom next to the enlarger − one may serve several enlargers; the information about the desired filtration and exposure time can be sent to the enlarger either electronically or by programmed magnetic card.

Handling and processing

Colour printing paper is panchromatic, and must, to all intents and purposes, be handled in total darkness. Sometimes a dark green safelight is acceptable; and there are others which use the very narrow spectrum of illumination from certain LEDs. It is possible to light the darkroom with infra-red light and use special goggles to see, but the cost of the equipment is very high.

Manufacturers supply their paper with a suggestion for an initial filtration, which can then be modified in the light of experience.

It is important that the light used to assess the print is of the correct colour. Tungsten lights have a warm colour, while some fluorescent lights do not emit a continuous spectrum of light and can have a slight green cast; even daylight varies from hour to hour and with the time of the year. Prints should be viewed under special fluorescent lights which emit a spectrum of light very similar to a standard daylight. Some prints have a milky blue appearance when wet, and they should be dried before being assessed for density and colour balance.

The last chapter emphasized the need for accuracy in time and temperature control to obtain consistent negative quality. The same is true with colour printing. Colour prints are processed by hand only on mobile assignments; and the occasions that this is necessary have been vastly reduced by the ability of wire machines to transmit colour pictures from negatives.

Processing machines maintain the solution temperatures and replenish them with far greater accuracy than can be done manually. A daily quality control strip can be processed and returned to the manufacturer of the processing system to check that the machine is functioning to specification.

Most machines are of the 'through the wall' type, with the feed table for the paper in the darkroom and the processed print emerging into a normally lit area.

Prints from negatives

Prints produced from negatives are processed in just two solutions. The first stage is the colour developer, when the developer reacts with the exposed silver halides to form metallic silver and oxidized developer, which then combines with a colour coupler within the emulsion to release a dye. The colour couplers used in each layer of emulsion are different to produce the dye of the appropriate colour. The paper is then bleached and fixed simultaneously − blixed − to destroy the silver, remove the unconverted silver halides and render the image stable. The resin-coated paper requires a brief wash, followed possibly by a rinse in stabilizer, before drying.

The most recent system for colour print processing delivers a dry print after three minutes; the Kodak version is described as Process RA-4, Agfa's is Process 94. They must only be used with paper compatible with this process. Typically the steps are as in Table 5.1.

Table 5.1

Step	Temperature (°C)	Time (s)
Develop	35 ± 0.5	45
Bleach/fix	30–36	45
Wash in running water	30–40	90

The need to maintain accurate control over time and temperature means that this process is suitable only for use in a machine.

It is possible to use separate bleach and fix baths, and to use a stabilizer rather than wash the print in running water.

An alternative, older, process takes eight minutes to produce a print. Kodak's process is called EP-2, Agfa's is AP92. The paper used is not compatible with the process described earlier. Typically the steps are as shown in Table 5.2.

Table 5.2

Step	Temperature (°C)	Time
Develop	33 ± 0.3	3 mins, 25 seconds
Bleach/fix	33 ± 2.0	1 min, 30 seconds
Wash in running water	33 ± 2.0	3 min

This is suitable for both machine and hand processing. For small-scale use the Photocolor II kit is highly recommended. It is all liquid and easy to prepare. The same chemicals are used for processing films and papers. A small quantity of additive is used with the developer when processing prints.

Assessing colour balance

The overall density of a print is easily assessed, and adjusted, either by increasing or decreasing the exposure.

Trying to assess the colour and degree of correction required is much harder and only comes with experience. There are filters through which a print can be examined to give an idea of how the colours may alter as the filtration is changed.

As a very rough guide, a print with a noticeable colour cast in only the neutral tones will require about 5 units of change, a print that has a slight cast overall will require 10 units of change, one where the stronger colours are correct, but the paler colours are wrong, 25 units, and a very strong obvious overall cast 40 units.

Some casts are more obvious than others. Generally we accept a print that is too red–yellow because it appears 'warm', more than one which is too blue–green, which appears cold. It is easier to assess the cast on neutral areas, rather than in strong colours. Adding to the filter pack will mean increasing the exposure and removing a filter means decreasing it; each filter has a factor by which the old exposure must be multiplied to obtain the new exposure; for the same increase in filtration, a cyan filter will require a greater change in exposure than a magenta, which in turn requires more than a yellow.

Table 5.3 Alterations to filter pack when using neg/pos process

If the print is too	Add this colour	Remove this colour
Magenta	Magenta	Yellow and cyan (green)
Cyan	Cyan	Magenta and yellow (red)
Yellow	Yellow	Magenta and cyan (blue)
Green	Yellow and cyan (green)	Magenta
Red	Magenta and yellow (red)	Cyan
Blue	Magenta and cyan (blue)	Yellow

Once the correct filter pack has been established for a particular film–paper–enlarger combination, the only changes necessary will be minor ones to take account of possible variations in lighting conditions.

Processing prints on a mobile assignment

On those increasingly rare occasions when colour prints are produced on mobile assignments they are invariably made from colour negatives and are processed either in a light-tight plastic drum or in two thin vertical tanks. Because of the difficulties in working in total darkness, dish processing is not used.

The vertical tank technique is popular as it requires very little equipment in addition to that which the photographer carries to develop the negatives; the tanks are usually built in to each side of the water bath used to keep the developer and blix at the correct temperature for film processing. Although the tanks are only two or three centimetres wide, they contain sufficient solution to ensure that there is no significant change in the activity of the developer from one print to the next. The print is agitated by periodically raising it slightly from the chemicals by means of a clip. Although some tanks have light-tight lids, the process has to be carried out in a light-tight room.

The drum technique is widely used by amateurs. The paper is held against the inside of the cylinder by clips. Once the lid is in place, all other operations can be carried out in daylight. The chemicals reach the paper through a light-tight entrance in the lid and are agitated by rotating the drum, either by hand or by machine. Temperature control is maintained by either pre-heating the drum or immersing it in a thermostatically controlled water bath. Most drums require about 50 cm^3 of chemicals; to obtain consistency of results, fresh developer should be used each time, but the bleach fix can be used two or three times without any adverse effects. Those processors which use a water bath usually have an area in which small bottles of chemicals can be brought to and maintained at the desired processing temperature.

The print is removed from the drum after blixing and washed in a tray. All the components of the drum must then be washed meticulously to avoid contamination. The print may be either squeegeed and left to dry naturally or dried with a hair drier.

Prints from transparencies

Newspapers have little need to routinely make prints from transparencies.

Conventional processing uses an initial developer to produce a black and white image in the three layers of emulsion. The paper is then fogged, either by light, or by chemicals within the next processing step, the colour developer. There is now a second latent image which can be processed by the colour developer to yield metallic silver and oxidized developer, which reacts with the different colour coupler in each layer of emulsion to produce three separate dye images. The paper is then blixed, washed and dried.

Colour transparencies have a greater contrast range than negatives, so the paper that they are printed on is softer, and hence has a greater latitude to exposure and filtration, than ordinary neg/pos colour printing paper.

The effects of changes in filtration and exposure are the reverse to those on the neg/pos process. This helps with adjusting the filtration; if the print has a colour cast, then remove some of the excess colour. However, if the print is too light, it requires less exposure; if it is too dark, then it requires more exposure.

Table 5.4   Alterations to filter pack when using pos/pos process

If the print is too	Remove this colour	Add this colour
Magenta	Magenta	Yellow and cyan (green)
Cyan	Cyan	Magenta and yellow (red)
Yellow	Yellow	Magenta and cyan (blue)
Green	Yellow and cyan (green)	Magenta
Red	Magenta and yellow (red)	Cyan
Blue	Magenta and cyan (blue)	Yellow

Because of the latitude of reversal paper, the changes in filtration required to correct a particular cast will be greater than that required to correct a similar cast on neg/pos papers.

Burning-in and dodging are a little more complicated. A dark area will need more exposure to bring out the detail, while highlights need less exposure to prevent them from being devoid of detail.

CIBACHROME

An alternative to producing the dyes in a reaction between the colour couplers and the oxidized developer is to place them in the emulsion during manufacture, and then to destroy them where they are not needed during the processing. This is known as 'dye destruction' or 'silver dye-bleach'. The only current material using this technique is CIBACHROME, which has the advantage of requiring just three processing steps at 24°C, and claims to offer wide latitude to exposure, filtration and processing times, excellent sharpness, high colour saturation and minimal fading of colour.

Table 5.5   Typical processing sequence for CIBACHROME

Step	Temperature (°C)	Time
Develop	24 ± 1.0	3 min
Wash	24 ± 2.0	30 s
Bleach	24 ± 2.0	3 min
Fix	24 ± 2.0	3 min
Wash	24 ± 2.0	3 min

The first developer produces a conventional black and white image. The bleach reacts with the silver formed and the dye present in the emulsion to produce chemicals which are either soluble or transparent. The fix then removes the unconverted silver halides.

The bleach used in the CIBACHROME process is strongly acidic, and the manufacturer's recommendations should be followed carefully when disposing of it.

CIBACHROME is a relatively expensive material. It is ideal for producing a special one-off print, but for large quantities, or routine uses, conventional reversal printing papers are preferable.

Photo colour transfer (PCT)

This process is unusual because the material exposed under the enlarger is not the same sheet as the finished print. It uses technology similar to that used to make instant prints, and can be used to make prints from both negatives and transparencies.

The image is projected back-to-front onto a sheet of PCT film which is then soaked in activator, and rolled onto a sheet of receiving paper. After six to eight minutes the two sheets are peeled apart to leave the finished picture of the receiving paper. There is no subsequent washing, and precise temperature control is not required.

Both negatives and transparencies can be used by choosing the appropriate PCT film. As with any other process, the enlarger light source has to be correctly filtered.

The PCT process is ideal for occasional amateur use, but is only of academic interest to the working press photographer.

Spotting colour prints

Colour printing is done with enlargers with diffuser light sources, so dust and marks on the negatives are less of a problem. It is possible to remove blemishes on the print with techniques similar to those used on black and white photographs, but it is much harder to match the colour of the surrounding area. It is possible to purchase dyes which can be mixed to match the required colour. Spotting colour prints requires a great deal of practice.

Duplicating transparencies

Slides can be duplicated simply by copying them onto reversal film. This can be done with a relatively cheap adaptor screwed to the front of a camera in place of its lens, and using either daylight or flash as a source of illumination.

Alternatively there is a range of purpose-built slide duplicators available. These have an integral light source, usually an electronic flashgun, of variable power. Some use a conventional 35 mm or 120 camera with a lens and bellows extension. Others are specialized cameras, use long lengths of bulk-loaded film in special magazines and have automatic film advance.

Copying transparencies onto normal reversal film can be disappointing, with the duplicates too contrasty and lacking the subtle colours of the original. This is because transparency film tends to compress tones in the extremes of highlights and shadows. Compressing them twice leads to results which may be unacceptable.

This can be overcome, either by slightly fogging the film, which reduces the contrast, or by using special duplicating film whose characteristics are modified to minimize this effect.

All duplicators give the user the opportunity to crop the picture, or to place filters between the light source and the original to correct colour casts.

Transparencies from negatives

It is possible to produce transparencies of a very high quality directly from negatives. The equipment needed is very similar to that needed to duplicate slides. However, the light source must be filtered – just as when making a print.

The film used has an emulsion similar to that found on colour paper, and is processed in conventional C41 chemicals. When processed, the film has a clear rebate.

Setting up a colour darkroom

Converting a newspaper's photographic operation from black and white to colour is a major undertaking. It is safe to assume that any news organization 'going colour' will be shooting on colour negative film.

Once the decision has been taken to 'go colour', then one of the earliest steps taken must be to start shooting all pictures on colour film, coupled with the purchase of an automatic processor.

This helps to build up some stock colour pictures, allays many photographers' natural fears of entrusting their film to an automatic processor and may assist in spreading expenditure and the disruption caused by the changeover. Colour negatives can be printed on conventional black and white paper, although on occasions the grain may be highlighted and the tones in the picture distorted slightly. Thought should be given about a back-up to the processor. Large operations will buy two or more processors, while smaller ones may have a conventional hand-tank available for emergencies.

It may be possible to convert black and white enlargers to colour merely by adding a colour head – or they may have to be replaced completely. Almost certainly the layout of the darkroom will have to be changed. Most black and white darkrooms contain several enlargers with a shared processing facility in the middle of the room. Because colour paper is handled in total darkness, each enlarger will have to be in its own room or cubicle. These may be off a central hall or lobby, which contains the darkroom-side feed to the paper processor.

The entrance to this lobby must be light-tight. A standard solution is a revolving door. This is a vertical metal cylinder which has a gap into which you walk; you rotate the cylinder through 180 degrees and walk out the other side. It has a metal escape hatch in case the door buckles in the heat of a fire.

The equipment found in a colour darkroom will vary with the newspaper's size, the anticipated workload and the money available. A national newspaper might need at least two automatic film processors; a machine printer, similar to those found in High Street photofinishers, to provide quick prints from an entire roll of film, possibly adapted so that the frame number appears on each picture; a daylight printer so that large numbers of prints can be quickly produced from the same negative; several enlargers with integral colour heads and analysers so that prints can be produced by hand; and one, or maybe two, paper processors. Duplicating the critical pieces of equipment minimizes the inconvenience caused by mechanical failures and allows adequate time for servicing.

Smaller newspapers or provincial agencies might manage with one film processor, two enlargers and a small paper processor.

Because virtually all commercial photography is in colour, there is a wide variety of equipment available for all levels of throughput and investment – far more so than with black and white photography.

One source of equipment is the small ads in the commercial photographic trade journals, where secondhand enlargers and paper processors can be found with considerable savings.

Anyone envisaging setting up a colour darkroom would be well advised to visit some of the trade exhibitions which specialize in such equipment.

6

The working photographer – 1

The American newspaper proprietor William Randolph Hearst is alleged to have said: 'News is what somebody, somewhere, doesn't want printed; everything else is public relations.' Thankfully most modern newspaper editors take a wider view.

Whether something is newsworthy enough to be included in a particular paper depends upon the editor's perception of its readers and their interests. For instance, the off-screen activities of television soap stars is of enormous interest to tabloid newspapers, but would go unrecorded in the 'quality' broadsheet end of the market, who in turn might be more interested in an atmospheric portrait of the new Governor of the Bank of England taken in its vaults. A provincial evening newspaper would probably not be interested in either – preferring to tell its readers about events closer to home.

News photographs may appear either in their own right because of their content – a plane crash, a family grieving at a funeral or a dog carrying in her mouth the kitten she has adopted; or because they illustrate the story which accompanies them – a schoolboy who rescued a family of three from a burning house, a well-known actor arriving at court to face a drunken driving charge or the Chancellor of the Exchequer walking through a London park with his family on the morning of Budget Day.

Both can be split broadly into 'hard' and 'soft' news. Hard news is unexpected and can happen any time, and a newspaper may require good contacts if it is to hear about it first; the photographer will merely be told what has happened and instructed to get there as fast as possible. Soft news can be anticipated, its value to the readers assessed and coverage arranged; a photographer will have ample time to plan possible picture ideas.

Hard news

Hard news includes explosions, fires, road, rail or aeroplane crashes, civil disturbances, sieges, and other such tragedies or misfortunes. Often the initial tip to a paper may come from a reader – the picture desk should always check the source as he or she may have pictures of the incident – or it may come, formally or informally, from the emergency services. A newspaper will always try to get one or more staffmen to the scene but if the journey is going to take some time, will probably hire a local freelance for initial coverage.

Figure 6.1   Poll tax rioter: The Anti-Poll Tax Rally turned into the worst scenes of civil disturbance seen in central London for several years. I arrived after the violence in Trafalgar Square and followed the protesters into London's West End. As soon as I had taken this picture, I removed the film from the camera and hid it in an inside pocket (© Press Association)

A photographer fortunate enough to arrive at the scene of an incident while it is still ongoing should take any pictures which present themselves. The content is what matters; improving the composition or finding a better viewpoint can come later. Take care not to hinder the emergency services as they aid injured people. More often than not the press arrives after the police have sealed off the area and the incident may be over, or, in the case of a siege or people being rescued from the wreckage of a plane or train, it may be continuing.

Although it may be possible to work from behind the police cordon, it is often worth a walk to see if there are any better vantage spots, either from another part of the cordon or from the window of any buildings which overlook the scene. It is not unknown for money to change hands, especially if a photographer wants the window to remain 'exclusive'.

On occasions the police press officers will arrange a facility for photographers to go closer to the scene of the incident. Sometimes this is for everybody, while at other times it is a pooled facility.

Be sure to photograph any senior policemen or eyewitnesses who talk to reporters. Try to discreetly ask eyewitnesses if they, or anyone they know, took any pictures of the incident or have any pictures of those involved. It may also help the production journalists laying out the page to photograph a sign with the name of the street, station, airport or wherever the incident took place.

Figure 6.2 Double IRA funeral: Covering the funerals of members of the IRA requires considerable discretion. At this one, two brothers who had been shot by the SAS were being buried at Loughnacrory in Co. Tyrone. Photographers were allowed to record the procession, but the majority were not allowed at the graveside. Standing on a wall gave a viewpoint which showed the black beret and gloves on the coffins and the writing on the wall of the house opposite (© Press Association)

Figure 6.3   Burnt-out vehicles in Belfast's Falls Road: After the extradition from the Irish Republic to Northern Ireland of an IRA man who had escaped from the Maze Prison several vehicles were hijacked and set alight in Belfast's Falls Road. I visited the scene later with two other photographers and found these children playing around the still-smouldering wreckage. Even though the troubles have brought the media from all over the world to Northern Ireland it is important to work quietly and discreetly, and to heed anyone who tells you that they would prefer not to be photographed. It is a prudent precaution to take only the minimum equipment and keep a driver sitting in the car (© Press Association)

A photographer at the scene should be able to advise the picture desk if it is worth chartering a helicopter or light plane to take aerial pictures of the incident. On one occasion the local Fire Brigade allowed photographers a lift in their hydraulic hoist to take aerial pictures of a train crash – it is always worth asking. For an event which looks like lasting some time, for instance a major siege, a newspaper might rent a scaffolding tower or platform hoist to give its photographers a better vantage point.

Finally people may have died at the incident, and it is incumbent upon all photographers to behave with decency and respect.

At civil disturbances, photographers are at risk from both sides, who may take a dislike to their activities being recorded. To be as manoeuvrable and as inconspicuous as possible, take the bare minimum of equipment, for example two bodies, 35 mm, 85 mm and 180 mm lenses and plenty of film. A camera bag can be a serious hindrance. Flashguns are very vulnerable to being snapped from the camera's hot shoe, and it is a good idea to have a couple of small spares in a pocket. Camera straps should go over the shoulder, rather than round the neck where they could be used to throttle a photographer.

After taking a particularly good picture on a film, it may be worth removing it from the camera and putting it safely in a pocket in case the subject comes and demands it. Although there is safety in numbers, too many photographers clustered together are conspicuous; try to work with just two or three colleagues

Figure 6.4   Boy at scene of Deal bombing: Dressed in the uniform of a Royal Marine, Scott Roberts, 11, arrives to place his flowers outside the barracks at Deal where the day before 11 Royal Marine musicians had been killed by an IRA bomb. The picture, which was taken by many of the photographers there and used by most Sunday papers, is clearly posed. How far it is acceptable for photographers to go in organizing and posing a situation like this is open to debate, but he did arrive in uniform, and he did lay his flowers; we merely asked him to turn around and salute (© Press Association)

you trust. If the situation starts to become particularly unpleasant, ensure that an escape route is available.

At least one photographer has been killed in recent years in the UK while covering a civil disturbance and several others have been badly injured. As important as the ability to recognize a good picture is the sense to realize that there may be times when it is better not to produce a camera and start taking pictures.

It is vital to keep in touch with the picture desk, who will be co-ordinating coverage and arranging to get the pictures back to the office. At a large incident they will know where other photographers are working from and avoid duplication of effort.

On hard news stories away from the office, facilities to process film may be limited. It is important to keep a mental note of the 'best' pictures and which roll of film they are on so that they can be developed first.

Court jobs

Snatching pictures of people arriving and leaving courts is a regular assignment for many photographers.

Figure 6.5 Bus crash: Road traffic accidents are routine events for press photographers. I was covering a school sports day when some of the competitors ran and told me that a double-decker bus carrying children was stuck underneath a bridge a couple of hundred yards away. Amazingly, very few children were hurt as a teacher had seen the imminent danger and shouted at them to duck. I arrived to see one of the youngsters who was shocked rather than seriously injured being comforted until ambulances arrived (© Herald Express Ltd)

Figure 6.6   Madonna arrives at Heathrow Airport: When the diminutive pop star Madonna arrived at Heathrow Airport it was every man (or woman) for himself. The amount of 'hype' preceding her arrival meant a large number of fans were waiting to greet her and most Fleet Street newspapers sent staff photographers – some as many as three or four – to record the scenes. The PR men were not disappointed. Her minders were typically short with any photographers who came too close, and, predictably, the scenes were compared in the next day's papers with the arrival at the airport of the Beatles some 25 years earlier. Such events are not for the faint-hearted – there is little alternative but to push and shove just that bit harder than everybody else. I used a 24 mm lens for this picture (© Press Association)

Section 41 of the Criminal Justice Act of 1925 bans photography inside courts and makes it an offence to photograph or try to photograph any party to the proceedings entering or leaving the court building or its precincts. The precincts are not defined in the Act, and the problems this causes are discussed in Chapter 10. Subject to any local guidelines, if you can see the person and they are not actually in the building, then take a picture.

Check with the photo library before going out on the job to see if the paper already has a picture of the person you are trying to photograph. It may help to identify him or her when they arrive.

Beware of photographing the wrong people. Court officials arriving for work do not like being hassled by photographers, and judges take a dim view of anyone trying to take pictures of jurors, whatever their intentions.

When there are several photographers milling around the entrance to the court, there is little chance of disguising the purpose of their presence. Ideal equipment is an 80–200 mm F2.8 zoom on one camera for when the person approaches the court but is still some way away, with a shorter lens, say a 35 mm, on a second camera with a flashgun, for when they are closer. When the person is leaving the court then an 80–200 mm F2.8 lens might be a little long. A 24 mm and a 50 mm lens might be a better choice.

Sometimes people will pose. They know it puts them in a better light and makes a less newsworthy picture than if they rush into the building with their hand in front of their face.

Photographers working alone outside court in the case of criminal proceedings are more vulnerable to harassment from court officials and friends of the accused than those in a group. It might be better to retreat a little from the doorway and use a longer lens.

It is possible to check the identity of the defendant once the hearing starts, either from the press bench, or from the public gallery; most courts do not allow photographers to take cameras into court, but provide somewhere for them to be left. If the photographer is sending the film back to the office, rather than

Figure 6.7   The rain man cometh: The fact that it poured with rain on the day that the government's newly appointed Drought Minister arrived to inspect a half-empty reservoir made sure his visit would be well covered in the next day's papers. It was necessary to ask him to hold the umbrella slightly to one side to allow what little light there was to reach his face (© Torbay News Agency)

Figure 6.8 Politics: Shirley Williams, David Steel and David Owen at an SDP Conference in Torquay. Wide aperture lenses are essential for photography at party conferences – especially as the light levels provided for the television cameras diminish with improvements in their technology. The big event of any conference is the set-piece speech by the party leader, and it is worth, if possible, having photographers covering it from different angles (© Torbay News Agency)

taking it back in person, it will help the editor looking at the negatives if there is a brief description of the defendant: 'Balding, glasses, dark suit.'

If the person is in custody, either before or after the case, then the tactics required differ. At most courts the defendants are driven into an enclosed secure courtyard before they are walked into the cells to wait for their appearance. On rare occasions it is possible to look into these courtyards from adjacent buildings; if it is a first appearance, there may have been a chance to see the defendant getting into the vehicle in a similar courtyard at the police station. There is no chance of breaking the law at the police station, but taking such pictures at the court is undoubtedly an offence. Elsewhere the defendant may be clearly visible as they are walked into court from a bus or taxi. Sometimes the escorting police and prison officers put the ubiquitous grey blanket over the prisoner's head. Sometimes they do not. Be discreet, and you may be lucky.

The only alternative is to try to photograph the defendant through the windows of the vehicle carrying him or her to court; a 'car shot'. The technique is to hold the camera and flashgun as close to the window as possible to minimize reflections, set the shutter at its faster speed at which it synchronizes with flash to eliminate any exposure from the daylight and use a wide angle lens for maximum depth of field. Some people use the automatic exposure facility available on most flashguns; others feel that there is too much chance of the flash bouncing back off the vehicle and fooling the sensor. They use the flashgun at full or half-power, and set the aperture for the distance at which they expect to work. It helps to have an auxiliary power pack to minimize the recycling time between flashes.

Sometimes it is possible to focus the lens by looking through the camera. At other times, it will be necessary to set the distance before taking the picture.

Think carefully where will be the best place to take the picture. A prisoner who does not wish to be photographed may cover his or her face when the vehicle is near the court; the police may stop the traffic to give the vehicle a clear run into the building. It may be better to go a few hundred yards along the street where the vehicle may stop at traffic lights and where the prisoner is not expecting a press photographer.

It is a bit hit and miss. On many occasions the windows are too dirty, there is a flash reflection in the middle of the picture, the picture is perfectly sharp and perfectly exposed, but it is of a prison warder, or the prisoner is covered by a blanket. But on the occasions that it works, it is worth all the failures.

Finally, if all your efforts are in vain, check with the senior police officer involved with the case. They may be prepared to release a picture of the prisoner if convicted. And they may have pictures of the scene of the crime or other relevant background material.

Collects

Sometimes it is not possible to take a picture of a person in the news, as they may have died or be in custody awaiting trial.

Calling on the relative of a person who has died, often in tragic circumstances, to acquire a picture of the deceased is a task no photographer enjoys.

Initially the call may be to the immediate family – parents or brothers and sisters – for whom the distress of the bereavement is the greatest.

A reporter frequently accompanies the photographer, and the reason for the visit should be explained as tactfully as possible, with due expressions of sympathy for their loss.

The reaction will vary. Sometimes you will be invited in and offered refreshment; the family may find it easier to talk about their loss with a complete stranger and want a fitting tribute to appear in the press or may be angry about the circumstances in which the death occurred. At other times the door will be slammed in your face.

Hopefully the reaction will be somewhere in between and the relatives will have some pictures of the deceased. The best picture is a balance between sharpness, image size, expression and the age of the picture.

Ask if it is possible to take the pictures back to the office where they can be copied better. Explain that you will return them at the earliest opportunity – but remember these pictures are precious to them, and make sure that you do. If they decline, you will have to copy them there and then. This is the time that having a close-up lens to screw to the front of the camera will be very useful. Try to copy the pictures using available light as it is easier to see if there are any unwanted reflections on the print. Check carefully the identity of anybody else in the pictures.

There may be occasions when it is not possible to contact the immediate family. Neighbours may be able to tell you where other relatives live. It is sometimes possible to make the initial approach to the family through a sympathetic neighbour.

Trying to collect a picture of somebody in police custody awaiting trial is harder as the family will resent the interest being shown by the press. It may help to find out a little about the person involved. If married, it might be possible to find some pictures taken at the wedding (but beware of copyright problems). The name of the church or register office and the witnesses will be on the wedding certificate, a copy of which can be obtained from St Catherine's House, Kingsway, London; if they have played a sport there might be a recent team picture; if they have left school or university recently there may be graduation pictures. Discreet enquiries may have to be made with neighbours or at the local pub.

Aerial photography

Aerial pictures can be used either by themselves, for example to show the progress of a new bridge across a river, or as part of the wider coverage of a news story like a train crash. They can also be used as 'fillers' to show an unusual view of a village or town and are highly saleable to readers.

Helicopters are ideal for aerial photography. Although the windows that open tend to be small it is quite straightforward to remove the door (provided, of course, that you ask the pilot to do it before you take off). Helicopters are more expensive to hire than fixed-wing aircraft but they are able to hover for precise positioning when taking the picture and to land almost anywhere. It may be possible to pick-up and drop-off a photographer at a site close to the office rather than going to and from the helicopter's base. Fixed wing aircraft suffer from less vibration than helicopters and are faster over longer distances. It is not worth taking aerial pictures through the plastic windows of any aircraft; they are usually dirty and are not optically flat, which means the picture will be seriously distorted.

Almost any helicopter is suitable for aerial photography, but check that the exhaust will not be blowing past the window or door you intend to work from; it will cause the picture to shimmer. If chartering a plane, ensure that the position of the wings will not obstruct the view from the passenger seat.

Private pilots are not allowed to carry out aerial photography for commercial purposes. A picture desk should have the name and telephone numbers of the nearest helicopter/aircraft charter firms to hand.

On major news stories, some newspapers share the cost of a helicopter charter. They may each put a photographer aboard or decide that just one photographer will go and shoot enough material for everybody to have some original negatives.

It is vital to brief the pilot about the purpose of the flight. He or she may have to file a flight plan or heed restrictions about flying in controlled airspace near airports or military installations. There are restrictions governing the minimum height at which aircraft may fly.

At some incidents the police may specify an 'exclusion zone', prohibiting aircraft from flying below a certain height within a given distance of the scene. The purpose is not to prevent the press from photographing the incident, but to allow helicopters owned by the police and other authorities to fly unimpeded. If the visibility is good it may still be worth flying above the exclusion zone.

The greatest problem facing aerial photography is the natural haze caused by dust, water vapour and pollutants which all tend to reduce contrast. With black and white photography it is possible to enhance the contrast by using a yellow or orange filter on the lens, deliberately underexposing the negative, extending the development time, and using a more contrasty grade of paper when the final print is made. These measures are not practical when shooting in colour. Ensure that there is an ultraviolet filter on the lens and see if a polarizing filter further increases the contrast.

A photographer can have no control over the weather when asked to fly on a hard news story. For a feature-type picture it is only worth flying if the conditions are right; work out, too, at what time of day the light will be coming from the best direction for the subject.

An 80–200 mm zoom lens is ideal for aerial photography as it enables the subject to be framed quickly and accurately but also take a shorter lens and a 300 mm and perhaps even a 500 mm. Use motor drives sparingly as it can be time-consuming trying to reload in a cramped cockpit. Try to keep cameras out of the slipstream of a fixed wing plane or the downdraught of helicopter rotors. If flying with the door open it goes without saying that all cameras, lenses and bags should be securely attached. The shutter speed should be 1/500th of a second or faster to minimize camera shake. There is little need to close the lens down more than a couple of stops as the subject is distant, photographically speaking, and there is no need for a large depth of field.

Take pictures on the flight to and from the subject as aerial pictures of landmarks and villages and towns make useful 'filler' pictures for local papers, are useful to have in the library and are highly saleable to readers.

FASHION

All newspapers use fashion pictures. Sometimes they are supplied directly to newspapers by the firms which make the clothes or they may be shot in the studio by the paper's own photographers. At other times firms may launch their latest range of swimwear, hats, underwear, winter coats or whatever at a photocall for the press and provide two or three models to show the clothes off to their best advantage. Photographers are also invited to attend fashion shows where the models parade the latest outfits along the catwalk and after the show there may or may not be the chance to take a model or two and some nice outfits outside and do some more leisurely pictures. And there is plenty of scope at certain jobs, for instance Ladies' Day at Ascot, or Henley Regatta, for photographers to provide their picture editors with the latest outfits worn by high society.

Good fashion pictures show readers either the unusual – a hat with a bowl of imitation strawberries and cream on top; the aspirational – an evening dress made from the finest silk costing thousands of pounds; or the paradoxical – a model wearing swimwear on the day that the country is under a foot of snow.

At a photocall where the organizers have provided a model, the clothes must be selected with care. Black reproduces badly and checked patterns can also be troublesome. If working in colour, both red and yellow will attract the reader's eye.

For a full length picture the ideal lens is a 180 mm F2.8 or longer, working nearly wide open to use differential focusing to eliminate the background.

Good fashion pictures need enthusiasm from both the model and the photographer. The model must not usually stand in a static position, but 'be doing something', be it walking down a set of grand steps, twirling a parasol, using a mobile phone or being sprayed with water from a hose by a park gardener.

When the models are parading along a catwalk, there are two possible techniques; either get a seat at the edge of the catwalk and photograph the models as they walk past or work from further away using a longer lens.

The first technique may give a greater sense of immediacy and capture more of the sense of the occasion. Expect to have to use flash, and several lenses, perhaps as short as a 35 mm. Arrive early to get the best position. Wait until the model comes 'into range' before taking the picture. Beware of fellow photographers beside you leaning out and blocking your view. It helps to work next to colleagues you can trust. The second technique may mean using a 180 mm or 300 mm lens, probably by available light, from head-on to the catwalk.

For photographers on those newspapers which usually print fashion pictures sent to them by clothing manufacturers and retailers, it may make an interesting change to ask local fashion boutiques if they might be able to help with half a dozen different outfits that could be used for a fashion 'spread'. The harder part is finding the models. The shop may know of some suitable girls, or if the newspaper can afford the fees, there may be a model agency in the town or city. Alternatively it may be worth checking who is the current local beauty queen. Good backdrops can be found anywhere. Although it may be better to start with a local park, stately home or marina, fashion pictures can be taken in the most unlikely of settings, provided that it is visually interesting.

SOFT NEWS

Soft news is just about anything which is not hard news, sport, or features. It is invariably an event anticipated through an entry on the diary and coverage can be planned in advance. Photographers from other newspapers would be expected to be there. This type of assignment is the staple diet of the press photographer and involves everything from the Slimmer of the Year competition, the local carnival, a customer winning one minute of free shopping in a local supermarket, the annual Trooping the Colour ceremony, the mayor visiting a local factory and the blowing up of a block of flats to the rehearsals of the local dramatic society.

The one common factor, as opposed to hard news, is that the photographer is usually assigned for the job in plenty of time to think out possible picture ideas. Sometimes the PR at the event will bring along a useful prop; in the case of the Slimmer of the Year, it might be a giant cutout picture of the winner taken a year ago when she was seven stone heavier. But on most occasions it is up to the photographer to think up the picture idea and come up with any necessary props. Some years ago I was assigned to photograph the Chairman of the House of Commons cycling committee campaigning during the general election in his

Figure 6.9 Daleks crossing the road: A newspaper's production facilities cannot cope if all the material for an edition arrives at once. Some pages are prepared for press earlier than others. So the earlier that a 'soft' picture appears in the Chief Sub-Editor's tray, the more likely it is to be used. Good public relations staff realize this, and ensure that photo-calls aimed at the national press happen before mid-morning. A preview of an auction of costumes from the television series *Dr Who* was a soft news story to which all national newspapers would be expected to send a photographer – and the Daleks were the stars of the sale. I arranged for two of the staff to push them across a busy road nearby. Using an 80–200 mm zoom lens at the longer end and nearly wide open at F4 meant that the distracting background was out focus but still recognizable as a London street. I also did pictures of the daleks waiting at the pedestrian crossing, but the picture of them 'on the way to the saleroom' was the one the picture editor preferred (© Press Association)

local constituency. But it needed more than just a picture of him cycling through the country lanes ... it needed him using a megaphone on the bicycle. A friendly school where I had taken some pictures a week or so earlier and which I passed on the way lent me their megaphone for an hour, and the picture was well published the next day.

On other soft news jobs it is a matter of deciding upon the best vantage point. Coverage of the local carnival will demand a number of pictures of people on their floats, but also a good 'general view' (sometimes known as a GV) of the procession passing through the town's main street. A trip along the route a day or two earlier will enable a photographer to pick out a good viewpoint and acquire any necessary permissions. And then keep a mental note of it for next year. Many soft stories are annual events – the mayor-making, the Oxford and Cambridge Boat Race, Derby Day, a marathon, swimmers taking a dip on Boxing Day and it is always worth having a look through the files to see what was published in previous years. Whether you do the same or try for something that bit different is up to you.

On any soft news story, the picture desk will expect to see a selection of photographs. Sometimes your paper will not be the first one to carry the picture – perhaps it is a weekly and there is an evening paper in the area – so it is essential

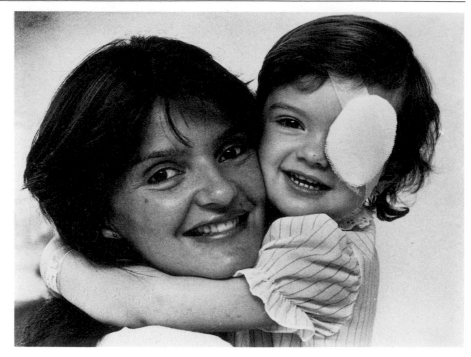

Figure 6.10   Anne and Amy Nolan: News about showbusiness personalities and their families is always of interest to tabloid newspapers and their readers. Little Amy, daughter of the singer Anne Nolan, was hurt during a shooting accident at a local fairground but was soon back home after treatment where I took the picture of the two of them with a single flash bounced off a large piece of white card. It was well published the next day in the national press, and we were busy for several weeks to come as fans of the Nolans wrote asking for copies of the picture (© Torbay News Agency)

to take two or three different pictures, so that the one which has already published can be discarded.

Some jobs, for instance the demolition of a bridge or an attempt to break the record for the most number of people sitting in a Mini, can be illustrated with a sequence of pictures. Alternatively the first, or last, of the series could be used as a 'teaser' on the front page to encourage readers to turn to the page with the rest of the pictures and story.

If possible, turn up early and stay at the job until you are sure that you will miss nothing further by leaving. Turning up early may give you the chance to set up a picture alone, find the best vantage point or discuss possible picture ideas with the organizer, winner or whoever. Leaving only when the job is over allows you to keep an eye on what the competition is doing.

At jobs like fashion photocalls or celebrities launching a new product where there are lots of photographers, it can be chaos if everybody tries to organize the picture simultaneously. If you are happy with the way that the session is going, fine; if not, do not hesitate to suggest a better way that the photograph could be taken, but it is courteous not to rearrange a picture until the photographer who set it up has taken it. At other times, when there are just a few photographers, each may take it in turn to set up a particular picture and it becomes a matter of

Figure 6.11 Sheep in the classroom: A friend who worked for a local radio station told me about a primary school where a lamb was being used to teach children about nature. Although they were mainly recording her weight during biology lessons, the picture I needed was the lamb sitting at a desk, reading a book and taking part in classes. The lamb required a certain amount of encouragement and we needed an enormous amount of patience before she was sitting comfortably. The picture was taken mainly with available light, but with a little bit of flash to clean up the shadows, and was well used locally and nationally as sub-editors wrote puns about how she wrote essays with sheeps pens and hoped to go to ewe-university after leaving school (© Torbay News Agency)

honour to change the picture slightly from one taken beforehand and not to come back for a 'second turn' and copy the idea of a subsequent photographer.

On any soft news job it is important to take a good portrait of the person at the centre of the story. It can be put in the library and used if there are subsequent developments in the story. And if the story that you are going to photograph involves any element of risk, photograph the participant beforehand. An example might be a teenager who is going to be a 'human cannon ball'; no picture editor would be pleased if the stunt went wrong, the teenager was injured and you did not have a 'before' picture.

Sometimes the organizer of an event has a specific idea as to the picture that he or she feels should be taken. Even if you think it has no chance of appearing in the paper, it is diplomatic to try to oblige them, and then rearrange the picture to suit your paper's needs.

ROYAL

Members of the Royal family are popular subjects for newspaper photographers.

A visit to a provincial town may mean the local paper deploying its entire photographic staff to provide a mass of pictures for special previews, supple-

Figure 6.12   Man with big sharks: This is one of those pictures which almost take themselves. *The Sun* asked me to photograph a man who claimed to have caught some record-breaking sharks by dipping his bait, a Cornish pasty, in a well-known brand of lager. There was an obvious headline:

LAGER AND LINE:
Heineken catches the sharks other beers can't reach.

I rang the man and we met by the harbourside. He had brought his fishing rod and on the way I had purchased a couple of cans of the lager, a Cornish pasty and a beer glass. The picture was taken with a 24 mm lens to accentuate the size of the beer glass and pasty. I also asked him if he had any pictures of his record-breaking catch, and he lent me a couple of photos that I could copy. From the time of the first call to the picture being on the wire was no more than three hours (© Torbay News Agency)

ments and the like. Although most royal visits start mid-morning, no effort will be spared to get the pictures into the earliest possible edition.

And if the visit is by a member of the family who they consider to be 'popular',

Figure 6.13   Mother and baby: A call from the local zoo alerted me to this colobus monkey and her baby – and fortunately the baby had white hair. Such a picture would be welcomed by a local newspaper – but would only have limited appeal to the nationals, unless it was accompanied by a particularly strong story. Keeping the lens close to the bars means that the bars and netting are so out of focus that they are invisible. A few prints to the keeper and the zoo's PR staff will be gratefully received and should ensure that the calls keep coming (© Torbay News Agency)

the national tabloids and those freelances who specialize in the coverage of the royal family will also be there. Although the national and local press may not be looking for the same kind of picture, their reasons for being there are the same – pictures of the Royal family interest the readers of newspapers and magazines.

Figure 6.14   Butterfly man: Placing the butterfly on the expert's face provided a sense of scale and involved him in the picture more than merely asking him to hold one of his collection. Although direct flash is not the best form of lighting, I used it because it provided good depth of field and brought out all the detail in the butterfly's wings (© Torbay News Agency)

Figure 6.15   Pedal car: This picture illustrated a story about a school which was selling the antique pedal car it had used for several years to teach children road safety. It is a good story for a local paper, and would also appeal to the 'heavy' national newspapers (especially if offered as a 'Sunday for Monday'), as well, perhaps, as the *Times Educational Supplement* and both motoring and general interest magazines. It is important to shoot several different pictures. As well as this one, I photographed the children polishing the bonnet and a wide angle picture of the car with the two pupils in front of their school building (© Torbay News Agency)

Figure 6.16   Cat for sale – free house: The cat was for sale for £40 000, and the house came free. It was a story which must have been used dozens of times before, and certainly it has been done several times since, but the tale of the pricey puss and the delightful Georgian mews house which came with him captured the hearts of many national newspaper picture editors. A picture story like this is only going to get in a national paper on a quiet day and needs to be offered in the morning to make an 'early' page. This story was discovered just after the New Year when news is traditionally very quiet (© Torbay News Agency)

Figure 6.17 Policeman wearing fume mask: On my way to buy a lunchtime sandwich I spotted this policeman wearing a fume mask as he directed the traffic. I popped back to the office, collected a 400 mm lens, and returned to the junction to take the picture. Within a few minutes I was joined by two other photographers; one had also been passing, the other had been assigned to the job after his editor, who was driving past, alerted his picture desk. The picture published well the next day, and has since been used by an environmental pressure group in one of their advertisements (© Press Association)

Figure 6.18   Little boys washing in bath: During one of our regular droughts newspapers had tired of pictures of empty reservoirs and it was a question of finding something that 'little bit different'. I thought that a picture of youngsters washing with water drawn from an old hand-pump would show that they were doing their bit to save water. Lots of people knew of old pumps or wells, but it took three days to find one which worked. The house where these two boys lived also had a tin bath in the garden, so the picture was made (© Torbay News Agency)

The rota

Because of the interest and number of photographers who wish to be present at an event, many of the Royal family's official engagements are covered by a rota. The rota is a representative selection of photographers (and print and radio reporters and TV crews) who are under an obligation to make their material available to other similar organizations. As well as royal events, some engagements carried out by government ministers and visits by foreign heads of state are covered by a rota party. The system is also known as 'pooling'.

Members of the rota are recognizable by a coloured pass, issued in the case of royal pictures by the Buckingham Palace Press Office. For a typical event outside London, there might be a pass for a photographer from the Newspaper Publishers Association (NPA) representing the national press, one for the Wire Photos Agencies (WPA) representing the Press Association, the Associated Press and Reuters, two or three for the Newspaper Society (NS) representing the local press and one for a photographer from the host organization. Sometimes there is a further pass, principally for colour agencies and magazines, which is shared between the Council of Photographic News Agencies (CPNA), the Periodical Publishers Association (PPA) and the Independent Photographers Association (IPA). On occasions when space is limited the number of passes issued is further restricted; in extreme cases there may be just one photographer in the rota.

Figure 6.19   Boat race cox thrown in the water: The traditional end to the boat race – the winning cox is thrown into the Thames by his team-mates. It is always a bit of a scramble to disembark from the press launch which follows the race onto the bank for the presentation to the winning crew. The next year we did not make it ashore in time after the press launch and its skipper were stopped for questioning by government inspectors and the river police! An annual event, the Boat Race has been covered from every possible angle from the sky, bridges, banks and even by a cameraman in a wet suit as photographers try to come up with a picture that is 'something different' (© Press Association)

As the name suggests, members of each of these bodies take it in turns to be the rota photographer at events they are interested in covering.

The rota party is usually conducted through a royal visit by a representative of the Central Office of Information (COI). The COI have offices in London, Bristol, Cambridge, Leeds and Birmingham. In Scotland, Wales and Northern Ireland, rotas are conducted by the Scottish, Welsh and Northern Ireland Offices.

From an editorial point of view rota pictures have an obvious drawback – they are not exclusive; all one's rivals can print them. The usual arrangement is that after an engagement the rota holder will issue a set of pictures to those who are entitled to them. The set can be just one picture, or several, but it must include any pictures that the rota holder intends to use in his or her own publication.

Fixed points

As well as the rota, many visits have specific fixed points from which photographers can work. Usually run by either the police or the COI, they may cover

Figure 6.20 Princess and admirer: The Princess of Wales receives a kiss on the hand from an admirer during a walkabout in the streets of Budapest. Sometimes walkabouts are planned during a royal visit, while at other times they happen spontaneously. Frequently they make better photographs than the more formal parts of the engagement. This picture was taken on a 35–70 mm zoom, an ideal lens for this type of fast-moving situation (© Press Association)

arrivals at airports and railway stations and planned walkabouts. These are run on a first-come first-served basis; sometimes passes are issued, while at other times a recognized press card is sufficient to gain access. Unlike a rota, there is no obligation to share pictures taken from fixed points. Fixed points can get crowded, and a small stepladder with two or three rungs will be very useful to look over the heads of one's colleagues in front.

The stepladder also comes in handy for a third way of covering royal events – from behind the public. Working behind the crowd has the benefits of not blocking the view of people who have waited, perhaps for many hours, to catch a glimpse of a member of the Royal family and that it is possible to move as the event or walkabout progresses. Some of the best pictures are taken from behind the crowd as members of the Royal family receive flowers or presents from wellwishers.

Unofficial engagements

As well as their official engagements, there are a number of other events which photographers who regularly cover the Royal family know they are likely to attend. These include the Windsor Horse Show, the Christmas Day Service at Windsor Castle or Sandringham, the Derby and Ascot week. Sometimes the organizers make special arrangements for photographers, while at others they can buy tickets like any member of the public.

Figure 6.21   Princess Royal in Soviet Union: The Princess Royal licks her finger after dipping it in a bowl of goats' milk during a visit to Arbizhil in Eastern Siberia, USSR. The local authority had organized a press centre in the town hall from where I tried to wire the picture back to London on the Soviet telephone system, but it took so long to get a line through to London and it was of such poor quality that a transmission was impossible. By a remarkable coincidence journalists covering the visit were staying in the same hotel as the advance party for the Camel Trophy Car Rally, and I was able to use their satellite telephone to transmit the picture to London (© Press Association)

Equipment

Most photographers on royal engagements work with three cameras, one with a 35–70 mm F2.8 zoom, one with an 80–200 F2.8 zoom and the third with a 300 mm F2.8 lens. When working at a fixed point, a 500 mm F4 is also useful. Some events call for even longer lenses. After the Trooping of the Colour, members of the Royal family watch a flypast from the balcony of Buckingham Palace. A photographer working from the Queen Victoria Memorial who was hoping for a reasonable close-up of two or three people would probably use a 600 mm lens and a 2 × teleconverter.

Overseas tours

Members of the Royal family on tour abroad provide colourful pictures for newspapers and magazines. Again, some photos are 'pooled' and others are taken at fixed points or from behind the crowd.

Photographers working for newspapers have to be aware of the time difference between London and where they are. From that point of view it is easier to work to the east, which is ahead of London, rather than to the west – America – which is behind. In years gone by, photographers had to find a local picture

Figure 6.22   Queen Mum at Dartmouth: The Queen Mother is a favourite with all press photographers. A true professional herself, she ensures that everybody has a chance to get a good picture. These two were taken when she took the salute and inspected the young officers passing out at the Lord High Admiral's Divisions at the Britannia Royal Naval College, Dartmouth. The picture of the equerry holding the royal handbag only works if the Queen Mother is kept in the picture, even if she does have her back to the camera. The other picture is strongly backlit – note the reflection coming off the officer's cap nearest to the camera – but this provided a pleasing soft light on the Queen Mother's face (© Herald Express Ltd)

agency to process and wire their photographs. Nowadays, although they will be delighted to find a one hour photo centre to develop the negatives, all carry their own processing facilities and equipment to wire the pictures from their hotel bedrooms. Some even carry satellite telephones to bypass the local telephone network. Magazine photographers have to negotiate with airline and customs officials to ship their precious films back to their offices.

Overseas tours can be testing times for photographers, moving every other night to a different hotel, working in a country whose language they do not understand, whose culture they may not appreciate and whose officials will certainly not have met the royal 'rat pack' in strength. The problem solvers are the diplomats from the British Embassy who understand the country, the language, the culture and the officials and the Buckingham Palace press officers who want the tour to be well reported, both back home and in the host country, and who strive to accommodate the needs of photographers and journalists.

ADVERTISING FEATURES

Many provincial newspapers regularly carry advertising features of a page or two, principally of fairly small display advertisements but with a modest amount of editorial copy, to promote anything from a new nightclub, supermarket or garage to the opening of a shopping precinct. Frequently a newspaper's photographic staff will be asked to provide the illustrations.

Sometimes the task is straightforward; for instance, a picture of the outside of a shop or hotel. Take it in decent light, ensure that the picture is not spoilt by parked or passing cars, try to keep the verticals upright and use a polarizing filter, if necessary, to remove any unwanted reflections from shop windows.

But there are other times when, for example, the owner of the premises insists on a picture of the interior of a huge nightclub, even though there is only space for a two-column picture, or there are workmen everywhere struggling to complete the project.

It is necessary to be diplomatic. Suggest that it may be better to show just some of the premises (from which the workmen can be cleared for a few minutes) and use members of staff as models, rather than a large empty room. Perhaps it might be better to use a picture of the owner standing by the sign outside so that potential customers can recognize the premises.

A tripod is vital for some interior pictures; two or three small flashguns with slave units can be invaluable for lighting larger areas and a star-burst filter can add sparkle to a picture of a nightclub or restaurant with lots of lights.

Press photographers do not think of advertising features as exciting work, but they are vital to a newspaper's revenue. An advertiser who likes the picture may order additional prints, and book another feature.

SPORT

All newspapers cover sport, and although some have specialist sports photographers, most cameramen will spend some of their Saturday afternoons on the touchline or boundary.

Any newspaper photographer would expect to cover cricket, football, tennis, golf, rugby union or rugby league, racing and boxing fairly regularly. Other sports, like sailing, bowls, athletics, ice hockey, autosports or swimming, might not be covered so often but they should not be ignored for unusual pictures.

Sports photography is a challenge – there is no asking a footballer to 'score that goal again'; competitive – top events attract photographers from all over the world; and technically demanding – low light, fast-moving subjects and minimal depth of field.

Sports photography is very much about capturing critical moments, a ball hitting a racquet, goals, a horse throwing a jockey or the bails flying; and the techniques required are honed with constant practice. It is also vital to have an understanding of the game, not only of the rules, but of how particular individuals play it.

The developments in lens technology in recent years have done much to assist sports photographers. Modern telephoto lenses have a maximum aperture and performance that would have been thought impossible by photographers working 20 years ago. But it is at a price, in terms of both hard cash and weight. Apart from a brighter image in the viewfinder, the advantages of using a 500 mm F4 as opposed to a 500 mm F8, or a 300 mm F2 rather than a 300 mm F4.5, are the chance to use a slower, more finely grained film, or to be able to work under poorer light conditions without using a faster film.

Sports photographers tend to avoid zoom lenses – especially for action pictures. They are slower, both to use and in the amount of light that they transmit, than fixed focal length lenses. And although, for obvious reasons, sports photographers mainly use telephoto lenses, wide angle lenses, especially super-wides like 15 mm or 20 mm, find favour for dramatic pictures from unusual viewpoints.

Film quality too has improved. It is not many years ago that High Speed Ektachrome was 160 ISO. Now transparency film is available at speeds of 1600 ISO. And although the need to produce high-quality materials for the mass market has meant that colour negative films have improved in quality, the users of black and white have not been neglected. Fuji produce a Neopan 1600 ISO film with a quality to rival the 400 ISO films of a decade ago.

However, sports photographers have little control over the light they work in. In spite of the latest advances in film and lenses there may be times when it is necessary to 'push process' the film by extending its development to compensate for deliberate underexposure. This is a technique with which all photographers should be familiar, and is discussed in Chapter 5.

Rain and the electronics found in modern cameras do not always mix. Professional photographers have to work in all weathers, and although most cameras are well sealed, it is essential to devise some method of keeping the camera and lens dry. There are purpose-made plastic covers available. Sometimes it is impossible and the only hope is to keep the front of the lens dry (a piece of chamois leather is ideal), and to dry the camera out as soon after use as possible.

All professional cameras either have a motor drive built-in, or can have one attached to the bottom. They enable the photographer to keep his or her eye to the viewfinder while the film is advanced and may help balance the weight of a camera and telephoto lens. However, they need to be used sparingly, or, as some can expose film at the rate of more than five frames-a-second, a photographer will spend more time reloading the camera than taking pictures. They can be used in 'bursts', for instance to photograph a horse clearing a steeplechase fence,

Figure 6.23   Bowled: An afternoon spent photographing local cricket can be most rewarding. The wickets often tumble quickly and the strokes are quite unorthodox. Whereas a 600 mm lens is probably the shortest usable for County and Test cricket, a 300 mm or 400 mm lens can be quite adequate at games played at a lower level. This picture was taken at a local league game in Devon, using a 400 mm Novoflex (© Torbay News Agency)

but they are no substitute for accurate timing in photographing a tennis player hitting the ball.

Cricket

Cricket is a great game to photograph as under most circumstances they stop playing when it starts raining or gets dark.

Naturally, the action is centred around the wickets in the middle of the pitch, so a good telephoto lens is a must. A 300 mm might be long enough at a small local ground; a 600 mm would be needed at a larger Test ground. A good compromise is a 300 mm F2.8 with 1.4× and 2× converters. Because cricket is usually played in good light, it is not essential to purchase expensive wide aperture lenses; several independent manufacturers offer 400 mm F5.6 lenses of very acceptable quality for a small fraction of a camera manufacturer's 400 mm F3.5. Whatever the lens, it should be supported on a sturdy tripod, and the shutter tripped with a cable release.

The one drawback of cricket is that after every six balls, there is a change of bowling and the action moves down the other end, and what was an excellent position to work from becomes less than ideal.

Figure 6.24   Tom Moody ties himself up in knots: A good cricket picture does not necessarily need bat, ball or stumps. Australian Tom Moody ties himself up in knots as he warms up to bowl during his team's match against Middlesex during their 1989 tour (© Press Association)

Figure 6.25   Lineker scores three: Sometimes a footballer's reaction after he has scored is better than the picture of the actual goal. Gary Lineker's delight at scoring a hat-trick while playing for England against Turkey was, I confess, my only decent picture in 90 minutes of rain-soaked football at Wembley, but it published widely the next morning. Floodlit football is a test of skill for any photographer. As light levels are low, the lens is usually wide open, and there is no margin for focusing error (© Press Association)

Figure 6.26   Mudlarks: Local games are excellent opportunities for good sports pictures – the enthusiasm, if not the skill, of the players is every bit as great as that found in higher levels – and a photographer has far more access and choice of positions. Dark winter days and nights may mean pushing the film – a technique of deliberate underexposure, compensated for by extending the development. Most films can be pushed one stop with only a minor increase in grain – beyond this, detail in the shadows starts to disappear (© Torbay News Agency)

At most local games it is possible to work from virtually anywhere around the boundary, other, obviously, than in front of the sight screen. And do remember not to cross the sight screen behind the bowler's arm. At County or Test grounds, the positions from which photographers can work are more restricted. Special areas may be designated for them so that neither advertising hoardings nor the view of the public are obstructed.

One of the best places to work from is a few yards around the boundary in a clockwise direction from a sight screen. From here there is a good view of the batsman when he is at the further set of stumps; depending upon the length of lens used, it may be possible to include the wicket-keeper and slips. When he is at the nearer step of stumps, the view is not so good for pictures of him playing strokes (other than down the leg side), but is excellent if he is bowled and the bails fly. Run-outs can occur at both ends of the pitch, and a photographer must be prepared to shift focus quickly from one set of stumps to another.

It is also possible to work from a position at right angles to the wicket. This provides a good view whichever end the batsman is at (although he will have his back to the photographer at one end), but unless the wicket-keeper is standing up to the stumps it can make for a rather 'loose' picture.

Some grounds offer photographers an elevated position from which to work. This means that there will not be any fielders between the photographer and the

Figure 6.27 Horse racing: Over the sticks at Newton Abbot: this picture was taken on a camera with a 24 mm lens placed on the ground next to the fence, and the shutter tripped with an electric cable release. As the viewfinder eyepiece was so low, I removed the prism of the Nikon F2 and framed the picture directly from the focusing screen. The spectators and grandstand add to the picture. Expect to use a shutter speed of at least 1/1000th of a second (© Torbay News Agency)

batsman, as sometimes happens when working at ground level, but makes for uninteresting pictures with just grass as a background. It is hard to tell whether the picture was taken at Lords or a local ground.

Elevated positions are safer, whereas ground positions produce much better pictures, but there is the chance that the view will be blocked by a fielder.

Some photographers deploy more than one camera. They operate one themselves, and fire another which has another view of the action by means of a wireless remote control. Clearly such a remote camera has to have an automatic exposure control.

Photographing cricket requires patience; every ball has to be watched, and an eye kept open for any other 'off the ball' incidents like protests from either players or spectators and streakers.

If the 'home' team is batting, then the photographer's job is easy, as some nice pictures of them in action at the crease will do fine; although do not totally ignore their team-mates who may be on the pavilion balcony to applaud their century-scoring batsman. But sometimes the 'home' team is fielding, and the newspaper's readers will not be very interested in pictures of the 'away' team's batsmen in action, and bowling pictures can be rather dull. It may help to shoot the action a little more loosely than usual to include any appeals from the wicket-keeper or bowler.

Cricketers' white clothes fool TTL exposure meters into thinking there is more light than there actually is. Provided that the photographer is not sitting in shadow, it is better to take an incident light reading from the camera position, or to use a spot meter and read the light from the player's faces. Alternatively, take a reading from the grass. On bright sunny days, the contrast range between a cricketer's whites and his face in the shade of his cap will be very high indeed, and careful darkroom technique will be needed to maintain detail in both. When using conventional black and white film, it will help reduce the contrast range if the film is overexposed and subsequently underdeveloped.

Captioning cricket pictures is not a problem provided the information is recorded carefully. At a local match, a photographer will usually be able to check the names of bowlers, batsmen and wicket-keepers with the scorers, or team-mates; it is a good idea to get all the names from the captains before the game starts, so that during the game no time is wasted checking spellings or first names. Against the number of every frame taken should be recorded the name of the batsman and the bowler and whether a run was scored or a wicket taken. As a cross-check it may help to jot down whether a batsman is right- or left-handed, or was wearing a cap or a helmet. To help with rapid editing some photographers expose a blank frame or take a picture of the scoreboard after a wicket falls.

At County matches, do not assume that the batsmen appear in the order on the scoreboard. Most scoreboards have the name or number of the batsman next to his total. At Test Matches, it may be possible to listen to the running commentary on a radio to determine the names of the players. Do not neglect the scoreboard as a possible picture. A picture of it is useful if a player or team in a Test makes a record high (or low) score.

Soccer

It is possible to take good football pictures with any lens from a 50 mm or 85 mm right up to a 500 mm.

Football may be about scoring goals, but today's sports editors want more – midfield action, sendings-off, celebrations, players receiving treatment and managers in despair. A photographer needs to be able to capture an incident anywhere on the pitch.

The 'traditional' place for football photographers to work from is along the goal line. Here the goalmouth action can be captured with any lens from an 85 mm through to a 300 mm, depending upon how near to the posts the photographer is. Too close to the posts, and it is hard to see the action happening the other side beyond the goalmouth; too close to the corner flag and there is the risk that a player or the referee will be in the way at the crucial moment. Try to sit a couple of yards in from the edge of the penalty box, from where a 135 mm lens will be ideal. As well as a shorter lens for goalmouth action, use a longer lens of 300 mm or 400 mm to capture action in midfield.

The goal line is ideal when a newspaper is primarily interested in the attack of just one team, but a photographer who needs to capture the goals at both ends may try to work from the side of the pitch, along the touchline. If sitting near the half-way line, then a 400 mm lens will be ideal for goalmouth action at either end. If the photographer is closer to one goal than the other, it may be best to cover one goalmouth with a 300 mm, and have a 500 mm for action at the other end. A second or third camera should have a shorter lens, 85 mm or 180 mm, to use for any incident close to the photographer.

At a local match it is usually possible to work from anywhere – but do not block the view of the manager or the trainer. At most professional grounds photographers are more restricted. They may have to work from behind hoardings (so the advertisements can be seen on television), or may have to lie down, so that the crowd can see. Usually they sit, either on camping stools or on lens boxes. At some grounds there are trenches in which photographers stand. Long lenses are best supported on a monopod. Tripods are not usually allowed. They are not popular with the clubs, whose expensive players might hurt themselves if they fell over them, or with other photographers, whose view they can obstruct.

To stop the movement of the players the camera shutter speed should be at least 1/500th and ideally 1/1000th of a second, and to provide some depth of field to minimize focusing errors, the lens stopped down to about F5.6. However, football is played under lighting conditions which vary enormously and although 400 ISO film may be more than adequate at the start and finish of the season, games played on dark winter afternoons or under floodlights may call for film speeds of 1600 ISO, 3200 ISO or greater, even with an exposure of 1/500th of a second at the lens's maximum aperture. Sometimes the film may have to be uprated or 'pushed', when it is intentionally underexposed and the development time subsequently increased. The technique is discussed more in Chapter 5.

The floodlights at many grounds do not light the pitch evenly – often there is a brighter area in the middle of the pitch and the goalmouths are darker. Photographers who regularly attend floodlit football matches at the same grounds will learn by experience what the appropriate goalmouth exposure is for their particular processing technique.

Captions are the responsibility of the photographer, although some newspapers have sports staff who can recognize all the members of their local Football League side. Some of the techniques are discussed in Chapter 9. In local games, the names of the players can be checked from the manager beforehand. At League or Cup games, changes to the team listed in the programme may be announced over the public address system, on an illuminated screen, or the club may provide a typed teamsheet for photographers.

Rugby

Rugby can be one of the easiest games to photograph, almost regardless of the level of skill of the players involved. As well as players tackling and scoring tries, there are also set occasions during the game, like line-outs and scrums, which give the photographer the chance to prepare for the action.

At all but the very top games, photographers can follow the action by moving along the touchline; occasionally they will be asked to crouch when taking pictures to avoid blocking the view of the crowd behind. A combination of lenses like 85 mm, 180 mm and 400 mm or 135 mm and 300 mm will be more than adequate.

At international games, the number of passes offered to 'runners' alongside the pitch are limited, and other photographers have to work from the public seats, either along the sides or ends of the pitch. In these positions, long lenses like 400 mm or 500 mm are essential, with a shorter one, perhaps a 135 mm, for any tries being scored.

As with football, a shutter speed of 1/500th or 1/1000th of a second is needed to 'stop' the action, but few grounds have floodlights, and at those that do, the light levels are very poor. Expect to be shooting virtually wide open, and to have to 'push' the film. However, the game is seldom played at night, and in mid-winter often starts earlier than football, which is helpful to evening papers trying to produce an early picture for their late Saturday sports edition.

Racing

Horse racing is either on the flat, or over the sticks (fences). The former includes the Derby, Ascot Week and Glorious Goodwood. The latter, the Grand National, the Cheltenham Gold Cup and the King George V Gold Cup, involves both steeplechasing, which is horses jumping over quite substantial fences, and hurdling, when the fences are somewhat smaller and less robust.

Steeplechasing and hurdling are photographically more interesting and the easier to do. The picture which usually publishes, in the absence of any incident during the race, is the winning horse clearing the last fence. It obviously improves the picture if there is more than one horse in shot. A little care needs to be taken when choosing a position; too head-on to the fence and there may be a big gap between adjacent horses coming over; too much to the side and the winner may be partially hidden by any other horses clearing the fence. Wherever a photographer is working from, it may help to stand on a pair of steps. These may enable the photographer to watch the horses approaching the fence, see how far across the fence the winner will jump, and how close the second horse is likely to be. Standing a few feet above the ground may help prevent the (dark) horse being silhouetted against the bright sky.

Most races do at least one complete circuit of the track. Do not ignore the first time they come past. They may be more bunched, with an increased risk of a faller; it may also be a good opportunity to shoot stock pictures of the horses in action.

Offbeat pictures can be taken with wide angle lenses placed at the base of the fences looking forwards or at the side of the water jump when there is not only the horse but also its reflection. Obviously these cameras have to be fired remotely – ideally by radio to avoid the hazard of trailing cables. When putting a camera on the ground, seek guidance from racecourse staff as to a suitable position, for the safety of both the equipment and the horses.

The best position for flat racing is head-on; where this position is depends upon the course. If the course is not straight, the horses, which always take the shortest line, will be on the inside rail. If the course is a straight sprint, then the horses usually stay on whichever side the starting stalls were. Working from head-on may mean working from a ladder or specially constructed stand. Aim to take the picture no later than 20 yards before the horses cross the finishing line – they tend to slow down and the jockeys relax as they cross the line. The horses go surprisingly fast – it is easier to focus on them running towards the camera with a 300 mm or even 500 mm lens than with an 180 mm or 85 mm.

An alternative way to photograph flat racing is to 'pan' the camera with the horses as they cross the finishing line. A shutter speed of 1/250th or slower will give sharp horses and a blurred background. Although less predictable than working head-on, the pictures can be extremely dramatic, especially if the distance between first and second is very small. Again, it is vital to know down which side of the course the horses run and to work from the opposite end of the finishing line. It is a technique which is improved with practice.

Captioning racing pictures seldom presents any problem. The racecard gives names and numbers of the horses running and the colours that the jockeys are wearing. Keep an ear to the public address system to listen for any changes. The names of the jockeys are usually displayed just before the race on a large highly visible board. It is useful to take a picture of this, both to save writing it all down and to identify the race being photographed.

Golf

Golfers and cameras do not mix. There is one golden rule of golf photography: do not take a picture until the golfer has hit the ball if there is any chance that the player will hear the shutter or motor drive. Most golfers have the kind of hearing that bats would envy. You have been warned.

Golf photographers carry their equipment for long distances, but golfers do not move fast and focusing is not a great problem so zoom lenses are ideal. A 35/70 mm F2.8 zoom, an 80/200 mm zoom, a 300 mm F2.8 lens on a monopod and a 2× teleconverter would be sufficient equipment.

Players driving from the tee make safe but dull pictures – until they react to their shot going astray. The pictures get more exciting when golfers are firing out of bunkers or the rough. And pictures of putting can be disappointing, with the players looking down until their ball stops on the rim of the hole, and they will it to drop in.

The nature of golf courses means that there is no 'right' lens or position. Although it is important to offer the sports editor good frame-filling pictures of players, do not ignore wider pictures which show the players and the natural features of the course – crossing bridges over streams – or a player and some of the watching crowd as he plays a stroke from out of the rough or the trees. There can be pictures too as golfer and caddy discuss the lie of the green in preparation for a putt.

Boxing

Photographing boxing looks easy, but is very difficult. It takes much practice, anticipation and expert timing to come away with a picture of a fighter at the receiving end of a good punch.

Most pictures are taken ringside, with the photographer pointing the camera either under the bottom rope, or between the bottom rope and the next one up; it helps to have a long neck.

The action can happen anywhere. When working from ringside, use two cameras, with 35 mm and 85 mm lenses. A third body with a 24 mm lens is useful at the knock-out if the boxer on the canvas is close to your position. A 180 mm can be used to photograph the fighters between rounds when they are receiving attention from their seconds in their respective corners.

At some venues it is possible to work from a balcony overlooking the ring. Such positions may be less cramped and more comfortable than ringside. The lenses needed obviously depend upon how far away the balcony is. As well as having a lens for tight fighting pictures, it is important to have one which will show the whole ring for the knock-down – just in case.

Some photographers working at ringside take boxing photographs by flash – usually with a 35 mm SLR but occasionally with a twin lens reflex camera, for instance a Rolleiflex, which uses larger 120 size film. The advantages of using flash are that its very short duration stops the movement; the lighting produced from the camera-mounted flashgun is better than the sometimes top-heavy lighting usually found in boxing rings and it is possible to stop down to F8 or F11, to minimize focusing errors. The attractions of using a Rolleiflex are: the leaf shutter synchronizes at 1/500th of a second, rather than the usual 1/250th of a second found on 35 mm SLRs, which means that there is less chance of a secondary exposure caused by the lights above the ring; there is less delay between pressing the release and the shutter firing than in an SLR which has to raise the mirror and stop the lens down before the shutter opens; and the larger negative size means that a portion of it can be selectively enlarged with less loss of quality than with the smaller 35 mm format.

Even at fights which are lit for television, expect to have to use film rated at 1600 ASA or faster. The light is very much over the fighters, although some may be reflected by the canvas to 'fill in' the shadows. It may be possible to take an incident light reading from within the ring before the fight starts. 1/250th of a second is too slow to stop the action; try to use 1/500th or even 1/1000th.

7

The working photographer – 2

COMPOSITION

Composition is an emotive word to press photographers, but it is really a few simple guidelines about what – other than the content – turns a mediocre picture into a good newspaper or magazine photograph.

The rules of composition are not hard and fast. They can occasionally be broken to good effect. How a photographer takes a picture by following or breaking the rules is his or her 'style'.

FILL THE FRAME

Pictures in newspapers, and, to a lesser extent, magazines have to compete with other items on the page for the reader's attention. Few are printed large (many pictures in tabloid newspapers are smaller than a postcard) and although printing processes vary, much of the detail and range of tones in the original will be lost in reproduction. Pictures must therefore be bold and simple.

A basic requirement is to ensure that the subject fills the frame and not to leave empty space in or around the picture. This should be done at the time the picture is taken, though additional cropping may be done in the darkroom when the negative is printed or by the sub-editor laying out the page.

WATCH THE BACKGROUND

Sometimes the background is an essential part of the picture and can be used to place the person photographed in context. At other times the content of the background needs to be eliminated. Filling the frame will help; there will be less background in the picture. Differential focusing is a useful technique for rendering a cluttered background inoffensive. It is particularly effective with portraiture and fashion. Move the subject as far away from the background as practicable, use a telephoto lens of at least 180 mm, and do not stop down beyond F4 or F5.6. The subject will be sharp, and the background almost totally out of focus.

EYE CONTACT

The eyes are the first part of a person we look at, either in real life or in a photograph. Sometimes all the people in a picture are looking at the camera, sometimes they are not. What appears strange is when some are, and others are not.

There are purists who would say that having people looking at the camera is unnatural; it shows that the photographer is intruding into their lives. But eye contact between, for example, a fashion model and the photographer (and thus the reader) adds enormously to the picture; it conveys involvement. A competent photographer should be able to organize or pose a picture either way.

With a little ingenuity a photographer should be able to turn the 'firing squad' pictures of beaming people giving away cheques, congratulating each other on winning awards or taking up a new office into something which has a little more animation. Often people insist that they want the formal picture taken. By all means do so, but then take the picture that will not only get into the paper, but will also be looked at by its readers.

TONES AND COLOURS

Photographers will quickly learn the shortcomings of their publication's method of printing. Most newspapers find it hard to reproduce shadow detail in dark tones. Fashion pictures frequently present problems. It is amazing how many public relations staff for fashion houses and clothing stores have not realized that trying to reproduce pictures of models wearing black clothing is a recipe for disaster. There really is no alternative to asking the model to change into another outfit.

Those photographers raised on black and white photography find there are different problems when working in colour. Colours need to harmonize rather than clash. Having more than one primary colour in the picture can disturb the eye. And merely rendering the background out of focus is not sufficient; it must be neutral in colour. Red pillar boxes or yellow waste-paper bins attract the eye just as much when they are out of focus as when they are sharp.

SHAPES

A picture can be any shape, but a quick scan of a cross-section of newspapers will show that those with a tabloid design prefer upright pictures, while broadsheet papers use pictures which are usually slightly wider than they are deep. It is not a coincidence, it is all to do with newspaper page layout. An unusually shaped picture may attract the eye – and by all means take it – but remember the sub-editor who has to lay out the page, and take one of a more conventional shape as well.

MOVEMENT

Cars, trains, runners, footballers, and anything with movement need space in the picture to move into. A Grand Prix motorcyclist, for example, racing from left to right, must not be cropped with the front wheel of the bike tight up against the right-hand side of the picture. Similarly, a batsman needs space into which to hit the ball.

CHOOSING THE LENS AND EXPOSURE

Sometimes the choice of lens is dictated by the situation – a telephoto lens when the photographer is unable to get closer to the scene and a wide angle when he or she cannot move any further back to get the entire scene in.

But there is more to choosing which lenses to use on a particular job. A wide angle lens appears to steepen perspective by accentuating closer objects, has an increased depth of field which makes it more tolerant of focusing errors and can be hand-held at slower shutter speeds. Telephoto lenses flatten perspective by compressing the planes in a picture, have a reduced depth of field, and need higher shutter speeds when hand-held to avoid camera shake.

The much appreciated introduction of wide-aperture zooms, typically 35–70 mm F2.8 and 80–200 mm F2.8, has meant that the majority of a photographer's assignments can be done with the same two cameras and lenses. A third body can be fitted with either a 24 mm wide angle or a 300 mm telephoto depending upon the job in hand.

Even when a photographer has decided what lens a picture is to be taken on, most have two cameras to hand – it is quicker to swap lenses between bodies than it is to change film.

A rule of thumb for the slowest shutter speed at which an SLR camera can be safely hand-held is the speed nearest to the reciprocal of the focal length of the lens fitted. For instance, a 500 mm lens can safely be hand-held at 1/500th of a second, and a 24 mm lens at 1/24th of a second; this speed falls between 1/15th and 1/30th of a second – for safety's sake it is better to use the faster of the two. Using a monopod reduces camera shake, and these times can probably be safely lengthened by a factor of four. With a reasonable tripod, camera shake becomes a problem only with very long lenses buffeted by strong winds.

Rangefinder cameras, like Leicas, can be safely hand-held at slower speeds than SLRs.

For any given amount of light falling on the subject there are a range of exposures which will provide negatives of identical density. 1/500th of a second at F5.6 is the same as 1/4000th at F2, or 1/30th at F22.

The choice depends upon the job. It is frequently a compromise which balances film speed, depth of field, subject movement and camera shake.

A boxer's right hook or a batsman diving to avoid being run out demand a shutter speed of 1/1000th of a second. This may mean working at or close to the lens's maximum aperture, which in turn limits the depth of field of the picture and requires the photographer to focus the lens accurately.

A portrait taken by available light of a mother and child living in a condemned flat may require a large depth of field to ensure that they and their surroundings are sharp. It may be necessary to stop the lens down to F5.6 or F8, and while subject movement is not a problem, the resulting shutter speed might be so slow that the photographer would have to use a monopod or brace the camera against a chair or wall to prevent camera shake.

A photographer 'snatching' a picture of a person arriving at court might be using flash, either as 'fill-in' or as the main source of light for the picture. The shutter speed chosen is the fastest, typically 1/250th of a second, at which the camera synchronizes with flash; the aperture set then depends upon the brightness of the daylight or the output of the flashgun. Ideally, it will be near F8 to allow for focusing errors.

For a fashion picture, when the photographer requires minimal depth of field, he or she will use the lens at or close to its maximum aperture. The shutter speed only matters if the picture requires 'fill-in flash' – when the photographer will choose the fastest speed available at which the camera synchronizes.

LIGHT

Light is essential to a photographer – no light, no picture.

In a studio the photographer has total control over the light – elsewhere we have to make the best of what there is.

There are occasions, for instance when covering a news event from a fixed point, when a photographer can do nothing about the light. If there is time and a choice of fixed points a photographer might be well advised to visit each to assess the direction and nature of the light at the time of the assignment before picking a spot.

On other assignments a photographer may be free to take the picture in the most appropriate lighting conditions, or to return later when the sun has moved, or the clouds have cleared.

COLOUR TEMPERATURE

Photographers who were used to working in black and white but who now work in colour have had to learn about the colour temperature of light. (Colour temperature is the temperature in Kelvins to which a black body must be raised to emit light of the same colour as the source in question.) Very simply this means that everything that the eye sees as 'white light' is not necessarily the same colour. For example, light from a tungsten filament has a lower colour temperature than daylight, and pictures taken by it on film balanced for daylight have a yellow–orange cast.

This is not a problem with negative film as the cast can be corrected at the printing stage. For transparency film it is possible either to buy a lightly tinted filter to screw on the front of the lens to make the appropriate correction or use film balanced for tungsten light. The light from electronic flashguns is the same temperature as daylight. Some fluorescent lights give a green cast with film balanced for daylight, but there are appropriate correction filters available.

What must be avoided is taking pictures under mixed lighting conditions. It will be impossible to avoid some part of the picture having a colour cast.

LIGHT OUTDOORS

Unless the picture would look wrong taken outdoors, most photographers prefer to work outside using daylight as their principal source of illumination. It is possible to see where highlights and shadows are and the contrast range between them; and daylight is even, unlike light from a flashgun, whose intensity diminishes as its distance from the subject increases.

Bright sunshine falling directly on the subject from behind the photographer is the worst kind of light. It gives bright highlights and dark, harsh shadows with an enormous contrast range which the film may not be able to handle. People screw up their eyes and faces may be half shade, half sunshine. If the photographer is close enough it may be possible to reduce the contrast range using the fill-in flash techniques described in Chapter 4 or use a reflector to bounce some light back into the shadows.

One answer to bright sunshine is to photograph into the light, with the sun behind the subject. This technique, sometimes rather grandly described as 'contre-jour', gives a soft light and is particularly effective for fashion, glamour or show-business pictures. It will usually be necessary to use a flashgun or a reflector to put some light back into the face and add some sparkle to the eyes, although sometimes natural reflectors, like snow, white walls or the pavement, will suffice. Try, if possible, to shoot against a darker background. When looking through the viewfinder, check for flare from the sun shining on the lens; if necessary use a hand to shield the lens.

Most photographers prefer to work outside with sun just hidden behind thin cloud which makes for a light which is bright but not harsh and provides just sufficient gentle shadow to give shape to the subject and a contrast range suitable for the film in use.

If the sky is totally overcast and the light has no direction, a very small amount of flash may provide the all-important highlights in the eyes.

Dawn and dusk, two times when light is in short supply, are not the exclusive preserve of magazine photographers. The slanting light at these times can have a pure, almost magical quality, especially at sunrise when the air is still and there is low mist or frost on the ground. Do not be afraid to use exposures of 1/8th of a second or slower provided that the camera is on a firm tripod. Unlike the human eye the film can build up an image over a long period of time.

LIGHTING INDOORS

Indoors, the choice is between using flash or making the most of the illumination available from windows or other lights. A flashgun mounted on the hot-shoe might be convenient, but available light is more natural and enables the photographer to see what the end result will be. If there is a suitable ceiling or wall, then bounced flash will add some modelling shadows and improve the quality of the lighting, but for immediate hard news, direct flash may be the only answer. Be careful when using hot-shoe-mounted flashguns for upright pictures; try to turn the camera so that the shadow is thrown behind the principal person in the pictures. Alternatively use a second or third flashgun to provide some more light on the subject from another direction or to illuminate the background. It is best to fire these with remote photo-slave units rather than have synchronizing leads festooned around the subject. A few experiments will quickly establish a successful technique.

If the photographer has any control over the picture, then it may be possible either to move the subject closer to a window, or use a slower shutter speed with the camera on a tripod. In both cases a reflector may help bounce light back into the shadows.

Some photographers carry a couple of powerful studio flashguns with stands and umbrellas to help them light interior feature pictures. As these have modelling lamps it is possible to see the lighting effect produced when the flashes are fired.

STUDIO

A studio is a room where the photographer has complete control over the subject, lighting and background. It is usually used for fashion or glamour pictures. The photographer may work alone, or with the help of an assistant to move lights or load cameras, a hairdresser, make-up artist and fashion editor.

Outside the national press, few newspapers have a formal photographic studio. Many have a set of studio lights which can be used on location for studio-type assignments. Certainly it is a useful skill to know how to organize a simple studio lighting arrangement.

Although some specialist studios intended mainly for portraiture are lit by daylight, electronic flash is by far and away the most popular source of illumination.

Studio electronic flashguns differ from the portable ones used on assignments. They are mains operated – which means that even at full power, they recycle in

Figure 7.1   Snooker player: I was assigned to photograph this young snooker player who was beating many of the adult players at his local club. There was no possibility of using natural light and direct flash would have burnt out the ball. His mother held my Metz flashgun on an extension lead to my left, and produced this pleasing half-lit picture. Of course I took a simple head-and-shoulders picture to keep in the files for the sports desk to use with any future stories (© Herald Express Ltd)

Figure 7.2 Ice hockey: Pictures do not have to be taken from eye-level. An elevated viewpoint for this ice-hockey match eliminated a messy background, and gave a pleasing vertical composition (© Herald Express Ltd)

Figure 7.3   Studio lighting equipment: A typical studio flashgun (centre) – from the Courtenay range – with its accessories (clockwise from top): 'soft-box' for almost shadowless lighting; reflective and translucent umbrellas for routine use; cap to protect flash-tube in transit; reflectors for a more directional light and for maximizing the light reaching the subject; snoot for creating a narrow beam of light

just a few seconds; have a modelling light so that the lighting effect can be seen before the picture is taken; have a variable output which can be adjusted between full power and, typically, 1/16th power; and have an extensive range of accessories – reflectors, umbrellas or diffusers – to enable the photographer to control the way the light reaches the subject.

Whereas the photoelectric sensors in modern cameras and portable electronic flashguns 'turn' the light off when the subject has received the correct amount of illumination for the chosen aperture, studio flashguns deliver a predetermined amount of light and the correct exposure is assessed beforehand with a flashmeter.

Flashguns can be fired directly at the subject with a rigid metallic reflector around the tube. This gives a harsh light. The light can be softened if the reflector is increased in size and a diffuser used to prevent any light reaching the subject directly. However, many people use an umbrella reflector to bounce the light from the flashgun back to the subject.

Some umbrellas are made from white nylon, or similar material. They transmit almost as much light as they reflect. Better, but slightly more expensive, are those umbrellas made from fabric coated with either silver- or gold-coloured foil; they reflect all the light. Although it does not make any difference to photographers working in black and white, the silver-coloured ones provide a neutral light, while the gold-coloured ones give a slighter warmer illumination.

The final accessory found in most studios is a snoot. It is just a tapered pipe which fits over the front of the flashlight and emits a narrow, fairly parallel beam of light.

There are many other accessories. 'Fishfriers' and 'softboxes' are large hooded diffusing screens through which the flash is fired to give a soft, shadowless light. Some diffusers use a honeycomb pattern to soften the light but prevent it from spreading too much. 'Barndoors' are movable flaps of metal mounted in front of the flashgun used to restrict the spread of light.

Rather than having yards of synchronizing cable trailing around the studio, one flashgun is connected to the camera and the others are fired by slave units which react instantly to the flash from the first unit.

Some flashguns have the facility to extinguish the modelling light after the picture has been taken until the capacitor has recharged and is ready for the next exposure. This is particularly useful with multi-flash set-ups as it provides visual confirmation that all the lights have fired and of when they are ready again.

Flashmeters almost invariably measure incident light. The most convenient ones are cordless. They are simply held at the subject facing the camera, the flashes are fired by the camera or the test button on the flash-head, and the exposure is read off. Others have to fire the flashguns themselves by means of a synchronizing cable.

LIGHTING WITH STUDIO FLASHGUNS

Classic studio lighting needs three or four lights.

The main or 'key' light is higher than the level of the camera, and at about 45 degrees to the subject. This is the main light by which the picture is taken. It could have either a metallic reflector or an umbrella. However, one light by itself makes for rather contrasty pictures.

A second light, to fill in the shadows, is placed closer to the camera. An umbrella would be ideal for this light, which must not be as bright as the main light: to provide a contrast range acceptable to most films, it should be between one and two stops less bright than the main light.

The intensity of each light can be checked with a flashmeter.

To add a little sparkle to the picture, fit a third light with a snoot and shine it on the subject's head from above and behind. This provides a highlight on the hair which adds depth to the picture.

Finally, it might be necessary to light the background with a fourth light.

STUDIO BACKGROUND

Some large studios have a plain background called an 'infinity curve'. Very simply this is a wall and floor joined in one continuous curve without a visible seam. Suited for photography of larger objects, like cars, it has the disadvantage that the only way to change its colour is to light or paint it.

A more common background is a roll of paper supported on stands at each end. The paper is available in different widths and colours and can also be arranged in a continuous curve between the wall and the floor. If the paper gets dirty it is a simple matter to cut off the soiled area and unroll some more.

STUDIO CAMERA

A photographer can use any camera in the studio. However, with the amount of light available and because the finished picture is usually closely scrutinized, it makes sense to use a large-format camera using 120 film. There is no risk of camera shake because of the short duration of the flash.

Many of the rules about photography outside on assignment are relevant to working in the studio. However, more attention has to be paid to detail. Annoying shadows or reflections of umbrellas on spectacles, marks on the background or anything wrong with the model's clothes will be very noticeable on the finished picture.

8
The working photographer – 3

BEING ORGANIZED

Press photographers ought to adopt the Scout motto 'Be prepared'.

Equipment should always be ready for use. Once a job is over, remove the exposed film, tear off the leader and put in a new film. (Some people wind the film straight back into the cassette which means that before the film can be processed the cassette must either be broken open or the leader extracted with a special tool – both of which take time.) A camera without film in it is dangerous; you may forget to reload before the next assignment.

Back in the office waiting for the next job check that every camera and lens has the appropriate body and lens caps in place; mine are painted yellow so that they will not be confused with those of other photographers, and I have glued two rear lens caps back to back to stop the lenses rattling against one another. Any equipment that has been used in the rain must be dried thoroughly. Surface moisture is easily wiped off, but internal condensation or dampness is harder to remove. Be wary of using hair driers or leaving cameras and lenses on radiators; too much heat can damage them. It is best to leave damp equipment overnight in a gentle draught of warm, dry air. Obviously anything which has been soaked or immersed in water must be taken to a specialist repairer as soon as possible.

Flashgun and motor drive batteries are best recharged overnight.

Once a week use a can of compressed air to clean the dust and dirt from inside the camera bodies, but do not direct the blower directly onto the delicate shutter curtain, and take care not to touch the mirror which is silvered on the front.

As lenses should be protected by a filter at all times, there should never be a need to clean the actual surface of the front element. A filter can be cleaned with a freshly-washed handkerchief or a piece of chamois leather. Dust on the rear elements can be removed with compressed air.

Any 'pool' lenses, kept in the office and used by all photographers, should be quickly checked before being taken out on assignment. Put the lens on the camera, look through the viewfinder and check that it focuses on infinity and stops down correctly when the depth of field button is pressed and opens up again fully when it is released.

Cameras and lenses do go wrong, either as a result of carelessness or fair wear and tear. Usually this means returning the equipment to the importer; some offer professional photographers a similar item on loan while the repair or service is completed.

There are some independent repairers who have access to spare parts and offer a faster, more personal service than that provided by some camera importers. For obvious reasons they tend to be in the larger cities.

CARS

To most photographers, their car is their office, and in it they carry a variety of indispensable items:

- Spare film.
- Notebook and several pens.
- Envelopes for shipping film.
- A set of small screwdrivers for tightening loose screws.
- A roll of sticky tape.
- Multi-function penknife.
- Spare set of batteries.
- Tripod and monopod.
- Aluminium ladder – for standing on behind crowds or other photographers or for keeping one's place.
- Waterproof coat and trousers.
- Wellington boots.
- Folding stool to sit on at football matches.
- Overnight bag containing a change of clothes, toilet bag, spare film, passport and chargers which may be needed for battery-operated equipment.
- Maps, both of the streets in the towns or cities in which they regularly work and Ordnance Survey maps of the area (particularly useful for finding footpaths and other vantage points, and routes around traffic congestion via side roads).
- Coins for parking meters – some cities have a range of meters which need different coins.
- Radio for monitoring hourly news bulletins on local radio stations – the frequencies can be found in any good motoring atlas. These broadcasts can be invaluable when working on a big story in an unfamiliar area. Many local radio stations have excellent contacts and pride themselves on their ability to respond to the 'big' story in their patch.
- Telephone directory. Sadly there are no longer directories in telephone boxes and Directory Enquiries will not release addresses. A local phone book will help you check addresses.
- Processing kit for jobs away from the office when a one hour photo centre is not available.

Photographers' cars may be a matter of personal choice, or they may be provided by the company. Either way, one with a boot is more secure than a hatchback. With several thousand pounds worth of easily disposable equipment inside, it is worth having an alarm fitted – the insurance company may insist. Some photographers keep their equipment inside a padlocked steel box which is firmly attached to the floor of the car boot. To avoid attracting thieves never leave any equipment in view in the car and never put equipment in the car and then walk away from it – you do not know who may have been watching.

Being prepared also means ensuring that the car is regularly serviced and starting the day with a full tank of petrol – stopping to refuel wastes valuable time on the way to urgent news assignments.

Photographers have a poor reputation with insurance companies, some of whom place us in the same high-risk groups as bookmakers, jockeys and entertainers and increase the premium accordingly. Nevertheless, those who use their cars for work should notify their insurance company and ensure that their cover extends to business use.

Finding companies to insure professional photographic equipment is not easy and the premiums are not cheap. Try approaching a specialist insurance broker or check the advertisements in professional photographic magazines.

DRESS

Many photographers let down themselves, their profession and the publication they work for by the way they dress.

For several years I covered the Passing-Out Parade at the Britannia Royal Naval College in Dartmouth. It is one of the highlights of the naval year with every button gleaming and every boot polished to perfection. At one point during the ceremony the photographers and TV crews were allowed to walk on to the parade ground to record the inspecting officer passing through the ranks. And we looked a shambles. Although some wore suits, others of us wore jeans and open-necked shirts, anoraks and trainers, most festooned with cameras and bags over the shoulder. Every year I went I was surprised that we did not finish up on a charge.

Press photographers should always dress in a manner relevant to the occasion and to whom they might meet; as in every other walk of life, it is first impressions that count.

Occasionally a pass or invitation to a particular job specifies what photographers must wear; for instance, dark suit or black tie. Not to conform is rude to the organizers and may mean that the photographer is refused admission.

Clearly there are jobs when it is inappropriate to wear one's best clothes and the lesson is always to have a change in the car or office. I once clambered up the outside of a church steeple in the same suit that I had been wearing when photographing the Duke of Edinburgh just an hour before simply because I did not have a spare pair of trousers in the car.

FINDING PICTURES

Although most staff photographers and many freelances are told by the picture desk which assignments they are to cover, those who can find their own jobs or picture ideas, especially when news is quiet, will rapidly become valued members of the team.

This is much easier to do when working on a provincial paper where the demand of pictures for each edition often outstrips the supply. On a national paper hundreds of images pass across the picture desk every day.

In the same way that reporters are the ears of the paper's readers, photographers are their eyes. Good photojournalism is about showing readers something which they have not seen before and which, when they see it in the paper, they stop and look at as something new.

As they spend much of their day driving from one job to the next, provincial photographers have a great advantage over their reporter colleagues who may spend their entire day in the office.

On duty, off duty or just between jobs, a photographer should always keep an eye open for the changes to landmarks or activities which reflect the time of year. The re-gilding of a church weathercock could provide enough pictures for a double-page spread. A picture of council workmen moving beach huts onto the seafront tells readers that it is the start of summer. The same men testing the lights on the civic Christmas tree outside the Town Hall might provide a picture in advance of the mayor turning them on officially a few days later.

A photographer cannot see everything; but he or she can be helped by those most precious and indefinable of assets, good contacts.

Contacts come with time. They are people you meet on jobs and with whom you cultivate a working friendship. They may be the press officer at the local zoo, a police sergeant, the Mayor's secretary, the head of the Parks Department, a local councillor, a farmer, the Head Porter at the town's only five star hotel, a pop singer, a football manager or the local fire chief. Often the relationship can work both ways; for whatever reason they want to get news and pictures of their activities into the paper, and you want to get them in your paper.

Sometimes a contact may ring with a picture idea or tell you that something newsworthy is going on; at other times you may ring him or her and ask if they know of anything that might make a picture, or suggest a picture idea.

Apart from the big exclusive stories that occasionally appear in national newspapers, contacts are paid little. But always send them some complimentary prints, and, depending upon the paper's policy, it may be possible to take them out to lunch from time to time or send them a bottle of whisky at Christmas.

It goes without saying that a photographer's contacts are valuable and their names and telephone numbers should be carefully recorded. And make sure they know how to contact you at any time. It is annoying to hear about a good picture opportunity which was lost because your contact could not reach you.

Do not ignore your own paper, or that of a rival, as a source of picture ideas. Reporters can write up a story as just a couple of paragraphs without realizing its picture potential; or their story might alert you to a good picture some time in the future. Scan the small ads and the personal columns. There might be a picture idea in those.

WORKING OVERSEAS

Travelling abroad can be one of the bonuses of the job, but there are pitfalls for the inexperienced.

Documentation

Any photographer who may have to work abroad at short notice should carry their passport with them at all times. Many countries require visitors to have visas, and although these can sometimes be acquired on arrival, it will save time if visa formalities have been completed before departure. There are different types of visas – tourism, business, multi-entry – and advice should be taken from the consulate as to which kind to apply for. Whereas reporters can pass themselves off as tourists, it is obviously harder for a photographer because of the accompanying equipment.

Any photographer travelling abroad frequently may find it worthwhile to apply for a second passport so that they are not prevented from going on an assignment because their passport is at a consulate for a visa.

Driving

A British driving licence is acceptable throughout Europe and in many other countries; the rest require an international driving licence, obtainable from the AA or RAC. If hiring a car abroad, it is vital to check what insurance the hire car company is providing – take the best and the most they can offer. A Green Card from the insurance company is necessary if taking one's own car, or that of the company, abroad. Check the local speed limits, and ask if there are any other regulations that might affect you; for instance, some European countries require drivers to carry snow chains in winter months on certain roads. The police abroad will have little sympathy with visitors who do not abide by their laws.

Health

Standards of health in other countries are different from those in the UK, and it may be advisable to have inoculations before travelling. Although it is possible to consult your local GP, the best advice may come from British Airways, who have travel clinics in many major cities which have up-to-date information about the health situation all over the world. Most people have regular vaccinations against tetanus, but travel to Third World countries may require inoculations against typhoid, cholera, yellow fever and meningitis. It is important to keep a record, ideally with your passport, of the vaccinations that you have received. There is no vaccination effective against malaria; instead tablets must be taken before and during the visit, and, just as importantly, for a month after returning from any affected area.

It is well worth having a simple first aid kit with adhesive plasters, antiseptic cream, aspirins, cough tablets, and anti-diarrhoea tablets. Medical facilities in some countries are a little primitive, and it is possible to purchase sealed packets of sterile syringes, needles and sutures.

In some countries it is not safe to drink the water; buy bottled water, and make sure that the seal on the bottle is intact. Beware of salads, which may not have been washed in bottled water, and peel all fruit. Form E111, available from local Post Offices, enables citizens of one EC country to receive emergency medical care when in another member country.

Customs

A photographer with a wire machine and three or four cameras and a range of lenses is probably carrying in excess of £30 000 worth of bulky and highly visible equipment. They are a Customs Officer's dream.

Within the European Community (which does not include all the countries in

Europe) there is no problem. The European single market, established in 1993, removed customs posts on borders between member countries. Equipment can be moved freely between one member country and another without any formalities. Passengers carry their bags which have labels with green edging through the Blue channel.

Outside the European Community, there are two hurdles to overcome: getting the equipment into the country you are visiting and then bringing it back into the UK.

The country which you are visiting is concerned that you are importing the equipment and will then sell it. They may insist on a carnet. This is an internationally accepted document which itemizes all the equipment carried with its serial numbers and value. It is issued by the photographer's local Chamber of Trade, and is in effect a guarantee, by means of a deposit with them, that you will export all of the equipment that you took into the country. Every time that you cross the border the carnet has to be stamped and formalities completed by Customs Officers on each side. Failure to do so leads to complications later on and the deposit may be forfeited. Carnets usually take 24 hours to issue.

Pushing the equipment straight through the Green channel, if the country has one, may work. It may be easier in the long run to go through the Red channel and explain to the Customs Officers what the equipment is and the purpose of the visit. It will help to have your letter on company notepaper itemizing everything, the serial numbers and value, with as many important-looking stamps on it as possible, as well as any kind of invitation or accreditation that you may have, and stress that you will be taking the equipment with you when you leave.

When bringing the equipment back into this country, HM Customs and Excise are concerned that are you either importing new equipment without paying import duty and VAT on it or are reimporting equipment which you have previously exported and have reclaimed the VAT paid at the time of purchase. It would then be possible to raise a false invoice, re-export the equipment, claim back the VAT for a second time, bring the equipment back in, and so on. The solution is to use the 'duplicate list' procedure. Prepare two lists of the equipment that you are carrying. When leaving the country, tell the customs officers that you wish to use the 'duplicate list' procedure. They may examine the equipment and check the serial numbers, before taking the one list and giving you a form which you surrender with the other list when you return.

Air travel

Recent terrorist attacks have made airlines more sensitive to the contents of passengers' luggage and most routinely ask if checked-in baggage being carried in the hold contains any electronic equipment or batteries. Their concern varies with the perceived level of terrorist threat at any time. Baggage containing electronic equipment may be X-rayed or searched by hand. Most equipment carried by photographers is straightforward, but it is worth ensuring that the mains cable for the wire machine is kept with it so that it can be plugged in and demonstrated in use.

Mercury thermometers are banned on aircraft – if they broke, the mercury would react violently with the aluminium from which the aircraft is made.

Occasionally, security staff take exception to photographic chemicals, but, provided they are securely packed and sealed, and they are aware that they are travelling in the hold, there should be no problem. If you anticipate travelling abroad regularly, consider using powdered chemicals which remove the concern about leaks – and save weight.

All cabin baggage carried on by passengers is X-rayed. There is no evidence that the machines used at airports in the Western World adversely affect 400 ASA films, even after at least six passes. If you are concerned, either because of the speed of the film or because of repeated exposure to X-rays, then remove the film cassettes from their plastic containers before leaving for the airport and place them in a clear plastic bag; at the security check, show them to the staff and insist that they are hand-searched rather than X-rayed. Outside the Western World, at airports where the equipment may not have been checked since the day it was installed, it is best not to take any chances. Remove all the film from the camera bag and insist that it does not go through the X-ray machine but is hand-searched.

Money

Try, if possible, to buy some of the appropriate currency before leaving. The exchange desk at the airport may be closed or airport luggage trolleys may require coins as a deposit.

Countries with a hard currency present few problems; travellers' cheques or sterling can be exchanged easily.

Elsewhere, the choice of cash or travellers' cheques has to be made more carefully. Both can be changed at the official exchange rate, but cash may also be exchanged on the black market at a better rate, though you dabble in that at your own risk. And some goods and services might be available only if payment is made in hard currency. Taxi drivers in Moscow, for instance, are not very interested in carrying foreigners for roubles; they want dollars. So it might be better, but riskier, to carry cash rather than travellers' cheques.

Credit cards are acceptable virtually all over the world and sometimes the exchange rate is better than you can get in the local money changers.

Electricity

Most countries have mains supplies of a voltage similar to that in the UK, but the plugs differ. The round plugs with two pins are almost standard throughout mainland Europe and adaptors are widely available in electrical or travel shops. Anyone anticipating travelling to America and Japan should check that their equipment can function on 110 volts. Much, but not all, electronic equipment has a manual voltage selector. When preparing for a trip abroad write yourself a reminder to change the voltage selector on arrival and stick it over the switch or somewhere similar. And do not forget to change it back when you return to the UK. For equipment which operates only on 240 volts, it is possible to use a transformer to reduce the voltage. The size, and hence cost, of the transformer is directly related to the current that the equipment draws. It is worth using a transformer for expensive items of equipment, like a modem or picture transmitter, but it is cheaper to buy a new hair drier or immersion heater than use a transformer to alter the voltage.

Moving the pictures

Wherever a photographer is abroad, there will be the problem of getting the pictures back to the office. It is a lucky person who is able to do the job and then take the films back to the office themselves.

An early priority is to assess the facilities for wiring. It may be that the photographer is covering an international summit, where the host government will have laid on telephones; or it might be a sporting event at which the paper has requested its own telephone line, or the photographer may have to wire from the hotel bedroom. Whichever, it is vital to check the choices, discover how to connect the wire machine and send a test transmission. There are countries with limited international telephone connections and sometimes it may be easier for the office to call the photographer every other hour, or at an agreed time, than it is for the photographer to try to get an international line. There may be other ways around the problem. In Moscow recently, photographers asking to call London were told that 'tomorrow is possible'; after 40 cigarettes changed hands an appreciative operator put the call through in 15 minutes. Hotels usually surcharge calls made through their switchboards and if wiring several pictures there are considerable savings to be made by asking the office to call the photographer when he or she is ready to start transmitting.

It is also worth thinking of back-up arrangements; are there any other photographers wiring, or is there a national or international agency nearby that has wire facilities?

A photographer will certainly have brought the equipment required to process film in the hotel bedroom, but is there a one-hour photo centre nearby which could process the film? Does it shut for lunch, or stay open late in the evenings? It can be worth putting a test film through to check the quality of their processing.

If it is necessary to process in the hotel bedroom, check the quality of the water. Almost any water can be used to dilute the chemicals and wash the film, but if the water is unfit to drink it may contain dirt and dissolved chemicals which will remain on the negatives after drying. The answer is to rinse the film several times in bottled water before it is dried.

If the film has to be air-freighted back to the office it is important to check the flight times and time taken to complete customs formalities at the airport. Although passengers are understandably wary of taking packets from strangers at airports, it may be possible to find someone travelling on the appropriate flight who is prepared to carry the film and be met at the airport at the other end.

Sometimes the aircraft crew can help; it may be worthwhile talking to the airline's station manager.

Other tips

Take a short wave radio to listen to the World Service. It is useful to hear what is news back home and it may be relevant to the job in hand. Try to find out if there is a local English-speaking radio station which carries news bulletins. There may also be local papers printed in English; if not, it might be worth asking someone in the hotel to translate any relevant stories.

9
Captions

A caption is a piece of text which accompanies a picture. It may be several paragraphs in length or as little as three or four words.

Captions in magazines and national and large provincial newspapers are usually written by the sub-editors who design, lay out and prepare the pages for publication. On smaller newspapers caption writing may be done by a sub-editor, a reporter or the photographer who took the picture. Whoever writes them, it is the photographer's duty to provide the relevant information accurately. If a reader spots an error in a caption, then it undermines the credibility of the rest of the newspaper.

A photographer who can return to the office with a picture and write a usable caption for it in good English, capable of being typeset with minimal editing, is valued by a newspaper's editor.

It does not mean that a photographer needs to accompany a picture of world leaders shaking hands with 500 words about the latest developments in East–West arms reduction talks. But it does mean that a picture of three local schoolchildren preparing for an exchange trip to Russia will have their names, ages, school and destination correctly spelt and that the photographer will know when they are leaving, how long their visit is for, and the name of the teacher at their school who can be contacted by a reporter who wants to follow up the story.

When time is short, a picture with a good caption readily available will go into the paper in front or instead of one whose caption needs further research or has to be deciphered from handwritten scrawl.

RECORDING THE INFORMATION – ACCURATELY

Caption information is recorded in a notebook so that it is available at a later date if there is any query about it, editorial or legal. A caption starts its life with the photographer out on assignment. The names of people photographed who are not so well known that they are instantly recognizable should be recorded, correctly spelt, in a notebook. The best person to check the spelling with is the person in question.

Examples of the many names which can lead to confusion include:

Ann/Anne
Brooks/Brookes

John/Jon
Keene/Keane/Keen
Leslie/Lesley
Martyn/Martin
Philips/Phillips
Rogers/Rodgers
Macdonald/MacDonald/McDonald

Beware of diminutives. There may be temptation to expand Bob to Robert, but some people are christened Bill, Bob, Reg, etc.

As well as recording a person's name, it is prudent to check their marital status. Some women prefer to be described as Ms rather than Miss. Married women may continue to use their maiden name for professional or business reasons.

Other information that may be relevant includes the person's age and where they come from. A local or regional newspaper needs more geographical information than a national newspaper. The Wadchester Gazette will localize a story by telling its readers that Mrs Brown, who is celebrating in London after winning the Slimmer of the Year competition, lives in Acacia Road, Wadchester. A national newspaper might be happy to describe her as being 'from Wadchester'.

It is vital to record telephone numbers: home telephone numbers, office telephone numbers and mobile telephone numbers. Particularly useful is a number where a person can be reached in, say, two hour's time when the photographer is back at the office and may have a query. A reporter following up a photographer's picture may be grateful for the number. Any telephone number which might be of the slightest use in the future should be recorded in the photographer's contacts book.

Any relevant titles, ranks or offices held, or awards being received, should also be noted. President is not the same as Chairman. The names of surgeons are not preceded by the word 'doctor'. And doctors are not only physicians, but also academics who have been awarded a PhD by a university. PhD is short for a Doctor of Philosophy, but it does not mean the holder is a philosopher. Barristers are not solicitors. Discover if a body is an Institute or an Institution. It is the Royal National Institute for the Deaf, but the Royal National Lifeboat Institution. Check apostrophes: it is the St John Ambulance Brigade not St John's Ambulance Brigade.

Honours and medals should be carefully checked: people who receive OBEs and CBEs are Officers and Commanders respectively of the Order of the British Empire. A frequent mistake is to omit the word 'Order'.

When there are several people in a picture, the photographer must devise a foolproof way of identifying each of them, usually recording their position from left to right, but must ensure that they do not move around between the picture being taken and the caption information being recorded. In some circumstances it may help to write down in the notebook a description of people or their clothes:

John Smith – wire frame glasses and check sports jacket.

Certainly it is wise to have a quick count of the number of people in the picture, and to compare this with the number of names in the notebook.

When locating people in a picture, *left* or *right* is as seen by the reader, and not as seen by a person standing in the picture.

A picture should never be captioned from right to left, but always the other way round. Positioning a person by reference to another one in the picture is always messy.

The location of the picture should be recorded; did the car crash happen in Park Street, Park Road or Park Avenue and was the dinner in the Hotel Royale, or the Royal Hotel? And while on dinners, the event which people hold in December is referred to as the annual Christmas party. That is a tautology – Christmas is an annual event.

Sometimes the information for the caption may be provided as a handout prepared by the event's organizers or their public relations advisers. This should be read carefully to ensure that it contains all the relevant information, and, if possible, checked against the person or people being photographed.

THE FIVE Ws

The photographer should then gather any further information thought relevant to ensure that answers can be given to the five Ws: who, why, what, where, when.

Clearly, when working with a reporter, it is not necessary for the photographer to come away with the same quantity of information as when working alone. But a reporter's presence does not absolve the photographer from knowing who has been pictured and how to spell their name correctly. The reporter may not be to hand when the caption is being written.

It may be useful to record the frame numbers for each picture taken to help with identification in the office.

SPORTS CAPTIONS

Sport can cause problems. The caption information for a team group can best be recorded by asking beforehand for the names of the players, the numbers on their shirts and the identity of any officials, and after taking the picture, asking the whole group to turn around so that another picture can be taken with the numbers showing. The list of names and numbers can then be used on return to the office to compile a caption.

Football, rugby, hockey, basketball and similar sports can best be captioned by dividing a notebook into five vertical columns, or using caption sheets printed for the purpose. It allows a photographer to use two cameras fitted with lenses of different focal lengths. When a picture is taken, the numbers of the principal players involved are written in the appropriate column. For the purposes of rapid editing, it can be a good idea to leave a blank after an important incident, or when a try or goal has been scored. Note that the photographer has used the first exposure of each film as an identifying frame to help match up the processed negatives with the caption sheet. The sheet also contains a space for any instructions from the photographer for the darkroom to extend the processing time of the film to take account of any intentional underexposure because of poor light. Despite the best intentions, it is not always possible to caption fully every picture during a fast-moving game. Sometimes it is possible to ask the

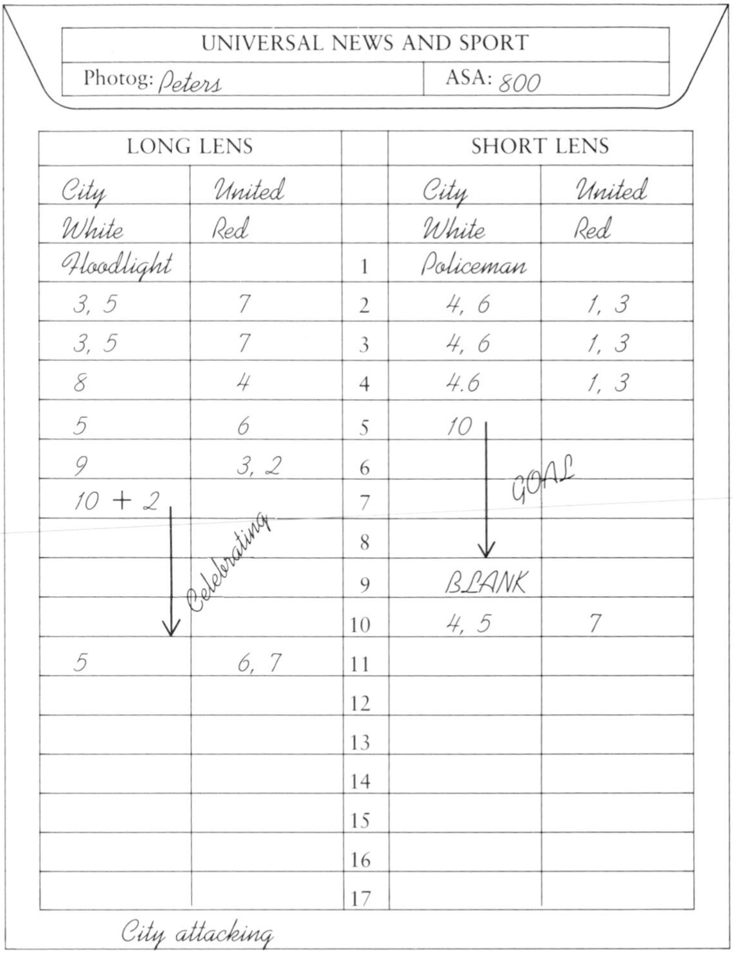

UNIVERSAL NEWS AND SPORT				
Photog: *Peters*			ASA: *800*	

LONG LENS			SHORT LENS	
City	*United*		*City*	*United*
White	*Red*		*White*	*Red*
Floodlight		1	*Policeman*	
3, 5	7	2	4, 6	1, 3
3, 5	7	3	4, 6	1, 3
8	4	4	4.6	1, 3
5	6	5	10	
9	3, 2	6		
10 + 2		7	*GOAL*	
		8		
		9	*BLANK*	
		10	4, 5	7
5	6, 7	11		
		12		
		13		
		14		
		15		
		16		
		17		

Celebrating

City attacking

Figure 9.1 Football envelope: A football envelope is an easy way of recording captions – and is really self-explanatory. The photographer has identified the individual films for the editor with a picture of a floodlight on one and a policeman on the other. The teams' colours, red and white, help the photographer remember which team is which and assists the editor who may be dealing with several games. The ASA tells the darkroom of any required adjustments to processing. Putting a blank after a goal helps locate it rapidly on the film during the editing process

newspaper's sports staff to help with the names of unidentified players. It is very sad that footballers only have their numbers on the back of their shirts, and not on their shorts, as in years gone by.

If it rains, a photographer should make every effort to keep the notebook dry as ballpoint pens do not write well on wet paper, and ink may run. A soft pencil or indelible marker similar to those used for gardening or marking laundry may help. Putting the notebook inside a large clear plastic bag will help keep it dry.

Sometimes the photographer will ship the exposed film back to the office by despatch rider or other means of transport. The information included must be clear to the caption writer at the office who does not have the benefit of having been at the job. For instance, the photographer may have been at the goalmouth being attacked by Arsenal, but the caption writer may have no way of knowing unless told on the caption sheet. Frequently photographers outside court take pictures of several people going in, and it will help the caption writer and picture editor if they are told that the accused is the third person photographed and was wearing a T-shirt with a Union Flag on it. The spelling of the accused's name should have been checked from the court listings.

WRITING THE CAPTION

Back in the office, with the print made, the photographer can start to write the caption material. In some newspapers' offices captions are written on specially printed sheets with perforations on them, which allow the caption to be stuck to the rear of the picture, but permit the text to be removed later for subbing and typesetting, leaving behind on the print the photographer's name and the date the picture was taken. It may be written on a typewriter – in which case it should be double-spaced – or prepared on a word processor, with a printed copy attached to the print and an electronic copy sent to the sub-editors, alerting them about the picture. Handwritten captions should be avoided at all costs – the chance of errors is too great.

There are many places to check caption information. Titles, honours and other personal details can be discovered in *Who's Who*. Details of MPs can be found in *Vacher's Parliamentary Companion*, and the spelling of towns and, villages can be obtained from a good gazetteer. *Jane's Fighting Ships* will inform you whether a warship is a frigate or a destroyer, and a good reference book will tell you the difference between the Welsh Guards and the Coldstream Guards from the number of buttons on their tunics. Details about footballers can be found in *Rothmans Yearbook*. The programme from a League or Cup game may have either team or individual pictures. It is important to use the most recent copy of any reference book. Picture libraries can be used to confirm the identities of people photographed and the newspaper's cuttings library can be a useful source of information for facts, and will probably have a greater range of reference books than the picture desk.

There is no excuse for wrong spelling in a caption. Anyone who is not sure how a particular word is spelt should consult a dictionary. If a name has an unusual spelling, let the subs know it has been spelt correctly by placing a tick over it, or put the word 'correct' in brackets afterwards:

Mr Roger Smithee, Chairman of Auldthorp Parish Council.

Mr Roger Smithee (correct), Chairman of Auldthorp (correct) Parish Council.

The word '(correct)' can be struck out later during the subbing process.

HOUSE STYLE

All newspapers and magazines have a house style book, which lays down rules which aim to ensure consistency in the publication, rather than to pass judgement on a particular use of language. The rules may relate to:

- Alternative spelling of words, e.g. jail, gaol.

- The use of abbreviations. Although most people know what the TUC is, many will not know what the EETPU or the GMBATU are. An abbreviation should only be used in a caption after it has first appeared in its full form. Particular problems in consistency occur with abbreviations of military ranks.
- Whether house numbers are printed in addresses.
- The Editor's personal preferences. For instance:

> Oldchester Mayor Billy Bloggs arrives at last night's council meeting.

may be unacceptable, and must be replaced by:

> Councillor Billy Bloggs, the Mayor of Oldchester, arrives at last night's council meeting.

- Trade names. The names of certain products may appear to have passed into common use in the English language, but manufacturers will be quick to send a newspaper a letter if they are printed without an initial capital letter, or are seen to refer to a rival's product. Accordingly use the alternatives:

Biro   Ball point pen
JCB   Mechanical excavator
Hoover   Vacuum cleaner
Portakabin   Portable building

- Forbidden words. All newspapers go through phases when budgets can't be 'slashed', jobs can't be 'axed' and 'union chiefs' can no longer hold 'top level talks' with 'management bosses'. And we should all be grateful.

Newspaper style books are a guide to writing good newspaper English. Time spent studying one on a quiet day will amply reward the photographer interested in writing competent captions.

LINKING THE CAPTION TO THE STORY

Newspaper picture captions are frequently no more than a line or two in length. Sometimes the picture's position on the page and the layout of text around it indicates the story to which it refers. On other occasions the picture and accompanying text are ruled off from the rest of the page in a separate box. Individual paragraphs of the text may start with a blob, or some other design feature – a crown, perhaps, for a story about a member of the royal family.

A caption should be adjacent to the picture where it can be found quickly by a reader. They should not have to hunt for it. Sometimes on a spread of pictures all the captions are lumped together, when the link between words and pictures can be confusing. 'Top left' is acceptable, but identifying pictures 'clockwise from the top' may baffle the reader. Sometimes it is possible to place a caption in a white block within the area of a picture if there is suitable redundant space.

The first few words of a caption are like the introductory paragraph of a story

– they have to attract the interest of the reader. They should form a link between the picture and the rest of the caption. Depending upon the house style, the introductory word or phrase may be set in bold type or capitals, and separated from the words following by a colon or a dash.

Suppose we have a picture taken at a garden show of a delighted man clutching a vase of chrysanthemums. The photograph may or may not be accompanied by a report on the event, perhaps with a list of winners.

BLOOMIN' MARVELLOUS

is a good link between the picture and the rest of the caption – but some papers may pedantically not permit the apostrophe.
But

BLOOMIN' MARVELLOUS – Peter Rodgers and his prize winning chrysanthemums.

tells us not much more that can be seen in the picture. Add some more of the facts that the photographer might have gleaned when speaking to Mr Rodgers and we can say:

BLOOMIN' MARVELLOUS – Peter Rodgers proudly displays the chrysanthemums which won him the Best in Show award at yesterday's (TUES) Annual Show of the Oldchester Flower Club. Mr Rodgers, 52, of Park Street, Oldchester, is a former Chairman of the Club, and won a Gold Award with five other exhibits.

Notice how the caption is written to appear in a newspaper the day after the show. (TUES) is included so that if the picture is held over to another day, a sub-editor will know when the picture was taken. An evening paper tries hard to print as many pictures as possible on the day they are taken, and would certainly use 'today' or 'this morning' where appropriate in a caption to convey to the readers the speed with which the picture has been brought to them. Unless a caption included the words 'yesterday' or 'last night', newspapers would probably remove any reference to when it was taken.

Captions are best written in the present tense – using the past tense reduces the immediacy of the picture. The first sentence in the caption above loses impact if 'displayed' replaces 'displays'.

Sometimes the past tense cannot be avoided:

WRECKED: The Ford Escort in which two people died last night (WEDS) after it rolled over a cliff.

but if there is a policeman in the picture looking at the car then we can write:

WRECKED: A policeman inspects the Ford Escort in which two people died last night (WEDS) after it rolled over a cliff.

The moral, which perhaps applies more to photography than to caption writing, is to make sure that something is happening in a picture.

Verbs should be active rather than passive:

WRECKED: The Ford Escort in which two people died last night (WEDS) after it rolled over a cliff is inspected by a policeman.

is laboured.

There are some phrases which should be avoided when writing a caption:

our picture shows
pictured yesterday
shares a joke with (this expression is normally preceded by the name of a member of the royal family)

These expressions can invariably be removed with a little thought, which will be well rewarded by the marked improvement in the resulting caption.

Caption writers should be wary of record-breaking achievements:

FLOWER POWER – John Grower measures the height of the sunflower in his back garden which has now grown to a record height of nine feet six inches.

may only bring calls from other sunflower growers. It is better to say:

FLOWER POWER – John Grower measures the height of the sunflower in his back garden, now nine feet six inches tall which he claims to be a record.

Some adjectives cannot be qualified. For instance, an item is unique if it is the only one. Even if there are only two of them, neither of them is almost unique.

CAPTIONS AND THE LAW

The legal problems in captions are discussed in Chapter 10. The principal pitfalls in the actual writing of a caption relate to libel and contempt of court.

People can be libelled, amongst other ways, if their marital relationships are incorrectly specified or they are misrepresented.

It is important to ensure that anyone who can be identified from a photograph must not be linked with imminent criminal proceedings. Some media even decline to use the word 'arrested', preferring 'led away'. Proceedings are imminent when a person has been arrested, or charged, or when there is a warrant out for their arrest.

NICKED – a rioter is arrested yesterday (TUES) after throwing a pot of paint at a policeman outside Downing Street.

will cause legal problems if the person can be identified in any way. It links the person with the offence and if they are released or cleared by the courts, there are grounds for an action for defamation. Furthermore it prejudices the chance of a fair trial and could place the newspaper in contempt of court. The picture and caption can be printed if the person's face is obliterated and rendered unidentifiable, or the picture can be used if the caption is rewritten, rendering it legally acceptable:

A person is led away by police yesterday (TUES) after a pot of paint had been thrown at a policeman outside Downing Street.

Implications of guilt should be avoided in pictures of car crashes:

Two people died last night (WEDS) after this Fiesta hit the Mayor's official limousine outside the council offices.

should be replaced by:

Two people died last night (WEDS) after this Fiesta and the Mayor's limousine collided outside the council offices.

NEWS AGENCY CAPTIONS

Freelance and news agency captions should be brief and self-explanatory. Picture editors do not have the time to read through an essay to discover the point of a caption/picture. If a longer story is needed, this should be attached to the print with a paperclip when prints are distributed.

Because of the international dateline and changing deadlines around the world, international news agency captions frequently use the day of the week, and omit references to 'today' or 'yesterday'. They assume less prior knowledge by the reader of the story behind the picture.

10
Law

WHY THE LAW MATTERS

An understanding of the law is important to a photographer working for the media. Ignorance can result in a fine, imprisonment, or payment of damages if the publication of a photograph lands a photographer in court. Knowledge will enable journalists to keep clear of the courts and to appreciate when threats against them or their newspaper are soundly based.

The purpose of this chapter is to give photographers and picture editors guidance on the problems they may face on a day-to-day operational basis. There are many books written about the full relationship between journalists and the law, and one should be on every picture desk. Particularly recommended is Tom Crone's *Law and the Media* published by Butterworth-Heinemann.

However, the law is not all black and white, but contains shades of grey. Frequently it is possible to use a picture if the caption is rewritten. There are occasions when the law is knowingly broken, when a newspaper or journalist is aware that the chances of a prosecution are low.

All newspapers should have access to a lawyer. They are often only consulted when things go wrong. If their advice is sought earlier, pitfalls may be avoided, and ways discovered of printing pictures and stories which otherwise would be spiked.

RIGHTS OF A PHOTOGRAPHER

A photographer is a citizen with a camera, and enjoys the same rights and restrictions as any other member of the public with a camera. On occasions privileges may be extended, for example to sit at the touchline of a football match, to attend photocalls closed to the public, or to work from areas designated by the police as being for the media. However, a photographer has no legal right to go anywhere from which the public are excluded.

A photographer may take a picture (provided it does not breach certain laws and guidelines discussed later) of anything visible from the public highway or of anything or anyone using it. There is no law of privacy in Britain, yet. The implications of the Calcutt report are discussed at the end of this chapter.

A news organization's management should be made aware of any legal problem encountered by a photographer. The defence for a libel action can be seriously prejudiced if an apology is offered without taking the appropriate legal advice.

CRIMINAL VERSUS CIVIL LAW

There are two principal branches of law, criminal and civil. Criminal law is enforced by the state, and covers offences like theft, murder, assault and fraud.

People accused of breaking the criminal law are dealt with in Magistrates' and Crown Courts, with appeals to higher levels. Those found guilty may be put on probation, fined or imprisoned. The Civil Law deals with disputes between individuals or companies, which are heard in County Courts, the High Courts and other specialized courts, again with appeals to higher levels. Typical actions heard in Civil Courts include matrimonial and custody proceedings, disputes over contracts, libel and negligence.

PRECINCTS OF COURT

Photographers frequently try to 'snatch' pictures of people arriving or leaving courts – this is covered by Section 41 of the Criminal Justice Act of 1925 which makes it a criminal offence to:

> take or attempt to take in any court any photograph … of any person, being a judge of the court or a juror or a witness in or a party to any proceedings before the court, whether civil or criminal, or to publish any photograph taken in contravention of this section.

It adds that:

> a photograph shall be deemed to be … taken in court if it is taken in the court-room or in the building or in the precincts of the building in which the court is held, or if it is a photograph taken … of the person while he is entering or leaving the … precincts.

The precincts, or surroundings, of the court are not defined in the Act, and can vary from court to court, or even from case to case. One guideline – though not a defence or a guarantee against prosecution – is to ensure that the court buildings do not appear in the picture. The precincts may be extended by a judge to include the route to or from court of the defendant. If a court leaves its courthouse to visit, say, the scene of an alleged crime, then the court's activity at that location is covered by the Act.

Where the photographer was when the picture was taken does not enter into the issue. The question is whether the photograph shows a person entering or leaving the precincts of the court, so the use of a telephoto lens from across the street is not a means of thwarting the law.

The Act does not forbid a photographer taking a camera into the court building, or even into the courtroom. It merely states that it cannot be used. Many courthouses do not permit photographers to take their cameras into the courtroom but, accepting that they need access to see proceedings, allow equipment to be left with an official at the entrance of the building.

It is an interesting question as to who exactly are parties to the proceedings, and when the proceedings are finished. The defendant is clearly a party to the proceedings during the hearing, but do the proceedings end once a verdict has been announced? And are people watching from the public gallery, who may be relatives of the defendant or others involved in the case, parties?

Anybody working at a court should familiarize themselves with local custom and practice (in itself no defence) which is a guide to the behaviour of photographers that officials at the court have tolerated previously.

Care should be taken that one is attempting to picture the right person. Members of the jury cannot be identified by the media under any circumstances. To photograph them, even inadvertently, is likely to lead to complaints to the judge, and a very stern rebuke to the photographers concerned. It could easily constitute contempt of court.

Prosecutions under the Act are infrequent, and although no photographer would ever try to take pictures inside a court, the letter of the law about people entering and leaving the precincts of the court is often ignored.

CONTEMPT OF COURT

Journalists may find themselves in contempt of court if they engage in behaviour which could interfere with the course of justice or is intended to sway the minds of a jury. The guiding principle is that evidence which will be introduced to the magistrate or jury must not be discussed or revealed beforehand.

A newspaper may be in contempt of court if it publishes a photograph of a person if the question of identity is to be raised during the trial. The risk to the prosecution's case is that the defence can claim that a witness did not recognize the defendant, for instance, at the scene of the crime, but from a picture subsequently printed in a newspaper.

On occasions, the police have told the media that issues of identification will feature in the trial and requested the media not to print any pictures of the defendant.

Care should be taken when printing pictures in which identifiable people may be involved in criminal activity, or have been arrested by the police following that activity. For instance:

> THUG – police arrest one of the football fans who attacked a group of rival soccer supporters outside Oldchester railway station last night (FRI).

accuses the person of the crime, clearly prejudices the chances of a fair trial and is also highly defamatory if the person is acquitted. Acceptable alternatives would be to either obliterate the person's face, rendering it unidentifiable, or to rewrite the caption:

> A fan is led away by police last night (FRI) after rival groups of soccer supporters clashed at Oldchester Railway Station.

It may be possible to use pictures of people indulging in illegal activity when the question of identity does not arise. If any charges arising from the incident are mentioned, then the caption must say that *a* man was later arrested, charged, bailed etc. and not that *the* man was later arrested etc. It would be prudent to take legal advice from a solicitor before doing this.

Taking pictures of people entering and leaving courthouses may also be treated as contempt at common law, because, in the eyes of the judiciary, defendants, witnesses and other parties have a right to go to and from court without being harassed by the press. In some cases the judges may make an explicit order banning the photographing of a party to the proceedings. Such an order should be obeyed. Reporters covering cases should ensure that picture desks are aware of any such orders imposed. Sometimes the order is exhibited in the courthouses.

POLICE PICTURES

On occasions the police may provide the media with a picture of a wanted person to accompany an appeal to the public to notify them of the person's whereabouts. It is acceptable to say that 'The police want to question the person in connection with . . .', but he must not be accused of committing the crime. A newspaper publishing the picture is protected from a libel by the privilege afforded to material issued by a Chief Officer of police under the 1952 Defamation Act. Although strictly speaking publication is contempt, the judiciary are aware of the services performed by the media in circulating the picture.

LIBEL

It is possible to libel someone both in a photograph and a caption. Libel is a civil matter heard in the High Courts in front of a jury, and damages are awarded, by the jury, against the defendant. In recent years, the level of damages has spiralled dramatically.

A photograph or a caption is libellous if it exposes a person to hatred, ridicule or contempt; lowers them in the estimation of right-thinking members of the community; causes them to be shunned or avoided; or disparages their reputation in trade, business, profession or office.

The principal pitfall for a photographer lies in failing to identify people in a picture correctly. If a caption describes two people as being Mr and Mrs Black, and Mrs Black is, in fact, Mrs Brown, or even Miss Brown, then that caption is libellous. To those people who know Mr Black and the real Mrs Black, it suggests, amongst other things, that Mr Black is bigamous. It casts aspersions upon the relationship between Mr and Mrs Brown, or suggests that Miss Brown is falsely representing her marital status. The message to the photographer is clear – captions must be taken down as accurately as possible, asking, if possible, the people in the picture themselves who they are, and clarifying any possible ambiguities.

A picture of an individual accused of or found guilty of criminal proceedings would be libellous if the caption was correct, but the picture was of the wrong person. This could occur because of a mistake by the photographer, or because the library was asked for a picture of, say, Peter Black, and insufficient checks were made to ensure that the picture supplied was of the correct Peter Black. If in any doubt the picture should be taken to the court to be checked against the real person.

Care should be taken with library or stock pictures. People's relationships do change. For instance, a beach scene from a few years ago might show a couple walking hand in hand along the sand. If that picture was used in a newspaper and the caption suggested that it was taken 'yesterday', but the relationship was no more, perhaps because one of them had married, or even remarried, then there are actions for libel.

RAPE AND OTHER SEXUAL OFFENCES

The identification of the complainant in rape cases is prohibited, other than in exceptional circumstances. The Criminal Justice Act 1988 removed the right to anonymity previously enjoyed by the defendant until he had been found guilty.

JUVENILES

Defendants under the age of 18 usually appear at a Juvenile Court, where they cannot be identified in any way, so they cannot be photographed. As these courts cannot deal with serious crimes like murder, the accused is sent for trial at a Crown Court, where there is no automatic ban on identifying the juvenile, but an order is usually made by the judge, under the Children and Young Persons Act 1933, prohibiting the identification of the defendant. This same act can be used to ban the identification of juveniles appearing as witnesses or victims in other courts.

POLICE AND CRIMINAL EVIDENCE ACT

It is becoming increasingly common after civil disturbances for the police to approach news organizations asking for access to the pictures or videotape that their photographers may have taken. The police hope that they can use these pictures to identify and prosecute offenders, and seek both published and unpublished material. Some branches of the media hand over their pictures voluntarily, feeling that their duty is to assist the police in apprehending criminals. Others feel that their duty is to their staff, who would be under real risk of attack during such disturbances if it were known that their material would be passed on to the police, and decline to help.

The police can apply to the courts, under the 1984 Police and Criminal Evidence Act, for an order forcing news media to hand over all material, both published and unpublished. Orders were obtained after disturbances in 1987 outside the News International printing plant at Wapping, and after the 1990 poll tax riots in central London.

The issue is an emotive one, but photographers working at a civil disturbance must now realize that the police will come looking for their pictures. If they find it morally objectionable, then freelances have the choice not to attend, and staff photographers should make their feelings about covering the assignment known to the picture editor.

Photographers are sometimes asked to hand over their film by the police at the scene of an incident. If the police believe that the photographer has committed a crime, or aided and abetted a crime, and that evidence of the crime is contained on the film, then they are entitled to seize the film and camera in much the same way as they would acquire any other evidence. If the photographer has merely taken pictures that the police would prefer not to have been taken, they have no rights at all to confiscate the film. If the police persist, then the matter should be drawn to the attention of a senior officer, and the photographer's picture desk informed as soon as possible.

There are some events, for instance pop concerts, which impose upon the public a condition of entry that the taking of pictures for publication without the consent of the organizers is forbidden. A press photographer who has gained admission legally and taken pictures at such an event is under no obligation to hand over the exposed film to the organizers. They may ask the photographer to leave, as a condition of entry has been broken, but their legal remedy is to seek damages against the photographer and newspaper through the civil courts. Alternatively, they could seek an injunction against the photographer and newspaper, restraining the publication of the pictures.

OFFICIAL SECRETS ACT

Section 1 of the 1911 Official Secrets Act makes it an offence if:

> ... any person for any purpose prejudicial to the safety or interest of the State –
>
> (a) approaches, inspects, passes over, or is in the neighbourhood of, or enters any prohibited place within the meaning of this Act, or
> (b) makes any sketch, plan, model, or note which is calculated to be or might be or is intended to be directly or indirectly useful to an enemy; or
> (c) obtains, collects, records or publishes or communicates to any other person any ... sketch, plan, model or article ... which is calculated to be or might be or is intended to be directly or indirectly useful to an enemy.

The Act goes on to define prohibited places. They include:

> any work of defence, arsenal, naval or air force establishment or station, factory, dockyard, mine, minefield, camp, ship or aircraft belonging to or occupied by or on behalf of Her Majesty, or any telegraph, telephone, wireless or signal station.

More recent acts have added to the lists places belonging to or used for the purposes of the United Kingdom Atomic Energy Authority, the Civil Aviation Authority, British Telecom, or any other public telecommunications operative.

Thankfully, prosecutions under the Act can only be started by, or with the consent of, the Attorney General, so photographers may continue to take pictures of the Telecom Tower or Heathrow airport – from the public highway, of course – without fear of imprisonment.

When the Act was introduced, there were no spy satellites. Now, when they must have discovered and photographed every installation in the country, it is hard to see why a spy would take his camera and look over the fence. Nevertheless, anyone using a camera in the vicinity of military establishments should expect more than a cursory interest from military patrols or police. These days the concern is more about the planning of a potential terrorist attack than a clandestine visit from spies of a foreign power. Common sense suggests that anyone intending to photograph a military base should contemplate explaining their intentions first.

Junior servicemen at the site of crashed military aircraft can sometimes suggest that the wreckage is covered by the Official Secrets Act. If they do, then a senior officer should be approached to establish precisely what, if anything, is genuinely covered by the Act.

Problems can arise at incidents when bomb disposal experts are present. As potential terrorist targets, these people have an understandable desire to maintain their anonymity, and any request to ensure that their faces do not appear in newspapers should be respected. Similarly, in Northern Ireland there is a convention that members of the security services will not be identified in news pictures.

DA NOTICES

In 1993 the system of D Notices (Defence Notices) which provided guidance to the news media about the publication of matters sensitive to the security of the nation was altered to reflect changing circumstances, including the break-up of the Soviet Union and the Warsaw Pact, the UK's involvement in smaller scale conflicts and the continuing terrorist threat.

The eight existing D Notices were replaced by six DA Notices (Defence Advisory Notices). They are made available – at one time even the context of D Notices were officially secret – to editorial executives by the Defence, Press and Broadcasting Committee, which consists of civil servants and representatives of news media. Obeying a DA Notice is no guarantee of escaping a prosecution under the Official Secrets Act.

OBSTRUCTION

The Queen's Highway – and that includes anything from a motorway to a public footpath – is for the purpose of travel, and not for the purpose of stopping, whether it be to admire the view, or to take a photograph. A group of photographers, or even an individual, working in a street, for instance 'doorstepping' a house in order to photograph a person in the news arriving or leaving, constitute an obstruction, and can be 'moved on' by the police. That nobody has been actually obstructed is immaterial. Failure to 'move on' could result in arrest, and a trip to the nearest police station. The process usually ends there as prosecution is unlikely. Common sense says that photographers should not block pavements, forcing the public on to the road.

Excessive harassment of people while trying to take their picture in the streets could culminate in an arrest under the grounds of 'behaviour likely to cause a breach of the peace'.

TRESPASS

The sign 'Trespassers will be prosecuted' is usually meaningless. Trespassing on someone's land is normally a civil matter, for which the remedy is an action for damages, to repair any harm done to the property.

The 1994 Criminal Justice Act introduced the concept of aggravated trespass: a criminal offence committed when on land with the intention of disrupting or preventing a legal activity.

Trespassing on the railway, and the property of some other statutory organizations, is a criminal offence.

Although not actually trespass, stopping one's car on the motorway to take a picture – even from inside the car – is a motoring offence. Taking pictures while driving a car could also bring a charge of driving without due care and attention.

COPYRIGHT

Under the Copyright, Designs and Patents Act 1988, the copyright of pictures taken by staff photographers is owned by their newspaper. Freelances submitting pictures, or employed on a casual or shift basis, own the copyright to their photographs unless there is a signed agreement to the contrary between them and the publication. Before 1988, the copyright was held by the person or organization who commissioned the work.

COLLECTS

When it is not possible to take a picture of a person – perhaps they are being held hostage abroad, have died in a disaster, or are the subject of criminal proceedings – photographers try to borrow pictures from friends, relatives or wedding photographers, and this can lead to copyright problems.

Pictures borrowed from the friends and relatives who took them should present no difficulties. To reproduce wedding pictures without legal complications, permission should be obtained from both the photographer who took them, who owns the copyright, and the couple who commissioned them, who have the right to control their circulation. This is not always practical – and picture desks should be made aware when a picture without full clearance has been obtained.

VIDEOGRABBING

Taking news pictures from television transmissions may not breach the broadcaster's copyright because of the 'fair dealing' provision of the 1988 Act which requires that the source of the material is acknowledged. Section 30 of Part 1 of the act states:

> Fair dealing with a work (other than a photograph) for the purpose
> of reporting current events does not infringe any copyright provided
> that ... it is accompanied by a sufficient acknowledgement.

The wording was tested in a dispute in the High Court in front of Mr Justice Scott after the BBC brought an action seeking damages and injunction against BSkyB for using their material from the World Cup in a sports review programme. The judge held that the material was being used for the purpose of reporting current affairs and with sufficient acknowledgement of the copyright owner, and dismissed the case.

However, some television companies take the view that their product is being used and may take a firmer line on videograbbed pictures.

The law provides protection to a photographer from a person making a direct copy of the print or transparency. There is insufficient case law at present to determine whether it also provides protection against the picture being imitated.

MISCELLANEOUS PROBLEMS

Although they may appear to be public, taking pictures in some London parks can be difficult as commercial photography is either banned, or allowed only with a permit from the relevant authority. Putting up a tripod is the fastest way of discovering the whereabouts of the nearest member of the parks police. Tripods are also banned in Trafalgar Square unless the user has a permit from the Department of the Environment.

Some shopping precincts do not allow any form of photography – again they may look public, but they are owned, or managed, by somebody who can impose whatever rules they like as a condition of entry.

ETHICS

Apart from legal considerations when going about their job, photographers also have to be aware of ethical problems. The law is black and white – perhaps with grey edges – and is the control by the state of the media's news-gathering and publishing activities. Ethics are less well defined, and are guided by the reaction of the public to the conduct of the media and its methods of operation.

Most photographers will have a gut feeling as to how far they can go in terms of subterfuge or intrusion to gain a picture or access to a location. Is it legitimate to don a white coat to enter a hospital to obtain pictures? Should one photograph and interview schoolchildren without a teacher or adult being present? How acceptable is it for *paparazzi*-style photographers to use telephoto lenses to snatch photographs of members of the Royal family in their unguarded moments? Are the rich, the famous, the powerful, the wealthy or those in the public eye entitled to privacy? How often are pictures and stories grandly defended as being 'in the public interest', when what is really meant is that they are merely 'of interest to the public'?

The irony is frequently that the public claims to disapprove of the way some material is obtained, but is none the less anxious to see it.

THE PRESS COUNCIL

The Press Council was a voluntary body whose purposes included adjudicating complaints about the conduct of newspapers and individual journalists. The complaint may have come from the person who felt wronged, or from anyone else who felt that the behaviour of the press had been inappropriate.

Its council was composed of equal numbers of lay members of the public and journalists drawn from the industry. It had no legal power, but after the submission of evidence either orally or in writing, editors were obliged to publish the Council's adjudication of the complaint.

Complaints about pictures to the Press Council usually involved either the methods used to obtain a picture, or the way in which a picture was used.

THE CALCUTT REPORT

The Calcutt Committee's report into Privacy and Related Matters was published in mid-1990, and came at a time of growing public concern about the standards and behaviour of journalists and newspapers. Journalists from a Sunday newspaper had entered the hospital room of Mr Gorden Kaye, an actor who had been badly hurt in a motor accident, and taken pictures of him. *The Sun* had paid huge sums in damages in an out-of-court settlement to the singer Elton John after printing allegations about his private life.

The report recommended that a new, smaller, Press Complaints Commission should replace the Press Council. The Commission would become a statutory tribunal if 'self-regulation' was not seen to be working. It proposed a new code of practice for the press. More controversially it advocated the introduction of criminal legislation to prevent journalists physically intruding into people's homes to obtain information, take photographs or tape-record them without their consent.

One of its more adventurous ideas was the establishment of a 'hot line' through which people who felt that they were being unfairly treated by the press could contact the Press Complaints Commission before a story appeared in print.

The press was put on notice by the government and opposition that it had 18 months to show that self-regulation would work.

THE PRESS COMPLAINTS COMMISSION

The Press Complaints Commission opened for business at the start of 1991. With the threat of statutory legislation hanging over it, the industry appears to be taking the code of practice to heart, and new laws restricting the freedom of the press do not appear imminent.

Some newspaper editors have appointed their own 'in-house' ombudsmen to receive and investigate complaints from readers. After an initial blaze of publicity, they do not appear to be stretched.

In August 1991 the Commission upheld a complaint made by the Buckingham Palace Press Office on behalf of a member of the Royal family. The *Sunday People* had published two pictures, taken surreptitiously, of Princess Eugenie, the 16-month-old daughter of the Duke of York, naked in a garden. He complained that the pictures were a breach of privacy.

After the newspaper had been told of the complaint, it reprinted the pictures and invited readers to participate in a telephone vote on whether or not they were offensive.

The newspaper defended the publication of the pictures on the grounds that they were charming, natural pictures of a little girl published good-naturedly and affectionately. In response to the complaint it claimed that under English law anybody is free to take a picture of anybody else.

The Commission stated that the pictures were in breach of clause 4 of the Code of Conduct which condemns intrusions and inquiries into an individual's private life, unless they can be justified as being in the interest of the public, and of clause 11, which states that journalists should not normally interview or photograph children under the age of 16 without the consent of their parents or an adult responsible for them. It considered that, by reprinting the pictures, the newspaper demonstrated contempt for both the Commission and the complaints procedure.

At about the same time, *The News*, Portsmouth, was censured by the Commission for taking and publishing photographs of a mother and her companion 'against their wishes' during a search for the woman's missing son.

The couple, it was claimed, had been asked several times if they could be photographed, and had declined. It was alleged that the photographer had trespassed to take the pictures, intruding on both privacy and grief. The paper said that their photographer was in a position which was not blocked to the public, that the pictures were a legitimate record of an event of interest to the public, and that the photographer stopped taking pictures when asked to do so.

Although the Commission accepted that the reporter and photographer had behaved courteously and were generally well restrained, it upheld the complaint, considering that the photography was in breach of the clause in the code of practice which calls for discretion and sympathy in cases of personal grief.

The Press Complaints Commission does not appear to be issuing as many adjudications as the old Press Council; libel payouts seem to be diminishing; perhaps the pendulum is starting to swing the other way.

In 1993 a self-regulatory Code of Conduct framed by the industry and ratified by the PCC (Press Complaints Commission) said that people on private property (which is defined as including hotel bedrooms and hospital wards and treatment rooms) should not be harassed or have their privacy intruded upon by long-lens photography. It also gave guidelines on photographing children under 16 while at school or on matters relating to their personal welfare.

11
The picture desk

THE ROLE OF THE PICTURE DESK

However large or small, the picture desk serves the same purpose – to plan and oversee the work of the paper's photographers and to marry their efforts to the needs of the editor. The picture desk of a big national newspaper or international news agency may be manned round the clock and have a dozen staff; at the other end of the industry, the picture desk of a small free weekly paper can be no more than a diary and in and out trays, overseen by the paper's news editor.

The staff of a picture desk need to be aware of the problems and difficulties faced by photographers but it is not essential that they have worked 'on the road' themselves. Sadly, photographers who turn to picture desk work are often disparaged by their former colleagues, usually quite unfairly, as 'failed cameramen'. Nevertheless a working knowledge of photography is needed by a picture editor.

A national newspaper will have a picture editor directly responsible to the editor for the photographic operations of the newspaper, aided usually by several deputy or assistant picture editors. One of these will run the diary – the paper's list of engagements – and another will be responsible for copy tasting – reading stories coming into the newspaper from its reporters, correspondents and agencies to which it subscribes. Until recently the transmission and reception of photographs over telephone lines was handled by separate staff in the paper's wireroom. Now, with changes in practice and technology, it is often undertaken by picture desk staff. The desk may also have a secretary to make travel arrangements and organize accommodation for the paper's staff photographers.

Larger provincial papers have simply a picture editor in whose absence a senior photographer may deputize. Smaller papers may not have a picture editor, but share the duties between the news editor and the chief photographer.

The extent to which picture editors have an influence on which photographs appear in a paper and the size that they are used at varies from publication to publication. It is greatest in quality broadsheet newspapers. The final choice of pictures used in national tabloid newspapers is largely made by the production journalists who lay out the pages, with the editor and deputy editor taking an interest in the front page picture and any others being used prominently inside.

Provincial picture editors have varied roles. As well as running the diary, assigning photographers and ensuring a continuous supply of good pictures to the editions, they may be responsible for photographers' equipment, overseeing the darkroom and maintaining stocks of photographic materials.

JOBS AND DUTIES

Every day a newspaper is aware of a large number of events which may merit a photographer's presence or to which one is invited. The responsibility of the picture desk is to ensure the right photographer is at the right job at the right time, and that the most suitable pictures are back in the office, by whatever means, in time to be processed, chosen, edited and prepared for the appropriate edition. As well as organizing the paper's own photographers, the picture editor assesses the pictures sent from agencies to which the paper subscribes and from freelances who offer material.

Each page of a newspaper has its own deadline which must be met. Not all pages are typeset and laid out simultaneously; some are early ones, and some are late. Tuesday lunchtime might be the deadline for an early page in a weekly paper which prints on a Friday; 2 a.m. might not be too late to squeeze in a picture for the last edition of a national tabloid newspaper. This must be borne in mind when planning the assignments.

The pages in a newspaper can be broadly split into news, sport and features. Feature pictures often accompany specific sections, such as the women's page, or particular topics such as fashion, and may be commissioned or organized by the features department. Similarly, the sports desk will know which are the most important matches to cover and will advise the picture desk on how resources may be best deployed.

Although some pictures can stand alone with only a brief caption, others will be linked to a story. To co-ordinate the activities of the photographers and reporters, the picture desk works in close contact with the news desk. On small papers this may mean the news editor looking at the diary and deciding which jobs must be covered. On larger papers the news and picture editors may sit at the same desk so that they are each aware what the staff of the other is doing. The contact may be formalized at daily editorial conferences, when heads of all departments gather with the editor or his or her deputy to plan the day's paper and discuss how particular jobs are covered.

Newspaper reporters are the ears of photographers since they are usually the first to hear of breaking news. They make regular check calls throughout the day to the emergency services, and also get calls from the police which can lead to stories which need a picture.

In their pursuit of picture ideas, most picture desks have a television set nearby in order to watch the news bulletins and keep an eye on the teletext services such as the BBC's Ceefax and ITV's Teletext. It is also worth monitoring the news output of local television and radio stations, which often have good contacts and hear early leads to news events.

WHERE PICTURES COME FROM

- *Staff* and *contract photographers* produce most pictures in a newspaper. Whereas staff photographers are permanent employees of the company, which usually provides their equipment and pays their national insurance and pension contributions, contract photographers are freelances hired to do either occasional or regular shifts. Staff and contract photographers are aware of a paper's deadlines and needs and style and their pictures are exclusive to that paper.

- *Agencies*. National papers take a service of pictures from international agencies which include Associated Press (AP), Reuters and Agence France Presse. These agencies have either staff photographers or local 'stringers' in virtually every country, although their strengths and weaknesses vary from place to place. Their pictures can be used for stories which would be too expensive to send a staff photographer to cover, or which would be over by the time they got there.

  Almost all morning and evening papers subscribe to the Press Association, Britain's national news agency, which supplies a service of news, sport and feature pictures from all over the country. Its photographers operate from London and six other centres throughout the country. For provincial customers it supplies a selection of international pictures from the service of AP.

  Obviously, agency pictures are not exclusive, nor are they taken to meet the deadline and style needs of a particular publication, but they may be the only ones available.

- *Provincial agencies* provide a service of pictures from a geographical area. They may be commissioned by a newspaper to take a picture or may take the picture first and offer it to whichever papers they feel will be likely to buy it. Most have wire machines to transmit the pictures over the telephone line. They live off their wits, and come into their own when a staff photographer is unable to reach the scene of a particular story because of time or distance. Alternatively they might offer a staff photographer the use of their processing facilities, for a fee.

  Provincial agencies respond fast to stories breaking in their area and can usually cover all but the largest story with more staff than a newspaper could spare. They should have good local contacts and the experience of where the best pictures of annual occurrences, like flooding, crowded beaches, summer traffic jams, etc., occur.

- *Other agencies* can cover a wide range of topics – for instance, personalities, sport, fashion, glamour, wildlife, military equipment, science or transport. Details of these can be found in the *Artists' and Writers' Yearbook* or in the *Freelance Photographer's Market Handbook*. Some charge a fee for looking for the material as well as a reproduction fee.

- *Other papers*. Some provincial papers whose circulation areas do not overlap may assist one another informally. For example, if the local Football League team was playing some distance away, it might be possible to get pictures of the match on the wire from the area's evening paper.

- *Library*. The newspaper's own library is a useful source of photographs. If an MP has eloped with his secretary or a pop star has died after a drug overdose, then the only picture available may be in the library. It is also useful for confirming identities of people for a caption.

- *Handout* pictures come from public relations officers in industry and entertainment. Some may be of immediate use, for instance the latest car from a manufacturer, while others, for instance the latest picture of a television newsreader, can be held in the library until they are in the news.
- *Rota* pictures are taken by a photographer on behalf of other publications which are unable, for various reasons, to send a photographer to the event. The rota system mainly applies to engagements by the Royal family, the prime minister and visiting heads of state, and is discussed in Chapter 8.
- *Videograbbed* pictures from television news programmes. Satellite technology and 24-hour news channels such as Ted Turner's Cable News Network and BSkyB bring pictures from all over the world to the picture desk faster than any news agency can. The quality may not be as good as a wire picture but it is better than no picture at all. Although it is possible to 'grab' an image from a broadcast, it is better to record the material and play it back to select the best material in terms of content and technical quality.

The technical parameters of television broadcasts vary around the world and equipment which works in one country may not work elsewhere.

Purpose-made videograbbing equipment has a recorder/player through which the tape can be advanced a frame at a time before the required one is output as a colour print from which the usual separations can be made. The print is produced on a thermal printer which uses heat to transfer dyes from a coloured film onto the paper rather than conventional colour photographic techniques and the whole process takes just a couple of minutes.

A much cheaper alternative is to mount a camera on a tripod squarely in front of a television set and photograph the screen. It is essential that all reflections are eliminated from the screen. A television picture in the UK is made up of 625 lines (a few at the top and bottom do not appear on the screen) which are scanned sequentially, 1, 3, 5, etc. to 625, and then 2, 4, 6, etc. The whole process takes 1/25th of a second. Using a shutter speed shorter than this will mean that the whole picture is not recorded; using a longer one increases the chance of subject movement and may introduce a bright band where subsequent scans overlap. The practical solution is to record the transmission, decide which moment is to be 'grabbed', freeze the frame on the video recorder and take several pictures using exposures of 1/30th and 1/15th of a second, and one will be all right.

Ricoh makes a camera with an exposure mode designed specifically for taking pictures from television screens. It provides the user with the correct shutter speed by having different settings for each of the three broadcast systems, PAL, SECAM and NTSC, in use in different countries around the world.

It is also possible to supply a video feed into a personal computer, equipped with the appropriate hardware, and 'grab' a picture. Software in the computer allows the picture to be enhanced before it is fed to an electronic picture desk.

Videograbbed pictures must be credited to the broadcasting company when they are published. Failure to do so breaches the 'fair dealing' defence under the 1988 Copyright Act which permits copyright material to be used. It states:

Fair dealing with a work (other than a photograph) for the reporting of current events does not infringe any copyright in the work provided that . . . it is accompanied by a sufficient acknowledgement.

However, some television stations consider that videograbbing their material is not 'fair dealing', but using their product, and may take a firmer line on the practice.

RUNNING THE DIARY

However large or small, a picture desk will always have a diary, a book into which are entered all the events happening on a particular day. It may be computerized, either on a small personal computer or as part of the office's mainframe system.

Much of the information arrives by post or fax and has to be scanned rapidly to find out if any action is required before the day of the event – it may be necessary to apply for a pass as soon as possible, or give the name of the particular photographer to whom the job has been assigned 48 hours before the event.

Only the briefest details are recorded. The full particulars, perhaps sent out in mailshot by a public relations company or a press cutting from a newspaper, are stored nearby, perhaps in a filing cabinet with folders for each date of the month or a set of trays with one for each day of the week.

On provincial papers many picture leads or 'requests' on provincial papers come from the reporters or the news desk. It helps if a simple form is printed on which these requests can be passed to the picture desk. As well as the person or event to be photographed, such a form should carry the name of the reporter, a contact number to help the photographer make necessary arrangements and a time at which the person or event will be available. A cautious picture editor will check these times; reporters and news desks have a habit of asking photographers to be at a job half an hour early 'for safety's sake'.

The diary will also contain reminders to organize passes for forthcoming events; details of events not 'announced', but whose date can be predicted, e.g. Budget Day, or the birthday of the local mayor or members of the royal family; anniversaries – one year since a train crash in which ten people died, or one year since a local child was the country's youngest-ever heart transplant recipient, etc.

Newspapers also have access to engagements of the local mayor, members of the Royal family and politicians. Some of these are supplied for 'operational use only'; the newspaper may use them to plan its coverage but must not, usually for security reasons, divulge them in advance of the event.

The diary can also be used for administration purposes, recording the names of photographers working various shifts, and which ones are on holiday, or unavailable until 11.00 a.m. because of a dental appointment and suchlike.

Some jobs require the details of the photographer covering the event to be sent to the organizer beforehand – usually for security reasons – and the diary editor, where there is one, will find it useful to keep a file of a few personal details of each photographer, including car type, colour and registration number, and passport number, date and place of issue and a supply of passport-size pictures.

As well as thinking about 'tomorrow's jobs' the picture and diary editors need to plan in advance for events needing special travel arrangements, overnight accommodation, or wire facilities for the photographer.

The diary list of the day is usually compiled the previous afternoon so that it can be used by the picture editor to choose which assignments to cover with which photographer.

PLANNING THE DAY'S COVERAGE

The full diary lists all events, within reason, which the paper knows about. The picture editor then selects which ones to cover and which to omit.

The criteria for selection are complicated and varied.

What jobs must be done

These include events which readers expect to see in the paper, and those which the picture editor expects rival newspapers to attend. Obvious ones are big state occasions, major news stories, a visit from a government minister, the local carnival and the mayor-making ceremony. Any worthwhile picture story which the paper has as an 'exclusive' must be covered. There may be in-house promotions and direct requests of 'expressions of interest' from editorial management. Local newspapers have close links with their readers who may be offended if the paper does not send a photographer to 'their event'.

Is it news?

Every picture editor has a different idea of what news is. Hard news – train crashes, fires, crime, courts, human tragedies and people on the snakes and ladders of life – is easy to define. Soft news is much hard to define. Winning £1 000 000 on the pools is clearly national news (although more common now), but is winning a holiday for two in Spain in a competition news – even for a local paper? Is the handover of the chain of office of the local rotary club news? Is it news that a local school is having a sponsored walk to raise money for the victims of an earthquake? Would it be more newsworthy if the sponsored walk was being done in fancy dress? Is news a cheque presentation for £100? £1000?

Is England's latest World Cup hero opening a supermarket news? Definitely, to a local paper. A national tabloid newspaper might be interested, especially if there is a good story to run with it – perhaps he had been sent off during a match the weekend before and this is the first time he has been seen since. But it probably is not news if he opened another one yesterday.

Some local newspaper editors believe faces sell papers, and do not worry too much about the news value of a picture provided it has the faces of as many people as possible who might buy the paper or even a copy of the photograph. That is sad. People might buy a paper once because their face is printed inside. But they will buy it every week or day if the paper contains good pictures.

What sort of picture?

Some PRs and personalities have a knack of knowing the elements needed to make a good picture – others believe that if they send out a fax with the name of a personality on it the subsequent picture from the event cannot fail to be published.

Picture editors and photographers will quickly learn which organizations can be relied upon to help, and which think that getting a picture in the paper is their right, rather than privilege.

Resources

Planning picture coverage means, especially on a local paper, balancing whether it is better to have a photographer doing one job which takes several hours but which might produce a brilliant picture, or have the same photographer at several jobs, all of which will produce a picture or two, but none likely to be outstanding. If there are several photographers available on the particular day, or the picture editor has a couple of feature pictures in the 'bottom drawer' which could be used if the brilliant picture does not materialize, then it is probably worth committing the photographer for several hours. If there is only one photographer available and there are holes in the paper which must be filled, then the more mundane jobs will have to be done.

Time

Evening newspapers are looking for early pictures so that they can be printed in the paper later that day. Daily papers need pictures to fill those pages which are prepared earlier than the main news pages. A good picture editor will organize a photograph of a heart transplant recipient celebrating the first anniversary of his operation as early in the day as possible. If it were done in the afternoon or evening it would be too late for an evening newspaper to use as a 'today' picture, and would have to compete against 'harder' pictures for a place on the news pages of a daily paper.

Fashion photocalls aimed at national newspapers, for instance, are invariably done around 10.30 a.m., as it means that the pictures are processed and on the desk of national newspapers before lunchtime, ideal for an early page.

Bear in mind that the time stated on the handout is not necessarily the time at which the job will be taken. It may say 10.30, but the picture may not be taken until 11.00. How long will it take the film to get back to the office, or for the photographer to process and wire the picture? Local sports organizations are notorious for asking photographers to their annual presentation at 7.30 p.m. and neglecting to mention that the award winners collect their trophies around 10.30 p.m., after the dinner.

Sometimes a feature picture session for the following day can be rearranged for the afternoon, when the pressure of deadlines for that day's paper is less.

Staff

It makes sense where possible to match photographers to jobs. Some enjoy fashion, while others may loathe it but enjoy sport. It may be that some have a particular hobby, for instance sailing, which makes them a natural for jobs afloat. Another may be a devoted soccer fan – so if there is a choice it would be better not to send him to a rugby match. A good picture editor makes the most of the strengths of his team.

Balance

The picture desk needs to be able to offer the editor a balanced selection of pictures. There may be six cheque presentations/fashion photocalls/village fetes tomorrow, but there is no need to do all of them. The art is in choosing the right jobs – not going to everything.

REACTING TO NEWS

Although diary jobs are important, hard news, by definition, can happen at any time and at any place. During the day, the picture desk will hear from the news desk, the reporters or through television and radio of important events which mean calling photographers away from their planned assignments and sending them elsewhere or arranging coverage by an agency. If the picture desk is not manned around the clock, calls at night may be taken either by a journalist manning the news desk or by the security or switchboard staff who will know how to contact the photographer or picture editor rostered for standby duty.

The skill of the picture editor comes in judging the importance of the event to the paper's readers, and then sending the photographers to the right places.

A motorway pile-up or train crash with several people killed might mean sending two or three photographers to the scene, one to each of the hospitals where the casualties are being taken and another to fly over the incident in a helicopter or a light plane. The picture desk might make a quick check with other papers to see if they would like to put a photographer on board and share the hire cost.

Initially, while news of a major story is still breaking and details are still sketchy, the picture editor cannot afford to pull photographers away from too many other jobs. If the story is not as big as first thought, then those jobs will be needed for the paper. It may be possible to check if they are being covered by an agency.

Meanwhile local freelances would be asked to cover the incident until the paper's own photographers could reach the scene. The television news will be monitored to see if there are any pictures available to be videograbbed.

The emergency services would be asked if they took any pictures of the rescue of survivors, and if so, when and how they will be released.

As news comes in of the names of those involved, photographers would be assigned to call on their families to try to 'pick up' a picture. The desk would also be checking to see if, by chance, any of the people are in their library files.

The desk must also think about the quickest way to get the pictures back to the office to meet edition deadlines. If there is time, the photographers might bring them themselves, but this would mean pulling them away from the incident. Can the films be brought back by despatch rider, or should the newspaper send a portable wire machine? On major disasters well away from London national newspapers wanting to use original pictures rather than wire prints might charter a plane to bring the exposed film back to the picture desk.

It is also worth checking with the news desk to see if any reporters know of eye-witnesses who have any pictures. Sometimes people ring in offering their photographs; although the quality may not be too good, the content may be excellent. Again, the picture desk will have to determine the best way of getting the pictures to the office – and keeping their rivals' hands off them!

THE RIGHT PHOTOGRAPH

The job has been done and the processed film is back in the office – now what?

On local papers without a picture editor, the photographers themselves will probably pick the best picture or pictures from a particular assignment by viewing the negatives with a magnifier, or putting them in the enlarger, before printing them to the paper's usual size, writing a caption, and passing them to either the news editor, the reporter who is writing the story which accompanies the picture or the sub-editor designing the page.

Experience will guide the photographer as to how many pictures a particular job will yield and how many the paper might use. A photographer covering a visit of a local MP to meet shopkeepers whose trade is threatened by a traffic scheme would probably offer just one picture, as it will be accompanied by reports of the remarks of the MP and the shopkeepers. The photographer should check, however, with the reporter to find out whose words to the MP are being quoted to ensure that the person is in the picture. A serious road accident, at which the photographer arrives while people are still being rescued, might merit three or four pictures. Carnivals, processions, flower shows and local dramatics are all topics which lend themselves to a 'spread' of several pictures in a local paper, and the photographer will be expected to provide a selection of perhaps a dozen.

Offering just one picture of an unusual shape – particularly wide or deep – can cause problems for sub-editors laying out pages in a hurry or against awkwardly shaped advertisements; a wise photographer will also offer an alternative of a more conventional shape.

Even on larger papers which have picture editors and a full picture desk, photographers may make their own selection of pictures to be printed-up by the darkroom before a final selection is made together with the picture editor of those to be offered to the sub-editors or page executives. The initial selection can be made either by viewing the negatives with a magnifier, or from a set of contact prints. Some people find contact prints easier to 'read', but a magnifier gives a better indication of sharpness.

Some organizations whose photographers shoot on colour negative film use a machine printer similar to those found in High Street photofinishers to produce a roll of en-prints from the photographers' films. These can be used for editing or planning a page layout while a hand print is made from the selected negatives.

There are also viewers available which use a miniature television camera to display a negative as a colour picture on a monitor screen.

Once the picture has been chosen, it should be clearly marked. This helps prevent the darkroom printing the wrong frame, and assists the library in identifying which picture has been printed. People who edit from negatives usually use scissors to cut the margin of the film into the sprocket hole. This immediately identifies the frame and makes it easy to find, simply by running the fingers along the edge of the film. Contact prints can have a hole punched through them.

Contact prints can be used to tell the darkroom how a particular frame should be printed by marking with a chinagraph pencil, which can be rubbed off if a mistake is made. Prints should not be marked in red, as it is invisible under the red–orange darkroom safelighting.

Photographers can be bad editors of their own work. They may want the paper to use a picture into which they put a lot of time and effort or one which their colleagues on other papers think was the best picture, rather than the one which, to a picture editor, appears to be the best, either technically or journalistically. A picture editor is able to keep an overview of the requirements of a paper's editor and readers, and can better judge how many pictures – and of what size and shape, if there is a choice – are needed to illustrate a particular story.

Sometimes the choice is simple – a matter of picking the best picture both journalistically and technically from those taken. It gets harder when the picture has to match the story. If, in a local football match, Wanderers beat Rangers 4–1, and Jones scored a hat-trick for Wanderers, there would be limited grounds for using a picture of Smith scoring Rangers' only goal – except if there was an edition which covered Rangers' area. And it is harder still when there are more good pictures than there is space for.

One of the hardest decisions is the balance between technical quality and content; for example, one frame might be pin sharp but the content is not as good journalistically as the frame next to it, which is spoilt by slight camera shake. There is no hard and fast rule, but news pictures are about content, rather than exhibition prints for a local camera club; a picture of poor technical quality can be electronically enhanced to improve its sharpness and tonal quality before the printing block or plate is made. Some hard news pictures, for example court snatches or the moment of explosion of a bomb, may appear more dramatic if they are not technically perfect. If it is a picture which the photographer has set up and has total control over, then there is no excuse for poor technical quality.

Choosing the right picture is an art, not a science.

COMMUNICATIONS

The picture desk has to contact its photographers effectively. Radiopagers are the cheapest way. Early ones merely 'bleeped', so the photographer had to ring the office for instructions. Current ones both 'bleep' and receive messages, which means the office can either send instructions to the photographer, or ask the photographer to ring, and can state the degree of urgency. Because the message is passed through a central bureau, either by telephone or electronically, radiopagers are ideal when different people need to contact the photographer. Both types have the drawback that there is no way of knowing if the message has been received.

Mobile telephones provide instant two-way communication between photographer and picture desk. These are becoming cheaper and lighter as manufacturers introduce new models. For freelances who need to be instantly available they are essential.

However, a telephone fixed in the car is of limited use, as the photographer obviously cannot be contacted if he or she is not in it.

LIBRARY

A well-run picture library is a useful editorial asset to a newspaper and a source of revenue.

Stock photographs may be retrieved from the library to illustrate a story when there is no time to take one. If, for example, there was a story about widening London's orbital motorway to reduce jams, a national newspaper's library would probably provide a choice of photographs of traffic jams on the motorway within minutes. It might take a photographer several hours to find a traffic jam, and then it might not be as good as one already in the library. Another example is where it is not possible to take a person's picture on the day because he or she is abroad or in prison.

Library pictures can remind readers of past events. The official report into a train crash might be best illustrated by a stock picture of the crash. Pictures from the library can illustrate 'before and after' features – for instance, after a major hotel has had a facelift or a new marina has been built.

Some provincial newspapers regularly trawl through their oldest pictures of local scenes and re-photograph the same spot to provide popular 'bygones' features. This can spur readers to send in their pictures and memories.

All libraries should be able to provide the picture desk with up-to-date portraits of government and opposition politicians, union leaders, sportsmen and sportswomen, members of the royal family and showbusiness personalities.

Readers sometimes ask to buy copies of pictures from newspapers. A newspaper can only sell those pictures whose copyright it owns. Such pictures sometimes have a reference number printed alongside. Requests for other pictures should be redirected to the copyright holder.

The key to an efficient library is the filing system. Prints and negatives should be filed and cross-referenced. Sub-editors laying out pages will want to see actual prints – perhaps folders of local MPs, royal visits, crowded beaches in summer, animals at the local zoo, and so on. On the back of each photograph should be its negative number to enable the darkroom to make a new print.

Some libraries have a book with an alphabetical index of the name of every person whose photograph has appeared in the paper and the relevant negative number.

Few newspapers have the space to keep every frame that every photographer exposes. After filing the negative for the picture used, many operate a policy of keeping all the 'over' negatives for six months and then discarding them.

The numbering system used for pictures should be as simple as possible, but it helps if every print is numbered before it leaves the darkroom. One way is to give an increasing number to each film that is processed. Every picture then has a unique reference number: the number of the film and the frame number, separated by a slash. For instance 12345/23A is frame 23A on film number 12345. If a photographer prints a picture from a second roll of film from that job, then its number starts 12346. The films are easily stored in numeric order. Each photographer enters in a master book the numbers for the film he or she has used. The reference number can be printed next to the published picture to assist with photo sales.

Personal computers have a role to play in the management of libraries and the retrieval of pictures and there is a range of software available. Ideally, captions should be written on a keyboard and held on a database along with the date the picture was taken and the photographer's name. When a picture of a topic or person is needed the computer searches the records for the relevant pictures. In buying a computer for a picture library, however, advice should be sought from a computer expert.

12
Using pictures

Once a selection of prints has been provided by the photographer, the darkroom or the picture editor, it is the responsibility of the page sub-editor, perhaps with guidance from the picture editor or another senior editorial executive, to decide exactly which picture or pictures to use, and at what size.

The opportunity for creative design varies with the style of each paper: the news pages of broadsheet papers like *The Daily Telegraph* and *The Times* are highly structured compared with those of a mass-circulation tabloid.

Pictures, like headlines, graphics, areas of text set in bold type and display advertisements, attract the readers' attention. The page must be designed and the contents laid out in harmony. Newspaper readers expect to start from the top of the page – so pictures with a strong visual content need to appear above the fold. This is particularly important for the front page: on a news stand, where the paper is sold in competition with and alongside others, frequently only the top half of the front page is visible to potential purchasers. Stronger, more visual material, is put on a right-hand page, where it is seen first when the page is turned. The left-hand page is kept for editorials, whole-page advertisements, and routine round-ups of news from abroad or outside a newspaper's circulation area. Pictures of scantily dressed young women did not appear on page 3 by chance. If they had been page 4 girls, they would have been much less noticed.

Newspapers use pictures to illustrate stories, as items of interest in their own right and as design features. Single column head-and-shoulder portraits can be used to break up what would otherwise be a large body of grey text. The need to marry pictures with the relevant stories is the responsibility of the newspaper's production journalists: it helps them if a story is marked 'With picture by ...', and picture captions contain the catchline of the story.

Within the news, sports and features sections, there is a need to distribute pictures evenly from page to page. Decisions have to be made as to which pictures will be printed in colour – in any newspaper, which pages can be printed in colour is not an editorial decision, but a production one, constrained by the configuration of the printing press. The sub-editors will also have to allocate pictures to pages which will change from one edition to the next.

Sometimes a page has to be designed before the page editor has seen the picture; it may still be being processed or transmitted. It is important that the photographer is asked as soon as possible what shape is the best picture from the assignment so that an appropriately proportioned 'hole' is left in the page. What is less acceptable is when the pictures are available from the assignment, but the page is laid out and a 'hole' left, so the designer has to use shape rather than content as a selection criterion, or even worse, make a bad 'crop' on a picture so that it fits.

The appearance of many pictures can be improved by placing a fine rule around the image: it also helps mask any slight misalignment in colour printing.

Designing pages and ensuring that the copy and pictures fit is a skilled task. It may help to have a selection of single column screened portraits of actors, politicians, royalty and sportsmen which can be kept near the area where pages are laid out so that they can be dropped in at a moment's notice if a story is too short.

PICTURE SPREADS

There are events – royal weddings, village carnivals and dramatic rooftop rescues – when pictures tell the story and a paper uses them to fill a complete page or more. As with laying out stories, one should be selected as the 'lead' or main picture and the others used at a smaller size. Pictures seldom stand totally alone: a headline can introduce the page, and some text, other than the captions, invites the reader to linger on the page.

When a spread is on the centre pages there is no problem with printing across the 'gutter' – the vertical space, usually blank, between the printed matter of

Figure 12.1   Scaling a photograph: Although a very few newspapers print their pictures to size, so that there is no need for enlargement or reduction during the screening process, and others handle pictures electronically, the vast majority require a picture to be 'sized' or 'scaled'. This means marking the rear of the picture to indicate the desired 'crop' and using the marks to determine the size of the scaled picture. First mark the area to be printed (ABCD), and hatch the area outside. Then draw a diagonal line across the rectangle. Most sizing is done to use a picture across a particular width – to match column size, so it is a matter of drawing the line FG parallel to AB so that it is the same length as the intended width of the picture. The other dimension of the picture will be the length of EG. If height is the important factor, rather than width, then the line EG is drawn first

facing pages. On other pairs of facing pages having a break caused by the gutter running through a picture is inadvisable.

CROPPING AND SIZING

The cropping of a picture starts when the photographer presses the shutter button, continues in the darkroom when the print is made and finishes when the sub-editor designs the page. Cropping is about removing unnecessary content to leave only that which is essential for the purpose of the picture on the page. How a picture is cropped determines its proportions when it appears in the paper.

If the picture has been printed by the photographer, or the markings made by the photographer and the picture editor on contact sheet have been followed correctly by the darkroom, then the picture may require little further cropping. If the picture has been printed 'all-in' – from the whole of the negative – then there may be scope for more creative cropping. The sub-editor must look carefully at the picture to assess its vital elements. Some people use two L-shaped pieces of card which can be placed on the print to examine the effects of a particular crop.

A very few newspapers produce photographs from the darkroom at the same size that they will appear in print: the benefit is that the pictures can all be screened together, which saves production time.

Figure 12.2   Boat race: Never take for granted that those people who have privileged press positions will capture the action. Every year while I was at university I went to watch the annual race on the Thames between Oxford and Cambridge. One year my brother and I were at the start early to get a position on the front of a large steamer which follows the race a quarter of a mile or so behind the two crews. The weather worsened, and Cambridge sank. It all happened very quickly, and the steamer, which was doing a fair turn of speed once the race had started, was soon very close to the scene, and we were able to photograph the crew in the water and their subsequent rescue. I assumed that all the photographers on the press boat had captured the incident, and went home. How wrong I was. Only Eammon McCabe, working for *The Observer*, who was in a press launch, and one photographer on the shore, had pictures of the event. Ours would have been worth a lot of money. Ah, well, put it down to experience!

Figure 12.3   Cropping: This picture of the Queen Mother inspecting young naval officers can be cropped so many ways that it is a sub-editor's dream. It could be a deep upright, a more conventionally proportioned upright or landscape, or just used big in its entirety (© Herald Express Ltd)

Figure 12.3 (*continued*)

Most newspaper darkrooms print their pictures on standard sized sheets of paper (8 × 6, 10 × 8, A4 or 15 × 12 are common sizes). The picture is further cropped on the back of the print by drawing a box around the area desired to appear in print and joining two opposite corners by a diagonal line. It is tempting, because it is easy, to crop a picture square to the original print's edges. Sometimes a better crop can be made on the diagonal: but beware of tilting lamp posts, houses or horizons.

When a picture is sized for reproduction, the final width is usually known – it will be across a certain number of columns – and the final depth can be assessed by measuring the final width out from the corner and from there drawing a vertical line parallel to the edge of the picture down to the diagonal. The length of this vertical line is the depth of the sized picture.

Sometimes the required width and depth are both known. In this case, a box is drawn of the finished size and the diagonal extended. Using a point anywhere along the diagonal will give a crop of the correct proportion.

Size and proportion are important. There is little point in printing a picture which contains important detail at a size where it cannot be properly appreciated by the reader. A very deep two column picture, or a shallow one across the entire width of one page, will attract the attention of the reader of a newspaper whose layout usually uses conventionally proportioned pictures over three or four columns.

CUTOUTS

Using pictures as rectangles of different shapes simplifies the design and production process. Sometimes, especially on feature pages where the text and picture are closely linked, a picture can have more impact when used as a cutout. The unwanted material around all or part of the subject is removed, either electronically or by a graphic artist, and the text arranged to 'flow' around the picture.

Modern photocopiers which allow an image to be enlarged or reduced by simple controls on the top panel are a useful tool in seeing how a cutout will appear when it has been scaled for publication.

DROPOUTS

The dropout – or bleach-out – process eliminates tones from a picture, leaving it as a stark black and white image. It is suitable for feature pages, especially for a picture in which the identity of the people involved needs to be concealed. Examples might be a photograph of a woman leaning into a car to accompany a feature on prostitution, or of a person injecting themselves with drugs.

REVERSING

A picture's position and content should not lead the eye out of the page. It is possible to reverse a picture left-to-right either electronically or when the screened bromide is made. This technique should be used with great care. Readers will notice if the face of a familiar person is reversed. Any picture which is reversed and contains letters or numbers, cars driving down the road or anybody wearing a wedding ring will also be spotted by the eagle-eyed. Even if the content will be unaffected by reversing the image it is embarrassing if two newspapers use the same (agency) picture and one reverses it.

NESSUNORMOUS

HE IS known as Fat Lucy in opera circles, but dieting Luciano Pavarotti vowed yesterday that soon his fans would not recognise him.

At 22-stone, he is nine stone overweight making him dangerously obese. And at last the 56-year-old has woken up to the fact that the opera could be over for him unless the Fat Lucy slims.

At a news conference on the eve of his Glasgow concert, he announced: "I'm on a diet. I have lost eight pounds and when you are going to see me in 28 days time I am going to wear a red carnation so you recognise me."

There was no doubt that, despite the humour, he was determined to crack his weight problem.

The reason he and his entourage are staying at the four-star Cameron House Hotel on the banks of Loch Lomond was that his first choice did not have a lift.

At present, he cannot even walk the 50 yards from his home to see his beloved horses — instead he has to squeeze into his red Mercedes to drive there.

The tenor already takes other aspects of his health very seriously.

A strip of sticky tape was laid on the carpet some six feet from where he sat, and photographers were ordered to stay on the other side of it in case they passed on colds or coughs.

Flowers were also banned from his hotel room — until botanist David Bellamy produced a selection of low-scented plants to soothe his famous throat.

Bellamy said yesterday there was no reason why Pavarotti could not surround himself with plants.

But he warned: "The danger in strong-scented plants is not the smell, but the pollen which releases huge numbers of allergens."

INCREDIBLE BULK: Health fear for Pavarotti

Picture: MARTIN GILFEATHER

Now Pavarotti is dieting hard in an effort to reduce his aria

Figure 12.4 Cutout: A cutout removes the background from a picture – as, for instance, in this picture of Luciano Pavarotti used in *Today*. The space 'saved' can then be filled with text. Sometimes the text is set over lines of varying length so that it 'flows' around the picture, rather than in specific columns, as in this case

RETOUCHING

The photographic retouching of pictures is usually limited to the removal of dust and scratch marks on the finished print. Once a picture has been selected for publication it may be necessary to perform further retouching, either manually or electronically. It is possible to airbrush out a distracting background, draw a dark line to accentuate the border between two areas of equal tone, subdue a highlight or lighten a shadow: in extreme cases, it is possible to remove a person from the picture completely or move two people closer together. It should be done discreetly. Airbrushing the background can make the main subject of the picture appear to be surrounded by fog: moving two people closer together

Figure 12.5 Reversing or 'flipping' a photograph: Reversing or 'flipping' a photograph may be done to improve the layout of a page, but it must be done with extreme care. That the picture in the *Daily Express* has been reversed is obvious, even without looking at the *Daily Mirror*, who used the picture the correct way around. People shake hands with their right hand – and gentlemen's jackets have a breast pocket on the left-hand side

could result in a legitimate complaint from those involved. If there is any doubt as to whether the effect appears overdone, then it probably is.

BY-LINES

By-lines are important. They are a way of establishing an identity for a newspaper's photographers in their dealings with readers, contacts and people whose pictures they take. They can be used as a newspaper's way of showing its news and picture gathering skills. A by-line for a newspaper's own photographer is a way of saying to readers, 'Look, we were there'.

If a newspaper can give a by-line to its own photographers, then it should use a by-line with agency pictures. Some credit the agency and the photographer; others credit neither; and some credit either the photographer or the agency – but how many readers know for what AFP or EPA are abbreviations? (Agence France Presse and European Press-Photo Agency.)

Sometimes news agency pictures appear with the by-line of a newspaper's own staff photographer. It would be nice to think that every time it happened it was an honest mistake.

It is not necessary to have a by-line on every picture – a guideline might be only on those used more than three columns wide. The style should be consistent. Some routinely use the photographer's name in small type along one vertical edge of the picture, other than for exceptional pictures when they use: *Picture by* . . ., at the end of the caption.

EXCLUSIVE

All newspapers like to obtain exclusive pictures. They are often indicated as such either in a strapline or through an in-house logo on or near the picture. Only tell the readers that a picture is exclusive if it is in no doubt. Sadly the word is overused; often it could be replaced by 'Look!'.

EDITIONS

All but the very smallest newspapers appear in several different editions.

The changes made from one edition to the next reflect both the area to which they are sent and any developments in live news or sports stories.

Typically a metropolitan evening paper might print three editions (although some have as many as 11). The first is sent to all outlets within its geographical area, but has a couple of pages with a strong bias towards stories in its rural areas of circulation. Many of the pages will be made up the previous day (usually described as 'overnight' pages), and the deadline for front page stories might be as early as 10.00 a.m. Because of the time taken to reach the rural newsagents, it is only economically viable to deliver them one edition a day.

In the second edition, which has a deadline of around 12.30 p.m., the two pages (change pages) of stories aimed at the paper's rural readers will have been replaced with stories relevant to its city readers and the opportunity taken to update any running stories on the front and page 2. This edition will go to newsagents throughout the city.

The final edition might have a deadline of 2.30 p.m., and go principally to newsagents in the city centre. As well as the two original pages which have been changed for the lunchtime edition, further changes may be made to reflect news which has broken since the first edition deadline more than four hours earlier.

Saturdays may be different. Those newspapers which depend almost totally upon casual sales – for instance, London's *Evening Standard* – do not print at all. Others print much earlier than usual and have a first edition on the streets in time to compete with the national dailies, and run off several other editions during the day before producing a special sports edition by about 5.30 p.m.

National newspapers have further to travel from printing press to reader, and editionizing has to reflect regional interest in both news and sport. Like local newspapers, national newspapers try to provide readers with stories from their area: people who buy a paper on Merseyside want to read about their local football clubs and may have less interest in events at London clubs. Editions may carry programme listings of the relevant local independent television stations, rather than print them for every region in all editions. Sometimes newspapers offer advertisers the chance to print in different editions, enabling them to link a campaign in a particular region with their television advertising.

The first editions of national newspapers are usually off press by about 10.30 p.m., and the deadline for the last may be as late as 2.30 a.m. The first editions are quickly swapped by Fleet Street news desks to discover if a rival has any exclusives which need to be followed up or to see how they have presented a particular story or picture to their readers.

In extreme cases, newspapers have been known to print just a few copies of an edition as a dummy to 'swap' with their rivals, before printing their main edition which has a major exclusive story. Their competitors, having checked the first edition, may not see this edition for several hours.

A photographer must be aware not only of the deadline for a picture to appear in a particular edition but also know how soon before the deadline the film must be in the office, to allow it to be processed and edited.

The production and delivery of a newspaper to its readers involves many people working to a precise timetable. In some cases the newspaper has to travel by plane. Editions, other than in the most extreme cases, do not wait for photographers.

PRINTING METHODS

An understanding of how newspapers are printed is not vital to a press photographer but it is useful knowledge, and may help him or her produce a print suited for a particular paper's reproduction methods.

There are two methods of printing in regular use in the industry: printing from a raised surface, called letterpress; and printing from a flat surface, called lithography. Intaglio, which is printing from an indented surface, is used only for the highest quality printing such as postage stamps or bank notes.

Both letterpress and lithography allow the paper to be either inked at full strength or not at all. The impression of tones in a photograph is given by breaking the picture up into dots of differing size. Close examination of any newspaper picture will show that it is the size of the dots which varies, not their density.

The dots are made by a process called screening, when the original photograph is copied onto film or paper behind a finely ruled glass screen to prepare it for printing. In traditional letterpress printing, the process resulted in an etched copper or zinc block. The size of the screen, measured in dots per inch, affects the ability of the reproduced picture to resolve fine detail. However, the finer the

Pavawetti fans left singing in the rain

By GEORGE PASCOE-WATSON

OPERA star Luciano Pavarotti's huge free concert turned into a washout last night as a downpour kept thousands of fans at home.

An hour before his London extravaganza was due to start, just 60,000 had turned up instead of an expected 250,000.

An area for 4,000 VIP guests was deserted with 90 minutes to go.

Rolling Stone Mick Jagger and his model wife Jerry Hall were among stars who stayed away from the tenor's Hyde Park concert, choosing instead to fly to their French villa.

But fans who had waited for hours in the rain wrapped themselves in black bin liners and huddled under a sea of umbrellas to keep dry.

Surprise

Pavarotti, 55, delighted early arrivals by appearing on stage for a 30-minute surprise warm-up, braving the wind in a tartan rug and white cricket hat.

Housewife fan Rose Berry, from Hastings, Sussex, said: "I can't afford to go to posh opera houses with toffs and fork out £100 a seat.

"This day belongs to the real music fans."

Organisers had hoped Pavarotti's 30th anniversary show would raise £100,000 for Prince Charles's Parks Tree appeal.

(a)

PAVAWETTI

120,000 hear him singing in the rain

By PETER WILLIS

OPERA star Luciano Pavarotti defied torrential rain last night to win the hearts of a massive open-air audience.

One of the heaviest downpours of the year failed to dampen the enthusiasm of 120,000 fans.

Even Prince Charles and Princess Di were drenched as they huddled together during the tenor's free Hyde Park concert — broadcast exclusively by BSkyB television.

LADY

The audience, wet through despite brollies and plastic sheets, cheered when Pavarotti sang an aria in Di's honour.

Before launching into Donna Non Vide Ma, he told Prince Charles: "That means in Italian 'I've never seen a Lady like that', which I dedicate, with your permission, Sir, to Lady Di."

Premier John Major sat

Continued on Page Three

Towel talk .. how BSkyB viewers saw John Major and Fergie at last night's Pavarotti concert

PAVAWETTI

Figure 12.6 Page changes as new material becomes available: These three edition of *The Sun* all carried the story of Pavarotti's anniversary concert in Hyde Park and illustrate how the picture content varied as different material became available. (a) The first edition was printed so early that it was unable to carry a picture of the event; (b) A later edition carried a front-page picture videograbbed from live television coverage of the event; (c) The last edition used a rota picture on the front and four pictures (three colour and one black and white) inside

screen, the higher must be the quality of the newsprint used. Some electronic picture desks can output pictures through a laser printer, sized, screened and ready for reproduction.

Traditional newspaper production methods involved assembling the entire page from lines of metal type and picture blocks. The metal page was assembled on a bench, which was at first made of stone, and subsequently of metal, and the journalist who oversaw the work and made last-minute corrections and alterations was called the stone sub-editor. The page was locked together in a forme from which a mould was taken to cast the curved lead alloy printing plate.

Typesetting in this 'hot metal' period was a highly skilled occupation, but the process meant that the copy was keystroked twice, first by a journalist and then by a printing keyboard operator. All photographs, graphics, cartoons, and special effects like tint or headlines printed 'white on black' had to be made from metal blocks. The whole process was highly labour intensive and time-consuming.

Modern newspaper production methods involve journalists – in the office and out on assignment – typing their copy into a computer and then transmitting the story electronically to the sub-editors. The sub-editors design the page, either on screen or on a layout sheet, and send the edited copy to a photo-typesetter. At those newspapers which use whole-page make-up on screen, the entire page is output from a photo-typesetter. More commonly, each story is output individually from the photo-typesetter and 'pasted up' in its place on the page. Cartoons, pictures, tints and reversed-out headlines are easily handled.

After the bromides for any pictures or half-tones have been added, a same-size film negative is made of the page which is then used to make a polymer plate for printing. The page negative can be transferred to a metal or heavy polymer plate for printing by letterpress. More commonly today it is used for the lithographic method.

Here the smooth printing plate relies on the simple fact that oil and water do not mix. The plate is exposed by shining strong light through the page negative. The plate is then processed so that the printing areas are receptive to the oily ink and the remaining areas are water receptive. During the printing process, the plate is mounted on a drum and alternately dampened and inked. The ink is rejected in the non-printing areas and retained in the printing areas, thus producing the page image as the paper prints.

Most lithographic printing is web offset – the plate deposits ink on a rubber roller or 'blanket' which then deposits the image onto the paper. There have been many recent advances in lithographic printing directly from the plate on to newsprint. Typically this may involve multi-metal plates made, for example, of copper, which is ink receptive, and unpolished chromium, which rejects it.

13

Electronic picture transmission and digital cameras

There are occasions, for instance evening sports events, overseas assignments or news stories in remote parts of the country, when it is not possible because of distance or time, to get a picture from a photographer back to the picture desk by car, motorcycle, train or plane to meet a deadline. The solution is to send the picture down a telephone line – a process which takes only a few minutes regardless of distance.

The technology used has changed enormously over the past few years as print transmitters – sometimes needing calibration with a tuning fork – have been replaced with negative scanners and laptop computers. It is possible to transmit pictures from almost anywhere in the world directly into the network of computers used to make up the pages of a newspaper.

Some newspapers no longer have darkrooms; once the picture has been selected, the negative is scanned into a computer, and the first time that it is seen as a print is when the newspaper comes off the presses.

The first pictures taken by filmless electronic cameras have already appeared in newspapers, and although there is still much work to be done to make them widely acceptable, they could be in regular use by the year 2000. For newspaper accountants there is the prospect of eliminating a costly film bill.

Photographers have had to learn new skills. In the 1980s, newspapers would deploy a three-person wire team: a photographer, a darkroom printer, and a wireperson to operate the transmitter. Now it is all done by the photographer. It can be as important to understand the workings of a modem as to be able to develop the film correctly.

To distribute their material to their customers, large international picture agencies such as Reuters, Associated Press, Agence France Presse and the Press Association in the United Kingdom now broadcast their pictures by satellite, rather than use the network of leased telephone lines of a decade ago.

TRANSMISSION FROM PRINTS

The first method of sending pictures down a telephone line involved wrapping a print around a drum which was then rotated at a fixed speed while a light and a photocell were moved parallel to the drum's axis. It was possible to imagine the print being unwound into a very long helix.

In the receiver, a light whose intensity varied in proportion to the received signal from the photocell, was focused on to a piece of sensitized paper. At the end of the transmission this piece of paper could be processed in the normal way.

More modern receivers use a laser and special paper that does not need processing; alternatively, the signal can be fed directly into an electronic picture desk. Transmission time depends upon the size of the print and the speed of rotation of the drum, but seven or eight minutes is typical.

The method is very susceptible to interference on the line, which shows up as marks on the received print.

COLOUR TRANSMISSION

Colour transmission is possible by making three sequential transmissions with a red, green and blue filter over the photocell to produce the appropriate cyan, magenta and yellow separations at the receiving end for printing the photograph. It is usual to put registration marks and a colour bar on the print so that the receiving end can identify the separations correctly. It may also be helpful to indicate the colour of an element of the picture – e.g. 'man on right wears blue sweater' – so that the production staff can confirm that the separations have been assembled correctly.

Sending a picture in colour can cause problems for those using it in black and white. Although they should first make it up in colour and then convert it to black and white either photomechanically or electronically, they may decide just to use one separation. This can cause the picture to have incorrect tones. The British Union Flag looks very different in each of the cyan, magenta and yellow separations, compared with its true black and white image.

NEGATIVE SCANNERS

Making a print, especially a colour one, can be time consuming if decent darkroom facilities are not available, and it is clearly possible to speed up the overall process if the transmission is done directly from the negative.

The first machine to win widespread popularity was the Nikon NT1000 transmitter which used either a black and white or a colour negative to produce an analogue output similar to that from a drum transmitter. Viewing and cropping were performed through a direct vision optical finder. The caption was prepared on a piece of paper attached to a drum that rotated as the negative was scanned.

The next generation of devices were able to transmit colour and came from Leaf, working in conjunction with the American wire service, the Associated Press; and from the Swedish camera manufacturer, Hasselblad. Both used a television screen to view and crop the picture and display the menus which controlled the machine. They were purpose-built devices, easy to operate and about the size of a large attaché case

All these negative scanners used a linear charge coupled device (CCD) which is moved relative to the negative by a precisely controlled step motor. A linear CCD is a line of solid state elements whose individual output varies with the intensity of the light falling on them. Although the Leaf and the

Hasselblad devices were initially used with an analogue output, their subsequent upgrades offered digital transmission.

Digital transmission means representing the density of a particular spot on the negative – measured by the output of an element of the CCD – by a number, which is sent to the receiver via a modem and then checked to ensure that it has been received correctly. If it has been received incorrectly, then the number is sent again. Such a check is not possible when varying the frequency or amplitude of the signal. Each discrete part of the picture which is inspected is called a pixel. The number of pixels in an image is one (among several) measurement of its quality – and will affect the transmission time. A typical digital image received over the telephone will contain between 3 and 6 million pixels, each with a value between 0 and 255.

A 35 mm negative has as many as 24 million pixels – the actual amount varies with the grain structure and hence speed of the emulsion: a high quality 10 x 8 colour magazine image about 8 million, while a quality black and white image might have less than half a million.

It is not possible to receive a picture digitally on a conventional analogue receiver. Instead, the images are received on an electronic picture desk (EPD) – a desktop computer – and viewed on a television monitor. They may then be printed on to paper, or passed electronically to the next stage of the production process.

The Hasselblad and Leaf scanners have some drawbacks. Initially at least, the Hasselblad had only a black and white screen, which made adjustment of the colour balance beyond that set by the machine almost impossible. Only in later versions of the Leaf is it possible to 'dodge' and 'burn' the image. Neither offered the user the chance to sharpen the picture or remove any blemishes on the negative before the picture was transmitted. Although both offered digital transmission, they used proprietary protocols that were mutually incompatible.

Although these two are both still in use in many parts of the world, other scanners marketed by Nikon, Kodak and Polaroid have since appeared. Apart from being much cheaper, the principal difference from the Leaf and the Hasselblad is that rather than containing all their own software, these three scanners are operated through a personal computer.

Current systems use 'open standards', where it is possible to select freely from the scanners, software and computers available, sure in the knowledge that they will interface successfully with one another.

The computer which has been adopted as standard is the Apple Mac range, – either as a desktop model for use in newspaper offices or at large events, or as a laptop model (known as a Powerbook) when on assignments. All the scanners can be used with DOS-based PCs running Windows applications, but the Apple Mac is the most popular choice because of its ease of use, and its widespread applications already within the newspaper and desktop publishing field.

Although some people have designed bespoke packages to combine the two separate processes of image handling and transmission, the vast majority of photographers use *Adobe Photoshop* to acquire, edit, caption and prepare the picture prior to transmission with a separate program, like ZTerm or Microphone, to handle the transmission. The scanners are usually sold only through fairly specialist shops but the computers and software are readily available off the shelf from any computer dealer.

Adobe Photoshop is a piece of picture handling software widely used within the newspaper industry, but it does contain many facilities of no use to press photographers. Sometimes 'cut-down' versions are published with fewer features but at significantly reduced price.

All three of these later scanners are driven by a piece of software known as a 'plug-in' which is shipped with the device and is installed by the operator into a folder used by Photoshop.

Computer users have been using modems and communications programmes to send data to one another for years. As far as the computer is concerned, there is no difference in sending a file, which when it is opened displays a picture, from sending one which represents the contents of a telephone directory. ZTerm is a shareware programme, which costs a few pounds and is available on many bulletin boards. Microphone is a commercially written product.

The three scanners referred to above share some common features. They all offer the operator a preview image with controls to adjust the colour balance, brightness and contrast; an outlined box of adjustable size to indicate the desired crop and the facility to control the size, in megabytes, of the final image. In the hands of a competent operator all are capable of producing scans of the highest quality. They are all connected via the computer's SCSI port.

There are pros and cons for each of the three scanners. The **KODAK RFS 2035** was the first one to be offered to photographers; now upgraded to the RFS 2035 Plus, it costs, at 1995 prices, about £6,000. It is about the size of a slide projector, weighs 6.6 kg, and uses a CCD chip, on to which the negative is flashed three times, with red, green and blue light. To preview and scan a negative to produce a 4 Mb file typically takes 60 seconds. It has two degrees of sharpening which the user can choose to apply to the picture.

The **Nikon Coolscan** was the next to be introduced and passed the negative once across a linear CCD to generate three separations. It was compact – a bit longer than a hardback book – weighed 1.9 kg and cost about a third of the price of the Kodak scanner, but was significantly slower. In summer 1995 Nikon launched the **Super Coolscan**, which is a similar size and weight to the original Coolscan, but several times faster. To preview and scan a negative to produce a 4 Mb file takes less than a minute. There is no opportunity to sharpen the picture before it is sent to the host computer.

The **Polaroid SprintScan 35** is about the size of a shortened shoebox, and moves the negative across a linear CCD. It is much faster than the original Coolscan, costs about the same as the Super Coolscan and weighs 2.5 kg. It takes about 90 seconds to preview and scan a 4 Mb file. It offers a range of sharpening and noise reduction facilities, performed as the image is scanned.

To sum up:

Kodak RFS2035 Plus: Fast, bulky, expensive.
Nikon Super Coolscan: Fast, compact, inexpensive.
Polaroid SprintScan 35: Fairly fast, fairly compact, inexpensive.

Figure 13.1   The Kodak RFS2035 film scanner

There is no perfect scanner for everybody. For anybody, especially those working in an office, doing many scans with speed and the highest quality being of the essence, then the one to buy is the Kodak RFS 2035. For those photographers, on the other hand, who would use a scanner infrequently, or for whom weight and size are critical, the choice is between the Polaroid and the recently introduced Super Coolscan.

There are many photographers who thought that the electronic transmission of photographs to magazines was a long way off and purchased Nikon Coolscans to test the waters. They found that the demand was much greater than they expected and they have now traded them in for the larger and quicker Kodak scanner or the Polaroid SprintScan which offers fast scanning at a cost acceptable to almost everybody. The new Super Coolscan gives a further choice.

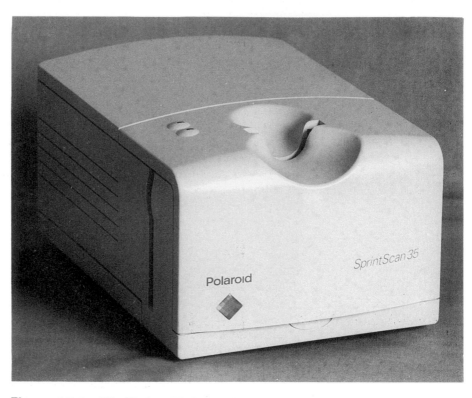

Figure 13.2   The Polaroid SprintScan 35 film scanner

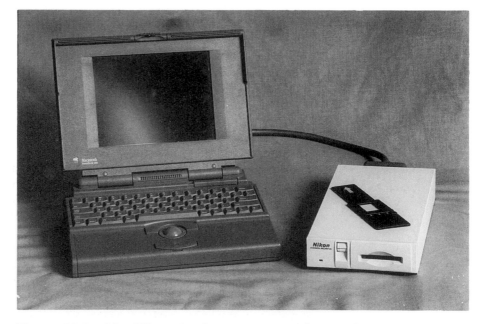

Figure 13.3   The Nikon Coolscan connected to an Apple PowerBook

CHOOSING A COMPUTER

Many newspaper and news agency offices may already have a Macintosh computer and in the first instance might consider using that to drive the scanner. It could be a mistake. Whereas a programme such as a word processor will run on a simple computer at a speed much more than adequate for almost every user, the handling of picture files containing 4 Mb or more of data makes a heavy demand on computing power. With an older, slower machine the user will spend a significant proportion of his or her time waiting for it to complete an operation.

So buy the best and fastest machine that you can afford – at the moment that means Apple's range of Power Macs for desktop use, and their 500 series of Powerbooks for use on assignment. The more RAM – the volatile memory used by the computer when the programme is running – the better (15 to 20 Mb will ensure good performance). Most software packages state their minimum requirement of RAM and processor. The size of the hard disk (where pictures and programmes are stored when they are not being used) is not as important, and most computers now come with plenty. It is not unusual to find as many as 300 Mb even on a laptop machine. Applications involving the long-term storage of pictures require special consideration about the hard disk space required.

Computers are available with a choice of monitors, and a good dealer will demonstrate the range available and explain if any additional cards are needed in the machine to drive the display. Those that can display the most colours are described as having a 24-bit colour capability – that is made up of eight bits for each of the red, green and blue parts of the image. The wider the range of colours and the greater the resolution available, the more memory will be needed for the monitor. A good monitor is important as it is the only way of viewing the scanned picture and assessing it for colour balance and tonal range. The highest quality ones are supplied with software to enable the brightness and contrast to be adjusted to give a repeatable standard.

CHOOSING A DEALER

As important as the choice of computer and scanner is the dealer from whom you buy your equipment. Do not necessarily choose the cheapest. Find one that has a significant turnover of the equipment that you are planning to buy and who will offer you some decent after-sales service. Sooner or later you will have a problem and you will need his help. If the dealer has sold many kits similar to yours, he should be able to cure your problem faster than someone less familiar with the system. And if he has a large turnover of stock, he may be able to lend you something to tide you over until your problem is fixed. But if you have forced him to shave his profit margin to the bone when buying the equipment, you cannot expect much in the way of 'free' help later. Even a manufacturer's guarantee is of limited use if it involves returning the equipment to his factory.

MODEMS

A modem (it is short for **mo**dulator **dem**odulator) converts a string of digital information into an analogue form suitable for transmission over a telephone. One is needed at each end of the line and they can stand alone (external), or on a card inside the computer (internal). Modems operate at various speeds or baud rates (measured in bps – bits per second – for instance 9600, 14,400 and 19,200) and use agreed protocols (for instance V32bis) to talk to one another. The process at the beginning of the call when they negotiate with each another to find a common speed and protocol compatible with the quality of the telephone line is called **handshaking**.

As well as using internationally agreed standards, some modems will use their own proprietary protocols when talking to another modem from the same manufacturer, which may result in a faster transfer. A fast modem means shorter calls – and lower telephone charges. It also means that more pictures can be sent in the same time than with a slower modem.

Modems have error – correcting and data – compression capabilities. The first means that they check the data received to ensure that it has not been corrupted during transmission, the second that they may be able to achieve a throughput greater than that expected by examining the data and seeing if it can be sent more efficiently. For instance if the same number occurred ten times in a row, it would be quicker to send it once – and tell the receiving modem that it should be repeated a further nine times.

Modems are plugged into telephone sockets just like ordinary handsets. Some external modems have a socket at the back for a handset so that it is possible to talk to the other end before or after the call – otherwise you may have to use a Y adaptor in the telephone socket.

The communication software which drives a modem handles dialling the number for outgoing calls and answering incoming ones. External modems have status lights on the front panel which inform the knowledgeable user what they are doing; some internal modems have a display which mimics the lights on the screen.

For the travelling photographer there is an obvious saving in weight in buying an internal modem. If you anticipate travelling abroad, check that your external modem will work at any voltage between 110 and 240: the same problem does not arise with internal modems, which run from the laptop's battery.

A good internal modem should be as reliable as its external counterpart, but as there is absolutely nothing that you can do to check it if there is any sort of malfunction, you should consider having an external modem available as a back–up – especially if you travel widely.

When buying a modem:

1   Stick to a well-known name – examples are Motorola, US Robotics or Hayes.
2   Buy one that operates to a wide range of standards and which offers the chance to upgrade at a later date to any standards which might be in the pipeline.
3   Ensure that the dealer from whom you buy it has sold them in the past and will able to give you competent guidance on setting it up and using it.

There are two speeds which are relevant in modem communications. The first, as already discussed, is the line speed and will depend upon the quality of the line and the protocols supported by the modems. The second is the speed at which the computer sends data from its serial port to the modem. This is known at the DTE speed and it is set by the communications programme. For efficient use of the modem's facilities, it must be greater than the line speed.

ISDN

Conventional telephone lines use analogue circuits between the subscriber and the exchange, and digital links between individual exchanges.

ISDN (**i**ntegrated **s**ervices **d**igital **n**etwork) takes the digital circuit right to the subscriber and is capable of data transfer at 64 Kbps, or even faster if two or more lines are used together. Instead of modems, there is a specific ISDN interface card inside the computer.

ISDN offers very rapid connection times, and although the installation and standing charges are higher than a conventional line, call charges are the same.

It is especially useful for newspapers and photographers operating from fixed sites. The need for additional cards and installations make it impractical for mobile assignments other than at frequently visited venues.

SOFTWARE

The cost of some software appears high, considering it comes on floppy disks that cost just a few pence, and it may be tempting to 'borrow' some one else's disks, or load it across from another machine. Do not. It is theft. Only use legally purchased software that has been correctly registered and licensed. By so doing you will get support from the manufacturers in the event of difficulties and hear about relevant upgrades. Software writers are as entitled to profit from their skills as photographers – and we get very upset if someone takes one of our pictures and passes it off as their own.

Keep your original disks in a safe place, but if you travel on assignment, make sure that you carry a copy of all the system disks and the programmes that you use regularly in case you have a hard disk failure and have to reload the software.

Imaging software – Adobe Photoshop

There are several 'independent' manuals on Adobe Photoshop available in the computer section of most good bookshops to augment and expand on those supplied with the programme. It is clearly beyond the scope of this section to compete with them.

However, these are my top ten Photoshop tips.

- *Files*

After a picture has been scanned, it appears on screen. Then, or at any subsequent time, it can be saved on to the computer's hard disk as a file for subsequent recovery or onward transmission. Press photographers deal in two sorts of files – Photoshop files which return the image completely unaltered; and JPEG files, which are smaller because they have been compressed according to an algorithm developed by the Joint **P**hotographic **E**xperts **G**roup. JPEG compression is lossy – the quality of the decompressed image is not as good as that of the original. The degree of image degradation is dependent upon the amount of compression – and that can be chosen by the user by moving a pointer along a sliding scale of image quality. The loss is not noticeable if the quality chosen is 'good' or better.

Saving as a JPEG file should be the last step in the image handling process before it is transmitted as repeating the compressing and decompressing process does lead to noticeable degradation.

- *Pixels*

Always work in pixels – they are a more relevant measure of the size of your picture than inches or centimetres, and can be selected from the units choice in the preferences menu. Photographers are only concerned with the amount of information in the picture, and pixels are the easiest way of determining this – the more pixels, the more information and the bigger the file.

- *Levels*

You may be lucky and get a scan which looks perfect on the screen. If you do not, one way to correct it is to go to levels in adjust section of the image menu (the keyboard short cut is to type Apple–L), and after ensuring that the preview box is crossed, click auto. This should correct the blacks and the whites – and you can adjust the midtones by changing the figure for the gamma (image contrast) in the middle box.

- *Master the magic wand*

The marquee, circle/ellipse and lasso tools enable you to select parts of the picture for further attention. The magic wand enables you to select parts with a similar tonal range. The degree of similarity or 'fuzziness' is chosen from the tolerance setting in the options offered to you when you double click on the wand tool. A small tolerance selects only those pixels close in value to the one you click on in the picture – a bigger one encompasses more.

You can add to your selection by holding down the shift key, and clicking elsewhere in the picture, possible after changing the fuzziness. The selection is surrounded by a moving dotted line (known universally as 'marching ants'). To turn off the marching ants, type Apple–H. When you have completed what you wished to do inside your selection, choose the marquee tool, and click once anywhere outside the chosen area.

- *Colour balance*

If part of the picture has a colour cast, you may be able to correct it by choosing the colour balance choice from the adjust section of the image menu (type Apple–Y). It offers you the choice of adjusting the balance in the shadows, midtones and highlights by sliding scales which permit you to add or subtract the three primary colours.

This adjustment can work well when used with the magic wand. You might, for instance, have a picture taken in winter with snow that appears a pale shade of blue. Use the magic wand to select the snow and then adjust the colour balance.

If you merely wish to alter the density – choose curves from the adjust section of the image menu (or type Apple–M), and drag the diagonal line up or down to achieve the desired effect.

- *Cloning*

The rubber stamp tool offers the chance to do an invisible mend on scratches or other blemishes on the negative. Select the tool, and then caps lock (this replaces the rubber stamp by cross hairs, which makes it much easier to see exactly what you are doing). Go to where you wish to copy from, hold down the option key, and click once, and move the cursor to where you wish to copy to, click and drag the cursor along the blemish. The tool will copy the pixels faithfully, rather like an old–fashioned pantograph.

Do ensure that you are using a brush with a soft edge – you can check that, and the size of the brush, in the show brushes option found through window, and then palettes.

- *Help, I have made a mistake*

You can always undo the most recent thing you have done by typing Apple–Z. The exception is saving a picture. If you are doing a complicated procedure to the picture (you shouldn't be!), it is worth saving a version at each stage of the process.

- *Scale down, not up*

If you have to, scan a bigger file than you need. If the preferred file size to transmit to your newspaper is 4 Mb, it is quite acceptable to scan a 5.5 Mb file, and reduce it using the image size control. The results, however, will not be as good if you merely scan a 2.5 Mb file, and increase it using the image size control. There be the same number of pixels as in the first version but the picture will contain less detail.

Always carry out repairs or retouching to the picture before down-sizing, and then make any adjustments to the tone or colour balance.

- *Use the densitometer*

Photoshop has a densitometer in the Show Info Menu, found under window, palettes, which displays the RGB components of any pixel on a numerical scale between 0 and 255.

It is most useful for checking that the whites are of the correct density. Put it on the very brightest part of the picture, perhaps a white shirt collar, and move it around a bit to get a feel for the values. They should never differ by more than 5, and all be within the range 244 to 250. If one is always more than the others, it indicates a cast in the picture which needs to be corrected.

- *Get it right from the scanner*

Photoshop is a very powerful tool, and it is possible to make some remarkable corrections of colour and tone. But it is best to try to get a scan which has a minimal need for further adjustment. Learn to use the controls and information provided in the preview scan mode to reduce the work you have to do in Photoshop.

The reason is that Photoshop can only work on the information in the scan – and there is always less in that than there is in the original negative. Brightening up a dark scan is never as good as getting it right in the first place.

COMMUNICATIONS SOFTWARE

Communications software sets up the modem, dials or answers the call and controls the flow of data from the remote site.

Many modems will work straight from the box, but others will need to be programmed. These programming instructions are called AT commands (because they start with the letters AT), and many, known as the Hayes commands after the company that first used them, are standard from modem to modem. AT commands are also used to dial and answer calls. The response on screen from an AT command is either OK, or ERROR.

Some communications programmes such as Microphone have specific commands, known as drivers, for a range of likely modems. Once you have highlighted your modem from the selection in the programme, it send the appropriate string of AT commands to initialise the modem.

Other programmes require the user to check the modem's manual to discover the correct string of commands, and enter them in a specific box for the programme to send to the modem.

The activities of the modem are reported to the user in the terminal window – and it is through this that you can watch AT commands being sent. You will also see information from the modem about the progress, speed and protocol of the connection, and any messages from the other end. Do not worry if you see all the commands appearing twice, eg: AATTZZ, it is because you have 'Local Echo On' – and means that the modem returns every character back to the screen to confirm it has received it. You will need 'Local Echo On' if you wish to see any messages that you type to the receiver.

Modem programming is outside the scope of this book – it is one of the areas in which you should receive support from your dealer – but there are four AT commands which every photographer should know.

ATZ   Return the modem's software to the state at power–up.

ATDTnnnn   Dial using tone, as opposed to pulse, dialling the telephone number nnnn. For pulse dialling, use the letter P instead of T. If you need a pause, perhaps while waiting a moment for an outside line, insert a comma between the relevant digits.

ATS0=n   The contents of the S0 register controls the number of rings before the modem automatically answers the call. Setting n=0 means it will not answer it, n=4 means that it will be answered after the fourth ring.

ATA   Answer the call. Type this if you see the words 'ring' appear in the terminal window. The modem will go off hook and initiate the handshake.

After handshaking the modem will report the speed and protocol of the connection and you can then send your picture. Zmodem is the most widely adopted protocol for file transmission. It takes account of the quality of the line, and will enable you to continue subsequent transmission of a partially sent file if the line is broken. Once transmission starts, a box will appear telling you, among other things, the time elapsed, the time left to go, the rate at which data is being sent, and the number of times that blocks of data have had to be re-sent because it was received garbled.

In addition to the AT commands above, find out how you can force the modem to connect at a specific line speed. Sometimes a modem may handshake and connect at, say 14.4 Kbps, but data transfer is unreliable. It may help if you can force the modem to connect at the slower speed of 9.6 or 4.8 KBps. The transfer rate will be slower but the overall call may be quicker if there are fewer errors.

All communications programmes have a directory to store and select frequently used telephone numbers. They also store the connection parameters relating to the serial port rate (that is the speed at which data travels between the computer and the modem), the size of the byte (normally set at 8 bits), the number of stop bits and the parity and the method of flow control.

Many modem problems are due to problems with flow control. In any communication, the receiving end has to pause occasionally to take stock of the situation, and therefore it has to be able to send a signal to the transmitting end to say, 'Wait', and another to say 'OK, start up again'. There are two methods of doing this. One is known as 'Xon/Xoff' and the other is known as 'Hardware handshaking'. The choice is made in the connection parameters box.

Sadly the two systems use differently wired but outwardly identical cables to connect the modem to the computer, and if you have the wrong cable for the method you are trying to use, you will have problems which will normally show up as a transfer with lots of repeats in it. Not selecting any form of flow control also causes problems, as the receiving end is deluged under data.

Once you have a modem setting that works reliably, copy it safely, both elsewhere in the computer and on to paper.

TELEFINDER

Telefinder is a programme to manage a bulletin board which users can access after they have supplied a correct name and password. According to their privileges they may upload or download files, browse through the material in the bulletin board or leave messages for others. Although users can access the bulletin board using ordinary communications software, the Telefinder user software provides a graphical interface which speeds and simplifies the operation.

The software logs callers, the duration of the connection and the material that they uploaded or downloaded.

Telefinder bulletin boards were the first effective on-line picture libraries.

CHOOSING A TELEPHONE LINE

Telephone lines have improved enormously in quality over the last few years and the days when it was necessary to book a special circuit to wire a picture are thankfully over.

The ideal line to wire from is the simplest possible exchange line. Switchboards, especially those in hotels, can be a source of interference as the pulses that are used to assess the charge for the call can interfere with the signal from a modem. In a hotel it is possible to use the fax line, which usually bypasses the switchboard.

Be wary of the telephones found in small businesses, where any phones can answer an incoming call and transfer it to another extension. These phones, which usually have several lights and buttons on top, are not straightforward, and the instrument cannot be simply switched with a modem.

Everyone anticipating wiring a picture should carry a small tool kit. In it should be selection of small flat and cross–headed screwdrivers, and one which lights up when placed on a live wire, a roll of insulating tape, a multi–function penknife and a pair of pliers.

Foreign countries tend to have their own domestic telephone socket. TeleAdapt, who have offices in the UK and America, offer a range of adaptors which have a local plug at one end and a BT socket at the other. They will supply either an individual adaptor for a specific country, a range for a particular geographic region (Europe/South America/Asia) or a set that they claim will cover virtually every country in the world. They can also supply a filter which will remove tax pulses in some countries which affect modem operations. In extreme cases, when no local plug is available, it may be necessary to use a pair of crocodile clips to connect to the telephone cables.

It is worth taking note of British Telecom's UK Direct service which operates in many countries and enables a photographer to make a transfer charge or credit card call via an operator in the UK through a local freephone number.

Some newspapers have their own dedicated freephone numbers from overseas, and others have arranged freephone numbers which will connect to the modems in their London offices. This is especially useful for an overseas sporting tour involving several venues.

MOBILE PHONES

It is possible to wire down conventional analogue mobile telephones, but the adoption of a universal standard for digital cellular phones by an increasing number of countries has led to new equipment becoming available.

The manufacturers of digital mobile phones have made a modem a little thicker than a credit card, which slips into the PCMCIA expansion port of a laptop computer and attaches by a short cable to the handset. The connection to the cellular base station is digital, leading to more reliable transfer of data. Ordinary communications software is used to drive the modem and the phone and a maximum speed of 9.6 Kbps is attainable.

SATELLITE TELEPHONES

There are parts of the world where telephones are scarce, and their links with the outside world of such poor quality that the possibility of wiring a picture is very limited. In these locations it may be possible to use a portable satellite telephone. These use the International Maritime Satellite (INMARSAT) network. The equipment is derived from that fitted to ships. There is an INMARSAT satellite in geostationary orbit approximately 20,000 miles over each of the Pacific, Atlantic and Indian Oceans.

A satellite phone has a parabolic dish, of about a metre in diameter which is either erected like an umbrella or slotted together like the petals of a flower. It must be pointed very accurately at the satellite. The phone has a signal strength meter or other device to let the user know when he or she is 'on target'. The associated electronics can come in more than one box, and all the equipment can weigh from 30 to 100 kg.

For normal use there is a telephone which may or not be highly specific to a particular manufacturer. It is important to ensure that also included with the equipment is a 'break out box'. This is connected at one end to the satellite telephone's electronics and has a conventional telephone socket at the other end into which a modem can be plugged. To the user the machine is just like a domestic telephone.

The signal from the dish goes up to the satellite and is bounced back down to one of several ground stations around the world, which forwards the call to its destination just like any other international connection. The ground station can be selected by the user; the choice is influenced by factors which include traffic levels and the distance from the ground station to the destination of the call. If this is great it may involve another satellite hop or a subsea cable, both of which could lead to degradation of the line, and subsequent loss of transmission speed.

Mobile satellite telephones have numbers just like ordinary telephones so is possible to call them from normal telephone networks.

Regulations vary from country to country about the import and deployment of such equipment because it deprives the local telecommunications operator of revenue for the international calls made, and because some countries are sensitive about a communication link which they cannot monitor or close down if they so desire or need to. If in any doubt, advice should be sought from INMARSAT, the equipment supplier, or the country's embassy.

Figure 13.4   The author using a satellite telephone on assignment in the Himalayas to transmit pictures scanned on a Nikon Coolscan and Apple PowerBook

It is possible to wire from a ship if it has an INMARSAT system installed.

Modems connect physically to INMARSAT terminals just like their terrestrial counterparts, but because of echoes and delays on the line, some adjustments to their internal programming may be necessary. Some modems may work better than others and it is advisable to carry out tests before using the equipment on an actual assignment.

Transmission speed over the INMARSAT A analogue network is effectively limited to 9.6 Kbps. They have two digital networks coming into service. INMARSAT B replaces the analogue service and offers 4.8 Kbps on a speech channel through a telephone socket and 9.6 or 16.0 Kbps though a data port. 64 Kpbs – the same speed as ISDN is available on both – but advice should be sought from the dealer.

INMARSAT M offers voice communication through equipment weighing less than 10 kg, and has a data port, but the maximum data transfer rate is 2.4 Kbps, making it unacceptably slow for picture transmission other than in an emergency.

ELECTRONIC STILL VIDEO

Several manufacturers have tried to produce a **filmless electronic camera**. At the time of writing, the most promising ones use a CCD chip similar to that found in the Kodak RFS 2035Plus scanner at the back of a slightly modified conventional Nikon N90 camera. One model has been developed and marketed by Associated Press, and a similar model by Kodak. Early in 1995 Canon also launched a similar product based on the top–of–the–range EOS1n.

As the chips in all are smaller than the full 35 mm frame, the viewfinder is masked to show the reduced image area. This increases the effective focal length of the lens by a factor of between 1.7 and 2.5, depending upon the model. This is a benefit for sports and similar photography, but disadvantageous for those situations needing a wide-angle lens.

The picture is compressed and stored on a PCMCIA card, which can be subsequently removed, inserted into a port on a laptop and read by a Photoshop plug–in. Alternatively, the camera can be connected directly to the SCSI port of a computer.

The image size produced by the Kodak DCS 420 is 1.5 million pixels, which is of the same order of magnitude as a typical wire print. Exposure has to be as accurate as for colour transparency. The DCS 420 can take a burst of five pictures in 2.5 seconds – and then manages a frame every three seconds. The Canon EOS.DCS 3 can manage a burst of twelve exposures in four seconds.

Nikon's latest digital still cameras – the E2 and its faster brother, the E2S – are based on a totally new body and have been produced in association with Fuji. They have internal optics to adjust the image size to the small chip so

Figure 13.5   The Nikon E2s electronic still video camera: Developed in association with Fuji, it uses a completely new body to accommodate extra optics so that there is no change in the angle of view when used with conventional Nikkor lenses. The storage card holds about 40 images

Figure 13.6 The Canon EOS.DCS3 electronic still video camera: Based on their top-of-the-range EOS1n, it uses a Kodak chip and has a buffer memory allowing a photographer to fire a burst of 12 frames in four seconds before downloading them to the removable disk

that lenses maintain their effective focal length, but this system also has an aperture which restricts all lenses to F 6.7 or smaller. The chip has 1,300,000 pixels and the E2S camera can take a burst of seven frames at three frames per second. A standard 15 Mb PCMCIA removable storage card typically holds forty-three images.

Canon are promising to introduce a model later in 1995 with a 6 million pixel chip.

Filmless photography is a compromise – making a chip the same size as a 35 mm frame is expensive. The bigger the picture file, the longer it takes to compress and store it – and that has to happen before the next picture or sequence can be taken.

That filmless photography will come is without doubt, but there is still much work to be done.

ELECTRONIC PICTURE DESKS

Electronic picture desks are the interface between incoming pictures and the newspaper's production process.

They were once purpose–built computers, but now that open standards like ZModem and JPEG have been widely adopted, they are conventional Macs or PCs running bespoke software.

As likely as not they may be several computers rather than just one linked together with the newspaper's production computers on an Ethernet. One may handle those pictures coming in via a satellite dish from the major picture agencies, while another may handle the modems which automatically receive the calls from freelances and the newspaper's staff photographers.

Any prints needed can be produced on a dye sublimation printer which produces a full colour print of a quality similar to that of the original negative in less than two minutes.

ELECTRONIC ARCHIVING

This is the next step in the electronic newspaper office and it is not one to be taken lightly. The storage itself is not a problem; there are hard drives whose storage capacity is enormous, or the information can be written on to optical discs.

The challenges are in cataloguing and searching for the pictures. The picture should be saved both as a JPEG file, and as a smaller preview–sized thumbnail and accompanied by a comprehensive caption which contains a narrative and keywords. The keywords can then be used as a basis for a search and the previews displayed for further perusal.

There are various manufacturers offering archiving systems; they should be consulted fully and an operational site visited before a commitment to purchase is made.

ETHICAL CONSIDERATIONS

Any alteration of a photographic print used to be fairly easy to spot. Competently done, it is invisible on an electronic image. It is now possible (although wrong) to add people to a picture or remove them, to move the ball to improve the composition in a sports picture, or in one celebrated case, to increase the number of chicken–pox spots on the face of a daughter of the Duchess of York.

In a conventional darkroom, a competent photographic printer used to adjust the tonal range of the picture by choosing of grade of paper and the exposure and 'burning in' or 'dodging' parts of the image. It seems unfair not to take advantage of similar facilities now offered in image-handling software.

Newspapers used to touch up prints to remove scratches and other marks on the negatives. It was also well understood that a picture looked sharper if it was printed on slightly more contrasty paper. Although some organizations will not allow journalists even to sharpen a picture, it seems sensible to permit any action which is a direct electronic equivalent to what used to be done in the darkroom.

It has been an accepted editorial practice in the past to remove the logos from advertising hoardings or footballers' shirts – though by doing that a newspaper could in theory run foul of the event's organizers whose sponsors have paid good money in the hope that their name appears in newspapers and on television. It may now be only a matter of time before event organizers ask photographers to sign an undertaking that photographs will appear in newspapers and magazines unretouched.

What to most people is unacceptable, however, is combining one or more pictures to produce another picture that a newspaper would liked to have, but unfortunately did not get. One case of this was in 1993 when a newspaper printed a picture of a monk walking down the street holding the hand of a girl. It quickly became apparent that the monk's habit was not in the original picture but was added later.

The final arbiter of such matters, unless they are blindingly obvious to the reader, is the editor, and he or she will make their own policy as to what is or is not acceptable in any particular organization.

A freelance should not make any alteration to a picture – other than to the tonal range and colour balance – before offering it to a newspaper.

The transfer and storage of electronic images also raises problems about copyright, especially when pictures may be available on CD or from on–line picture libraries. A print has, or should have, the name and telephone number of the photographer stamped on the back. Most proprietary electronic image transfer protocols do include a file containing the name of the photographer and caption details which accompany the picture wherever it is sent. But such safeguards are not in place on most 'open systems'.

Some picture libraries put an electronic 'watermark' on their low resolution pictures so that they can be used as dummies in a layout, but if they are needed for reproduction by a client, then a clean, high resolution image has to be downloaded separately, and charged for.

14
Careers

SO YOU WANT TO BE A PRESS PHOTOGRAPHER?

Lots of people want to be press photographers; they imagine it to be an exotic lifestyle, rubbing shoulders with the rich and the famous and travelling first class around the world at someone else's expense in search of tomorrow's scoop.

It is not like that. And there is a world of difference between taking pictures as a hobby, and earning a living through professional photography.

For every photographer gathering around the celebrities at Cannes, there are scores, if not hundreds, preparing for a day on a weekly newspaper when they will maybe visit a handful of fetes, photograph the mayor visiting a school, record a couple of cheques being handed over to a charity, and stand alongside the proverbial one man and his dog on the touchline of a local league football match. After doing as many as a dozen assignments, the photographer will then return to the darkroom to develop the films, print the pictures and write the captions.

There are training courses for aspiring photographers, but the demand for places is high.

FINDING A JOB

There is no formal career structure in press photography. Whether you end up in Cannes or at the installation of the president of the local Rotary Club or anywhere you choose in between is up to you, your ability, drive and personality, and as much luck as you can muster.

The hardest part is getting the first job.

Almost all photographers start as trainees on a local newspaper. These jobs are rarely advertised, even locally, as editors receive a steady stream of letters from applicants hoping to become press photographers. When a vacancy arises, these letters are scrutinized to provide a short list of candidates for interview. Sometimes one of the staff photographers on the paper may know of a suitable candidate.

When writing to an editor:

- Address the letter to him or her by name rather than just sending it to 'The Editor'. The newspaper's switchboard will be able to give you the correct spelling.
- Be sure that you know the correct title of the publication.
- Enclose a Curriculum Vitae, which should give details of your academic achievements, and any journalistic or photographic experience that you have. Examples of this might include taking

pictures for the school magazine, being a member of a photographic society or having done some work on a newspaper while at school. Try to show that you take an interest in current affairs and in the local community.

- Send some photographs. They do not have to be large prints (8 × 6 inch would be ideal) but should be of subjects similar to those which appear in newspapers, rather than family snapshots. Sport, unusual weather conditions, car crashes and local dramatics are all material within most people's reach. And if you want them back it is only courteous to enclose a stamped addressed envelope.
- Spread your net as far and wide as possible. *Benn's UK Press Directory* and *Willing's Press Guide* list all the newspapers in the country. You should find both publications in your local library. The further you are prepared to travel in search of a job, the greater will be the number of editors to whom you can apply and the greater will be the chance of striking lucky. If you are prepared to move home to take up a job, let the editor know, as it will be taken as an indication of your enthusiasm.
- Include a daytime telephone number, so that if there is a vacancy and interviews are in progress you can be contacted quickly.

It goes without saying that a letter of application should not contain any spelling mistakes or grammatical errors. If your handwriting is poor, type the letter.

Be prepared for disappointments. The training of press photographers and reporters in Britain is overseen mainly by the National Council for the Training of Journalists (NCTJ) who estimate that the industry annually recruits about 50 trainees. You will have been incredibly fortunate if you get a job after writing just one letter. You will have done very well indeed if you succeed after fewer than a dozen.

You can do a lot to help yourself. Try to get some work experience at your local newspaper. Find out the name of the editor or the chief photographer and approach either. You will not be paid, but you will get some priceless experience and maybe some pictures published that you will be able to talk about at any interview for a trainee post. Offer your local newspaper some pictures. Earlier chapters in this book will help you take interesting pictures, correctly processed and captioned.

Make sure that you can drive. Press photographers have to travel in all weather conditions, often with expensive equipment, and the ability to drive is vital. Motorcycles may be fine in the summer, but the protective clothing required in the wet and the cold does not create a businesslike impression.

INTERVIEW

When you are called for an interview, be presentable and arrive punctually. You may soon be representing the newspaper, and these are both qualities that an editor will expect staff to have. Ensure that you have read several copies of the paper – if necessary ask the circulation manager to send you some. Make sure you know what is in the news that day, both nationally and locally. If you did not send any pictures with your application, take some to the interview. And take your cameras and other equipment. If nothing else it shows that you do carry a camera with you, but you may be asked there and then to go out and take a picture for the paper.

EDUCATIONAL QUALIFICATIONS

The NCTJ requires direct entrants to the industry to have a minimum of five GCSEs at grades A–C of which one should be English. There are press photographers these days with university degrees, but they are the exception. Newspaper editors are not looking for an impressive list of qualifications. They are seeking staff who have enquiring minds and an interest in events around them and who can get on with a wide range of people. The formal educational requirement may be modified or waived for adult entrants and those who have some previous experience elsewhere within the newspaper or photographic industries.

TRAINING AND PROFICIENCY TEST

Once accepted by a newspaper, a trainee photographer in Britain will serve a six month probationary period, with the ultimate aim of passing the NCTJ's National Certificate. Direct non-graduate entrants take the Test two years after entry, and graduates after 18 months.

As well as receiving on-the-job training while working on their newspaper, British trainees under the NCTJ scheme attend two eight week block-release periods at Stradbroke College, Sheffield, where they receive intensive tuition in Photographic Knowledge, Law, Caption Writing and Newspaper Practice. There are preliminary tests in these four subjects which must be passed before the National Certificate can be taken.

As well as theory sessions, photographers attending the block-release courses have practical sessions, both in the studio and outside, taking pictures under the kind of pressure found in newspapers. The block-release courses are valuable not only for their formal content, which may introduce photographers to techniques such as colour that they do not use on their newspaper, but also for the informal mixing of photographers from different newspapers and backgrounds.

The National Certificate is in three main parts. Photographers have to provide the examiners with a portfolio of work taken over their indenture period. The subjects covered include sport, news, royalty, features, fashion or glamour, and pictures taken by flash and by available light. The photographers also submit a feature project which they not only shoot, but for which they write the caption and lay out the pictures. Finally, on the day of the test they attend the college to cover three jobs which have to be taken, processed and captioned against the clock.

PRE-ENTRY COURSE

As an alternative to the two block-release periods, there is under the NCTJ scheme a 36 week pre-entry course at Stradbroke College, which starts in September each year. This aims to cover the same material as found in the two block-release courses and to give its 12 students a working knowledge of press photography similar to that acquired by direct entrants. At the end of the course, students have to apply to newspapers for trainee positions in the same way as direct entrants. The college maintains links with newspaper editors and picture editors which help with job hunting. Pre-entry students take the National Certificate 18 months after joining a paper.

Applicants for the pre-entry course need one A-level and four GCSEs. One pass should be in English. Application forms for the course are available from the NCTJ at Latton Bush Centre, Southern Way, Harlow, Essex CM18 7BL.

Press photography also forms part of several in-house training schemes run by a number of newspaper groups, some operating outside the NCTJ scheme. Applications should be made direct to newspaper editors.

OTHER COURSES

The School of Media and Management at the London College of Printing offers two courses of interest to photojournalists.

The Postgraduate Diploma in Photojournalism is a one year full-time course which looks at the theory and practice of photography and journalism, the way that pictures are used and reproduced and their relationship with the written word. It examines the interaction of photojournalism with society today, investigates photojournalism as a process of communication and also teaches business studies and media law.

Applications for the course are invited from graduates in photography, journalism and media studies but graduates with first degrees in English, History, Politics, Sociology and other similar subjects will also be considered. In addition, the college will consider applications from non-graduates who have significant experience in photography or journalism.

The college also runs a series of 'Special Lectures in Photojournalism' over 20 evenings between October and March, aimed at professional photographers, teachers, photojournalists, writers, picture librarians and picture researchers.

The lecturers include well-known photojournalists, and the course covers a wide range of photographic techniques as well as copyright law, fee scales, markets for pictures and contracts.

Applicants require five GCSEs or equivalent and have to show a submission of professional or published work.

Details of both courses can be obtained from the School of Media and Management, London College of Printing, Elephant and Castle, London SE1 6SB.

Details of other courses in the UK can be found in *Art & Design Admissions Registry* and *The Adviser's Handbook*. Overseas courses are listed in the *Commonwealth Universities Yearbook*. These publications should be available in any careers library or good public reference library.

WORKING FOR A NEWS AGENCY

Instead of starting your career working for a newspaper, you might consider working for a provincial news agency. There is usually at least one in every large city and they supply stories and pictures to both local and national newspapers. They may have a contract to do all the photography for a local paper. The disadvantages are that the hours may be even longer and the initial pay somewhat less than on a local paper, but the advantages are that you will gain broad experience of press photography very quickly and your work will be seen by a wide range of picture editors. News agencies are commercial organizations, and if you take good pictures which sell well, you can expect an appropriate increase in salary; if you do not come up to scratch, then you will be quickly looking for alternative employment. Staffing levels are tight, and few can afford to have a photographer away for block-release courses, so you may not be able to take the NCTJ's National Certificate at that time.

MOVING ON

With a National Certificate or its equivalent and a good portfolio under your belt, the next step is up to you. You may want to move onto a larger paper – perhaps a metropolitan evening or a regional daily. A job may be advertised in the newspaper which has the vacancy, in the trade's weekly paper, the *UK Press Gazette*, and occasionally in the *British Journal of Photography* or the media pages of *The Guardian*. You may hear of other vacancies through contacts you made with fellow photographers at block-release or pre-entry courses.

FREELANCING

At some stage you may consider freelancing. There is an increasing tendency for provincial newspapers to use freelances because they need only be hired when there is work to be done and they carry no overheads in terms of pensions, equipment, cars or sick pay. For the freelance there is the outlay of equipment and a car, the uncertainty of not knowing where the next job is coming from and all the hassles of keeping accounts – but this is balanced by being one's own boss, and by finding, shooting and selling one's own photographs. Successful freelances may find that there is more work than they can handle, and in turn have to hire staff.

It would be a brave photographer who started a career as a freelance; far better to gain some knowledge, gather some experience and make a few mistakes while working for someone else.

Many provincial freelances are staff photographers who became frustrated while working for their local newspaper, did not wish to move away from an area that they knew, and in which they were known, but felt that they would like to 'be their own boss' and thought that they could find enough work from a variety of publications to make a living.

It is important when deciding to quit a staff job and become a freelance to estimate the amount of work available. Will you be in competition with another agency? What sort of a reputation do they have? How many local papers are there who might use your services and how large is their budget? Do you expect to get any work from the paper you are leaving? Where do you expect to get your news from? Are there good local radio and television stations in the area? Does the local paper provide good leads for pictures? Do you have good contacts – and will they still help you when you are working for yourself?

Almost every freelance has a different 'spread' of customers and way of going about things. Some work almost exclusively for the national press, others mainly for several local newspapers. Some work alone while others find it helpful to have a link, formal or informal, with a freelance reporter. It may be possible to work from home if you have space for an office and a darkroom, or it may be more practical to rent premises, equip an office and build a small darkroom.

As a freelance you have to have your finger on the pulse of your area, knowing everything that is going on, and constantly looking for that different way of photographing the story to make it interesting to national newspapers. It is important to know what nationally is the news of the day and to see if it can be linked with people and events in your area.

Every freelance needs cameras, a car, a telephone and a darkroom. In addition, any photographer hoping to work for the national press should own a wire machine.

- *Cameras*. A good 35 mm outfit, perhaps with a 120 roll film camera if you envisage doing any commercial work.
- *Car*. Should not present any problem.
- *Telephone*. Although it is possible to work totally alone with an answering machine at base and carry a mobile telephone, it is useful to have a telephone manned at all times, regardless of whether you work from home or from an office.

  It is not a good idea to rely on a mobile telephone. You may wish to turn it off on occasions (at a court case, for instance), or its constant ringing may interrupt an assignment.

  You may be fortunate and have a relative who is willing; otherwise you may have to hire someone to man your office.
- *Film processing*. You should be able to produce black and white prints in your darkroom – and be able to process colour negatives there and at the scene of a news story.
- *Transmitters*. Daily and evening newspapers now take it for granted that any freelance will have the facilities to transmit pictures. Speed is of the essence, so you will be looking initially to buy equipment that you can take with you to transmit from as close as possible to a news event rather than having to return to your office.

  Although there have been major changes and improvements over the past five years, they may have reached a plateau. The time taken to transmit a colour picture has been reduced from 25 minutes to two or three. Even if someone produced newer technology that reduced it to just 30 seconds, it would not be as big as saving in time as has already been made.

  For the computer, look no further than the Apple Powerbook range. As explained elsewhere in this book, image handling is a heavy user of processing power and computer memory. Additionally, you will want to ensure that your pictures look at their best before you send them, so you will want a good screen.

  For the scanner, look at either the Polaroid SprintScan or the Nikon Super Coolscan. They are very similar in price and speed, but the Super Coolscan is significantly smaller.

  For a modem, those from the 326X range from Motorola are expensive, but very good and rapidly becoming the industry standard; for other external modems, consider those from Hayes and US Robotics. I have also used the Powerport Mercury internal modem with success.

  As your business grows, you may wish to buy a desktop Mac to store pictures, or to receive them from your staff and colleagues in the field before forwarding them to newspapers. Then may be the time to buy a Kodak RFS2035 scanner, and install an ISDN line.

A freelance is a photographer, picture editor, caption writer, wireman and despatch rider all in one. It is essential to make the most of every picture and story which comes your way.

Even if you are working all by yourself, consider giving your business a name. Eventually you will, you hope, establish a reputation, and picture editors will know the area you cover. In the meantime, it may help put you physically, if not metaphorically, on the map if you are known as 'John Smith – Anytown Photo News' or 'Westshire Photo Agency'.

Before starting business, circulate a letter to every picture editor who you think might, at some time in the future, be able to use your services. It need be no more than a few introductory paragraphs mentioning your experience, when you start, the area you intend to cover and any particular expertise and facilities you can offer and, most importantly, your telephone number. Include a separate card for a box file with the same details.

Do not expect the telephone to ring continuously on day one. But whereas a staff man gets paid if he or she does not work on a particular day, a freelance does not. Initially it is an uphill struggle, looking for stories, spending money on equipment, materials, petrol and telephones with little money coming in.

If you are lucky, local newspapers will know you and ring and ask you to cover certain stories for them. Do not be surprised if they are the ones on Friday and Saturday evenings. What is harder is trying to find stories for the national newspapers, because, to start with, they mostly will not ring you. But as a professional journalist, and one who reads the papers, you should have a shrewd idea as to what is news to the national press.

If you are not sure if a particular national paper might be interested in a certain picture, then ask. It will cost you nothing; all papers accept transfer charge calls, and most have charge-free telephone numbers you can use.

It is important to know when to ask. Picture desk staff are more receptive to calls about an orphaned tiger cub being hand-reared in mid-morning after conference, but before the early pages start to be prepared, than in the late afternoon when the production of the next day's paper is in full swing. If six people are dead after a coach full of pensioners left the road and fell into a river, then ring them any time.

For any hard news story, it is always better to tell the picture desks that you are on your way, than to ring when you get there. They may have already organized their own coverage, and your trip may be in vain, or a rival agency may ring while you are en route, and you will lose the business to them.

For a soft story, like the tiger cub, if you are new to the business and especially if you have the exclusive story, it is probably best to take the picture first and be sure that the film is safely hanging in the drying cabinet before offering it to the picture desks.

Occasionally there is some confusion between a picture 'order' and a 'commission'. An order usually implies that you offered the pictures and that that particular paper would like a look at the same set as you might be offering to

Figure 14.1 Man shearing house: Before the start of the summer season at Torquay's Model Village a maintenance man uses a pair of shears to trim the real thatch on the houses and tidy up any damage done by the birds. I shot the picture first, and then offered it to *The Times*, who wanted it as a 'Sunday for Monday'. With parliament and the courts not sitting, Sunday is traditionally a bad day for hard news, and a wise picture editor will gather a few exclusive 'soft' pictures during the latter half of the previous week which can be used if needed. *The Times* preferred to have the original negatives and make their own print, rather than use a wire print. Although British Rail's Red Star or the Post Office's Datapost or Registered Post are very reliable, do not commit all your negatives or prints, but hang on to a few in case of any unforeseen problems (© Torbay News Agency)

other papers. A 'commission' implies that the paper has asked you to take those pictures specifically for them, and that they do not expect to see them in a rival publication. A 'commission' should pay more than an 'order'.

Generally, national newspapers are fair payers and have a good knowledge of what a picture is worth. They are not going to pay over the odds but it is not in their interests to leave you feeling short-changed. Your next picture may be 'the big one' and they would not like you to take it to their rivals.

Do not ignore local newspapers outside your area. If their football or cricket team is coming to play near you, then ring the local evening or daily paper to see if they would like a couple of pictures 'on the wire'.

Many London-based magazines are desperately short of quality material from around the country. Women's magazines are always interested in an offbeat feature picture. And there are a whole host of magazines that you will never see on the shelves of your local newsagent. Described as 'controlled circulation', they are targeted at particular professions: doctors, chemical engineers, farmers, garage proprietors, surveyors, etc. They are always interested in hearing about the activities, professional or recreational, of their targeted readership. You can find out the titles in *Benn's Press Directory* in your local library. If you have already sold the picture to a local or national newspaper then a further sale to a specialist magazine is a bonus.

COMMERCIAL WORK

It is worth contacting local public relations firms to offer your services. You may know some of them already from your time as a staff photographer.

PR work frequently pays better than press photography and many PR firms like using photographers who have newspaper experience because they know how to take a picture that will publish, and are used to handling people and gathering the relevant information for captions.

PR pictures need to be of a high technical quality – pin sharp, grain free and well lit. It is easier to achieve such technical excellence with a camera which uses 120 size film and produces larger negatives than conventional 35 mm equipment. If the PR side of the business increases it is well worth investing in a larger format camera. Hasselblads are expensive, but are very well built and hold their value; Mamiya makes both an SLR which produces negatives 6 × 4.5 cm and which has a comprehensive range of lenses, and a TLR which produces square negatives but has a smaller range of lenses. Other choices come from Pentax and Bronica.

Most PR companies expect to see a set of contacts from a job before ordering prints; they are usually supplied as part of the job fee, but the prints ordered are charged additionally.

The only drawback with PR work is that it is usually a firm commitment which cannot be dropped if an important news job arises.

WORKING FOR A NATIONAL NEWSPAPER

For some photographers, working on the staff of a national newspaper is their ambition. Like papers in the provinces, the nationals are also using more and more freelance or contract staff. Many national newspaper photographers would have worked for a paper or news agency near London or Manchester from where they could show their work to picture editors. They will probably have started on a national newspaper by working casual shifts, which means coming into the paper at a set time to work specifically for that publication. During their eight or nine hour shift they may do one job, or several, or, if it is very quiet, none at all – but they will be paid the same. Initially it may be possible to combine an occasional shift with a job elsewhere, but there will come a time when it has to be one or the other. Some photographers do a shift several days a week for a morning paper, and then one on Saturday for a Sunday paper, sometimes in the same group. Eventually they may be offered a staff job, or the promise of a number of regular shifts every week. Casual shifts are not only for photographers; the picture desk may need extra manpower which is similarly hired in.

The principal difference between freelances in the provinces and those doing shifts for national newspapers is that the former tend to offer pictures that they have taken or are intending to take to a range of papers, although they may sometimes be commissioned by an individual publication, while the latter work for only one paper at a time and are assigned to jobs by the picture editor.

AGENCIES

The Press Association, Britain's national news agency, employs staff photographers in London and in the provinces, while three international agencies, Associated Press, Reuters and Agence France Presse, have staff photographers based in London who are supplemented by freelances as the need arises.

MAGAZINES

There are far more magazines published than there are paid-for newspapers.

Some large magazines employ their own staff photographers, often with particular skills such as food or fashion photography, but smaller ones may use only freelances. These freelances may receive regular commissions from the magazine and their relationship comes close to that of a staff photographer. Many magazines cover just one topic, for instance sailing, golf, angling – and there is a far greater chance to specialize than when working for a newspaper.

As in other areas of press photography, it is a matter of knocking on enough doors, showing editors your portfolio and eventually somebody will publish your pictures or offer you work – and the rest is up to you.

Glossary

24-bit colour A system where each of the three separations is made up of eight bits, giving each pixel a choice of more than 17 million colours.

120 film Film with an opaque paper backing supplied on a spool (as opposed to in a cassette) and used by larger format cameras like Hasselblad and Rolleiflex; has space for twelve 6 × 6 cm images.

220 film Similar to 120 sized film, but without the backing paper, permitting twice as much film to be on the spool, allowing twenty-four 6 × 6 cm images.

35 mm film Most popular film format for press photographers, supplied in various lengths in light-tight cassettes; maximum number of 24 × 36 mm exposures possible on one film is usually 36. Ilford experimented with a film with a thinner base which was twice as long and allowed for 72 exposures, but most frame counters and processing equipment are designed to cope with the film accommodating 36 exposures.

Aberration Failure of a lens to perform as predicted by simple optical theory. It leads to distortion and a loss of sharpness at the edge of the picture. Six main aberrations are chromatic, spherical, curvature of field, coma, pincushion and barrel, astigmatism.

Acetic acid Main ingredient in stop bath which is used to halt the action of the developer (an alkali) before the film is fixed.

Additive printing Colour printing technique which uses three successive exposures through red, green and blue filters.

Advertising feature Mixture of paid-for advertising and editorial copy/pictures.

Agence France Presse French state-owned international news agency.

All-in Uncropped.

AM – Amplitude modulation Method of sending an analogue signal from a wire machine when the strength of the signal varies with the density of the picture.

Amidol Developing agent.

Ammonium thiosulphate High-speed fixing chemical.

Analogue transmission   Method of transmitting pictures over a telephone line in which a parameter of the signal varies continuously with the density of the picture.

Anti-halation layer   Coating on the back of a film to prevent scatter from light passing through the emulsion which might otherwise create a 'halo' around any highlights.

Anti-reflection coating   A layer – there may be several – on the surface of a lens to minimize reflections which might otherwise cause flare.

Aperture   Hole which can be varied in size to determine the amount of light passing through a lens.

Aperture priority   Method of semi-automatic exposure when the photographer selects an aperture and the camera's built-in exposure meter determines the correct shutter speed.

ASA   Arithmetic measure of film speed overseen by the American Standards Association; numerically identical to ISO.

Associated Press   International news agency.

Astigmatism   Aberration in which horizontal and vertical lines are focused in different planes.

AT commands   A set of instruction sent manually or automatically to a modem from a computer communications programme.

Autofocus   Lens/camera system which can focus unaided by the photographer.

Back-lit   Picture taken with the main light behind the subject.

Ball and socket head   Tripod head with one control for both vertical and horizontal movements.

Barrel distortion   Aberration when straight lines near the edge of the frame are bent outwards.

Baud rates   The rate at which data is transferred from one device to another – measured in kilobytes per second.

Bayonet mount   Method of rapidly attaching an interchangeable lens to a camera body. Mounts from one camera manufacturer are generally incompatible with those from others.

Bit   The basic unit used in computing – it is either 1 or 0.

Bleach   Process of removing the silver from a processed colour negative or transparency.

Bleach out   Reduce a picture to black and white with no grey tones.

Blue   One of the three primary colours.

Bounce flash   Technique to diffuse and soften the light from a flashgun by reflecting it from a surface such as a ceiling.

Broadsheet   Newspaper with large pages.

Bulletin board   A computer offering material that can be downloaded by callers.

Burning-in   Giving extra exposure to part of a photographic print to increase its density.

By-line   Credit alongside a picture to identify the photographer.

Byte   An aggregation of bits which represent a number.   For example an eight bit byte can represent any number between 0 and 255.

C41   Name for a particular processing sequence in common use for developing colour negatives and prints.

Cable News Network (CNN)   American television network which pioneered 24 hour news programming.

Cable release   Threaded cable which screws into a socket on a camera and contains an inner core used to trip the shutter. Useful when the camera is on a tripod and to minimize vibration when using a long shutter speed. Some cameras have a similar facility, but use a switch at the end of an electric cable which can be of (almost) indefinite length.

Cadmium sulphide (CdS)   Compound whose resistance varies with the intensity of light falling upon it. Used in exposure meters.

Calcutt report   An inquiry into privacy and the press which recommended, amongst other things, the formation of the new Press Complaints Committee and a code of conduct for journalists.

Capacitor   An electrical device to store electricity.

Caption   Descriptive type under or near a picture.

Caption sheet   Information gathered by a photographer and sent back to the picture desk with the film. It may be printed or ruled to assist cross-reference between frame numbers and subject.

Carnet   Official document issued by the local Chamber of Trade and Commerce which is stamped by customs officers when a photographer's equipment crosses an international border. Not needed when travelling from one EEC country to another.

Car-shot   Picture taken through a window, usually by flash, of a person in a car (or van or bus).

Catchline   Two or three words at the top of a story used to identify it during the production process but removed before it appears in print.

Centre-weighting   Through-the-lens (TTL) exposure measurement made from the whole scene, but biased towards the middle.

Changing bag   Light-tight bag for loading a developing tank or freeing a jammed camera in daylight. Access is by two elasticated arm holes.

Charge coupled device (CCD)   An electronic device whose output varies with the amount of light falling upon it.

Chromatic aberration   Inability to focus light of different wavelengths onto the same plane. It appears as colour 'fringes' around white objects towards the edge of the picture. It is particularly noticeable on telephoto lenses – which was why ED (extra-low dispersion) glass was developed.

Chromogenic   Photographic materials in which the final image is made of dyes, rather than silver. All colour film and paper is chromogenic.

CIBACHROME   Trade name for a reversal printing process when the dyes are present in the paper before exposure. Processing removes the dyes from the areas where they are not needed. It produces prints of excellent colour saturation which are highly resistant to fading.

Close-up lens   Accessory screwed into the filter thread of a lens which reduces its minimum focusing distance.

Cold-cathode light   Light source used in large-format enlargers. It is even, runs at a low temperature, does not require a condenser and provides a diffuse light which minimizes scratches or other marks on the negative.

Collect   Picture of a person who it is not possible to photograph acquired from a relative, friend or neighbour.

Colour analyser   Device to assess the required filtration when making colour prints. It assumes that the picture integrates to grey, and can be fooled by scenes with one predominant colour.

Colour cast   Overall tint of a particular hue to a print or transparency.

Colour temperature   Measurement, in kelvins, of the warmth/coldness of the light from a source. Colour reversal film is intended for use with light of a particular colour temperature.

Coma   An aberration when objects off the lens axis appear to have a 'tail'.

Compact cameras   Small 35 mm cameras with a potentially high level of automation and the minimum of controls used by the majority of amateur photographers.

Complementary colours   Two colours which when mixed together in the correct proportions form white or grey: cyan, magenta and yellow are the complementary colours to red, green and blue.

Composition   Rules which determine the visual structure of a picture.

Concave lens   One which is thinner in the middle than the perimeter. It makes rays of light diverge.

Condenser   Large lens placed below the enlarger lamp to project the light through the negative carrier. Some enlargers use two condensers.

Contact   Press photographer's source of information and assistance.

Contact print   Same-size print made by exposing the printing paper in contact with the negatives. Useful for editing and filing purposes.

Contempt of court   Acting (or using a camera) in a manner contrary to the instructions of a judge or magistrate or in a way likely to influence the course of legal proceedings.

Contrast   Differences in brightness between one area of an image and another.

Contre-jour   Picture taken with the light behind the subject.

Converging verticals   Illusion that a building is toppling backwards when a camera is tilted upwards.

Convex lens   One which is thicker in the middle than the perimeter. It makes rays of light converge.

Copyright   Legally enshrined right to make copies of a picture – or other intellectual property – owned by the person who took the picture or their employer.

Covering power   Ability of a lens to provide a usable image over a given area.

Crop   Edit the content of a print before publication to maximize its impact.

Curvature of field   Inability of a lens to focus an image onto a flat surface.

Cutout   Technique used when designing pages which removes the background of the picture.

Cyan   Complementary colour to red: colour of one of the filter sets used in subtractive printing.

D Notices   Series of informal guidelines for editors from the government over particular areas and topics which concern national security.

D76   Kodak's classic metol-hydroquinone developer which gives fine grain, good tonal range and full emulsion speed.

Darkroom   Light-tight room for processing films and making prints.

Deadline   Time by which a picture or story must be in the office, or other editorial function completed.

Dedicated flashgun   One built for a specific camera or range of cameras to link into their internal shutter and exposure control electronics.

Defamation   To damage the personal or professional reputation of an individual in speech (slander) or in print (libel) by words or pictures.

Depth of field   Area in front and behind the subject which appears acceptably sharp.

Developer   Chemical which renders the latent image visible by converting the exposed silver halides into metallic silver.

Developing tank   Light-tight container, made of steel or plastic, into which the processing chemicals are poured. Alternatively, the chemicals are kept in large tanks and the films are transported from one tank to the next.

Diaphragm   Hole which can be varied in size to determine the amount of light passing through a lens.

Diary jobs　Routine newspaper assignments whose time and place are known beforehand.

Diffraction　Phenomenon observed when rays of light bend as they pass the edge of a solid object.

Digital transmission　Method of transmission when the density of each pixel is assigned a numerical value and the picture is transmitted, with a modem if necessary, as a stream of numbers.

DIN　Logarithmic measure of film speed overseen by the Deutsche Industrie Norm (German Standards Organization).

Dispersion　Phenomenon observed when a beam of white light passing through a prism is split into its component parts. It occurs if a material's refractive index varies with the wavelength.

Dodging　Giving less exposure to part of a photographic print to reduce its density.

DOS　Disk operating system – the software at the operating heart of most non–Macintosh computers.

Doubler　Lens which is placed between the camera and the prime lens which doubles the size of the image; also known as a teleconverter.

Dropouts　Reducing a picture to just black and white, with no mid-tones.

Drying cabinet　Heated cabinet with a filtered air supply for drying films.

Drying marks　Deposits remaining on a negative after drying caused by dirty water; areas of varying density caused by uneven drying.

DX coding　Metal/paint pattern on film cassette which is interpreted by electrical contacts inside a suitably equipped camera to assess film speed and number of exposures.

E6　Substantive processing sequence for colour reversal films.

ED glass　Extra-low-dispersion glass used to minimize effects of chromatic aberration in wide aperture telephoto lenses.

Editions　Differing versions of a newspaper published on the same day but changed to take account of the geographical locality of the reader or later-breaking news.

Electronic flash　Electronic device which stores electricity in a capacitor before discharging it through a tube filled with inert gas. It may be battery powered and mounted on the camera's hot-shoe or mains powered and used in a studio.

Electronic picture desk　Device used to receive, edit, store and transmit pictures. Prints are stored on magnetic discs and viewed on video screens.

Electronic 'watermark'　An electronic overlay embedded in a picture to indicate its ownership and prevent unauthorized use.

Embargo Undertaking or instruction not to publish material before agreed time.

Emulsion Layer of gelatine and other materials containing a suspension of light-sensitive silver halides.

Enlargement Print bigger than the negative.

Enlarger Optical apparatus to project the image of a negative on to a sheet of photographic paper.

Exposure meter Electronic instrument containing a sensor whose properties vary with the intensity of the light falling on it used to assess the required shutter and aperture needed for a correct exposure. Can be hand-held or built in to a camera.

Extension tube Metal tubes fitted between camera and lens to reduce the minimum focusing distance enabling the photography of small objects.

Features An article other than news or sport – typically editorial or columnists' opinions, or matter aimed at a particular group of readers.

Fill-in flash Flash-light used to illuminate the shadows in a picture thereby reducing the contrast to a level the film can handle.

Filters Coloured pieces of glass mounted in circular metal holders which are screwed onto the front (or, occasionally, into the back) of a lens to absorb light of different colours.

Fish-eye lenses Extremely wide angle lens capable of an angle of view in excess of 180 degrees. The image is distorted and appears circular.

Five Ws Who, what, where, when and why; a quick checklist of the questions to ask when finding the information for or writing a caption.

Fixer Chemical which removes unexposed and undeveloped silver halides from the emulsion, rendering the silver image stable.

Flare Non-image-forming light scattered from the surface of the lens and inside of the camera body which degrades the image.

Flashmeter Exposure meter used to assess the F-stop required when taking pictures by electronic flash.

Flash synchronization Arrangement whereby the camera fires the flashgun when the shutter is fully open.

Flat Lacking in contrast.

Floppy disk Inexpensive magnetic storage device of limited capacity which is inserted into a computer.

FM – Frequency modulation Method of sending an analogue signal from a wire machine when the pitch of the signal varies with the density of the picture.

Focal length Distance from the plane of focus to the optical (rather than physical) rear of the lens. Image size increases with focal length.

Focal plane shutter   Shutter of two blinds which travel across the film. The film exposure is determined by the speed at which the blinds move and the gap between them. Used in SLR cameras as they cover the film between exposures, permitting the lens to be changed.

Focus finder   Aid to assist focusing an enlarger. It reflects part of the image onto a ground glass screen or cross-wires where it can be examined through a magnifier.

Focusing screen   Ground glass or plastic screen on which the image from the lens is projected so that it can be examined visually for composition and sharpness.

Fog   Uniform density across the negative caused by incorrect processing or accidental exposure to light.

Fresnel lens   Lens which serves the same purpose as a condenser, but which is made of concentric stepped rings, each with a convex surface, thus saving weight.

F-stop   Photographic measurement of the light-gathering power of a lens, derived by dividing the focal length of the lens by the diameter of the effective aperture.

Gallium arsenide phosphide photodiode (GaASP)   Photovoltaic material used in exposure meters.

Grain   Individual clusters of silver or dye which make up the image. The faster the film, the larger the clusters.

Green   One of the three primary colours.

Guide number   Measure of the output of a flashgun. It varies with film speed and is quoted either in metres or feet. The correct aperture can be calculated by dividing the guide number by the flash-to-subject distance.

Gutter   Margin between two facing pages.

Half-tone   Photograph which has been screened for reproduction.

Hard disk   Magnetic storage device usuallyfound inside computers which holds the programmes, operating systems and data files. The information is retained when the machine is turned off.

Handshaking   The initial contact between two modems when they try to establish common operating speeds and protocols.

Hardener   Chemical added to fixer to strengthen the emulsion against physical damage.

Hot-shoe   Place to locate accessories, especially a flashgun, on top of many cameras. It has electrical contacts to synchronize the firing and may also provide the additional dedicated links with the camera's circuitry.

House style   Guidelines laid down by a newspaper to ensure conformity by journalists over layout, spelling and titles of individuals.

Hydroquinone   Developing agent.

Hypo   Abbreviation for fixing chemical sodium thiosulphate.

ID 11   Ilford's classic metol-hydroquinone developer giving fine grain, a good range of tones and full emulsion speed.

Incident light measurement   Exposure assessment by the amount of light falling on the subject, as opposed to that reflected from it.

Inert gas   Chemically inactive elements like xenon and krypton which are used in the discharge tubes of electronic flashguns.

Infinity   Distance at or beyond which rays of light reaching a lens are considered to be parallel.

Intaglio   Printing from an indented surface; also known as photogravure. A process used for banknotes, stamps and other high-quality printing.

Interchangeable lens system   Range of lenses of differing focal length which fit the same camera.

Internal focusing   Focusing a lens by moving some elements relative to one another internally, rather than moving the whole lens relative to the film plane.

Inverse square law   Physical law which states that the intensity of light reaching a surface is proportional to the square of its distance from the source.

Inverted telephoto   Design of wide angle lenses for reflex cameras which allows space between the rear element and the film to accommodate the mirror. Also known as retrofocus.

ISDN   Integrated services digital network – a telephone system which is totally digital to the subscriber's apparatus, and capable of carrying data at high speeds.

ISO   Arithmetic measure of film speed overseen by the International Standards Organization; numerically identical to ASA.

JPEG compression   A method of reducing the size of a picture file using a mathematical algorithm developed by the Joint Photographic Experts Group.

Latent image   Invisible image present in an emulsion after it has been exposed to light and before it has been developed.

LCD (liquid crystal display)   Electronic display, parts of which can be rendered opaque by application of a charge. Many modern cameras have dispensed with conventional dials and knobs and display the shutter speed, exposure mode, film speed, aperture setting and similar information on an LCD.

Leaf shutter   Shutter between the elements of a lens. Found in compact cameras and some large-format cameras.

Lens   Optical device to form an image.

Lens hoods   Shade attached, either by bayonet fitting or into the filter ring, which prevents light from outside the picture area entering the lens.

Letterpress   Printing from a raised surface. Traditional newspaper letterpresses used plates cast from metal; modern letterpress uses polymer printing plates.

Libel Damage the personal or professional reputation of a person in print.

Light Visible part of the electromagnetic spectrum of radiation.

Light-emitting diode (LED) Electronic component which glows when a voltage is applied to it. Now largely replaced by the liquid crystal display which permits more complicated designs.

Line break Horizontal line on a wire print caused by an interruption between transmitter and receiver.

Lithography Printing from a flat surface, part of which is ink-receptive, and part ink-rejecting.

Local echo When a modem returns to the display screen the characters sent to it from the computer keyboard.

Macro lens Lens capable of focusing closer than usual for photographing small objects.

Magenta Complementary colour of green: colour of one of the filter sets used in subtractive printing.

Masking frame Device to hold paper flat during enlargement. The arms which keep the paper in place leave a white border.

Matrix metering Through-the-lens (TTL) exposure measurement which assesses the brightness of different areas of the pictures and compares them with likely distributions before calculating the correct exposure.

Megabyte A million bytes; it can be used as an electronic measure of a picture's size.

Metol Developing agent.

Microprism Focusing aid of small pyramids on the viewing screen of a reflex camera which break up the image and cause it to shimmer when it is out of focus.

Mirror lens A lens which uses mirrors, rather than lenses, to focus light. Mirror lenses do not suffer from chromatic aberration and are much shorter than their conventional counterparts as the optical path is 'folded' internally. They have a fixed aperture.

Modem (modulator-demodulator) Electronic apparatus used to transmit digital information along a telephone line – one is needed at each end. If information is corrupted because of noise on the line, it is automatically sent again.

Monopod Extendable metal stick with a thread on top used to support camera and lens.

Motor drive Electro-mechanical accessory (sometimes built-in) to advance film between exposures.

Mug shot Picture of a person's head.

Multiple exposure Exposing the same frame two or more times, usually to achieve a special effect.

National Certificate   Examination taken by photographers and reporters at the end of their period of training under the NCTJ scheme.

National Council for the Training of Journalists (NCTJ)   Body which oversees journalists' training in the UK.

Negative transmitter   Machine to transmit picture from a processed negative rather than a print. It may transmit digitally using a modem into an electronic picture desk.

Neutral density filter   Grey filter to reduce the amount of light entering a lens without affecting the colours of the picture.

News agency   Commercial organization which sells stories and pictures. Customers may subscribe to its services, or it may offer them material for payment on use.

Nickel cadmium battery   Rechargeable electrical cell used in flashguns and cameras.

Non-substantive film   Film in which the colour-couplers which react with the developer by-products to form the dyes in the final image are not in the emulsion, but in the processing chemicals. Such films, like Kodachrome, are usually returned to the manufacturer for processing.

Official Secrets Act   Legislation preventing, amongst other things, photography of sensitive military areas.

One-shot developer   Processing chemical used once and thrown away.

Open standard   A protocol or method of working that is understood and freely available to all writers and users of software.

Orthochromatic   Sensitive to all colours of the spectrum except red and deep orange.

Overnight pages   Pages for an evening paper prepared the previous day.

Pan and tilt head   Tripod head with independent controls for both vertical and horizontal movements.

Panchromatic   Sensitive to all colours of the spectrum.

Para-phenylenediamine   Developing agent.

Pentaprism   Five-sided glass prism placed in a reflex camera above the focusing screen which enables the image to be seen through the eyepiece both the right way up and laterally correct.

Perspective control lens   Lens which can be moved parallel to the film to prevent the camera having to be tilted to photograph tall buildings.

Perspective   Appearance of three-dimensional objects when recorded on two dimensions.

Phenidone   Developing agent.

Photocall   Invitation to photographers to attend an event primarily staged for them.

Photovoltaic   Material which generates electricity when light falls on it used in exposure meters.

Picture desk   Department which co-ordinates a newspaper's picture-gathering activities.

Picture editor   Editorial executive with overall strategic control of a newspaper's picture-gathering activities.

Pincushion   Lens aberration which makes straight lines near the edge of the frame bend inwards.

Pixel (picture element)   Smallest discrete element from which a picture is built up. An image's technical quality is directly related to the number of pixels it contains.

Plug-in   A piece of third party software which is inserted into another programme to add extra functions – usually relating to the import and export of pictures and data.

Polarizing filter   Filter which only passes light vibrating in a particular plane.

Police and Criminal Evidence Act (PACE)   Legislation which enables police in possession of a judge's order to seize photographic material to assist them with their investigations.

Pool   Arrangement whereby a few press photographers, or even just one, gain access to an event on the understanding that their material will be made available freely and rapidly to all other members of the pool.

Potassium bromide   Used in developer as a restrainer to prevent developer affecting unexposed silver halides.

Potassium carbonate   Used in developer as an accelerator to speed up the action of the developing agent.

Precincts of court   Legally undefined area around a court in which photography of parties to the proceedings is forbidden under the Criminal Justice Act of 1925.

Press Association (PA)   Britain's national news agency which supplies words and pictures to national and local newspapers, radio, television and other non-media customers.

Press Complaints Commission   Took over from the Press Council in January 1991 after the Calcutt Committee's report on privacy and the press.

Press Council   Voluntary body whose primary purpose was adjudicating on complaints about the conduct of newspapers and individual journalists. It was replaced in 1991 after the Calcutt Committee's report by the Press Complaints Commission.

Primary colours   Red, green and blue.

Programmed exposure   Decision by camera's exposure meter and electronics of both shutter speed and aperture. There may be bias from the user towards higher shutter speeds or maximizing depth of field. Some systems also take into account the focal length of lens fitted and whether a flashgun is being used.

Protocol   Agreed standards to which hardware or software conforms.

Push-processing   Intentional overdevelopment of a film to compensate for previous underexposure.

Rag-out   An illustration with jagged edges which gives the appearance of having been torn out of a previous edition to remind readers of the newspaper's coverage of an earlier event or topic.

RAM   Random access memory – the area of a computer used to hold programmes and data while they are in use. The information is usually lost when the power is disconnected.

Rangefinder camera   Camera with a rangefinder as an aid for focusing. A second view of part of the subject is superimposed in the viewfinder via a mirror whose orientation varies with the distance at which the lens is focused. The subject is in focus when the two images overlap precisely.

Recycling time   Time taken for an electronic flashgun to be charged and ready for the next exposure.

Red   One of the three primary colours.

Red-eye   Bright red spots in the eyes of people taken by flashlight caused by light reflecting off the retina at the rear of the eye and back into the lens.

Reflector   White card, piece of foil or fabric used to reflect light into the shadows of a picture: metal dish surrounding a light source to control its direction.

Refraction   Change in direction of a ray of light as it passes obliquely from one medium to another.

Refractive index   Measure of the ability of a material to bend light.

Replenisher   Mixture of chemicals added to used developer to maintain its activity.

Resin-coated paper   Photographic printing material that has a paper base coated on either side with a thin layer of polythene to minimize the absorption and carry-over of chemicals from one solution to the next and permit rapid washing and drying.

Reticulation   A mottling effect on the finished print caused by the emulsion on the film swelling or shrinking when it is transferred from one solution to another at a significantly higher or lower temperature.

Retouching   Photographic retouching is limited to the removal of blemishes on prints caused by dust, dirt or scratches on the negative. Further retouching may take place for editorial purposes.

Retrofocus   Design of wide angle lenses for reflex cameras which allows space between the rear element and the film to accommodate the mirror. Also known as inverted telephoto.

Reuters   International news agency.

Reversal film   Film whose processing steps include fogging and redevelopment to produce a positive image.

Reversing   Transposing a picture left to right to improve the aesthetic appearance of a page design.

Rota   Arrangement whereby a few press photographers, or even just one, gain access to an event on the understanding that their material will be made available freely and rapidly to all other subscribers to the arrangement.

Safelighting   Illumination in a darkroom of a colour and intensity that will not affect the sensitized materials being handled.

Satellite telephone   Portable telephone which transmits via a satellite in geostationary orbit, rather than along conventional wires.

Screening   Copying a picture through a ruled grid onto high-contrast material so that it is composed of dots of differing size.

SCSI   Small computer systems interface. An industry standard for connecting computers to peripheral devices like scanners and external hard disks.

Selenium   Photovoltaic material used in early exposure meters.

Separation   One of the three component parts of a colour picture which are subsequently printed with yellow, magenta and cyan ink.

Serial port   An interface between a computer and another piece of equipment – usually a modem or a printer.

Shareware   Software that is freely available from bulletin boards or libraries for which royalties are usually sent directly to the programmer. Much cheaper than commercial software.

Shutter   Device used to control the duration of an exposure.

Shutter priority   Method of semi-automatic exposure when the photographer selects the shutter speed and the camera's built-in exposure meter determines the correct aperture.

Silicon photodiode (SPD)   Photovoltaic material used in modern exposure meters.

Silver halides   Light-sensitive compounds formed between silver and bromine, iodine or chlorine.

Single lens reflex cameras (SLR)   Camera which uses the same lens for viewing and taking the picture.

Slave unit   Electronic accessory which triggers a flashgun when it receives a pulse of light from another one.

Smudge   Photographers' slang for picture.

Snatch picture   Picture taken without the subject's knowledge or approval.

Snoot   Cone-shaped shield used to control the spread from a light.

Sodium sulphite   Preservative in a developer to prevent premature oxidation of the developing agent.

Sodium thiosulphate   Fixing chemical.

Software   The coded instructions which make a computer perform desired functions.

Spherical aberration   Aberration caused because rays of light passing through different annular zones of the lens do not come to a focus at the same distance from the lens.

Split-image rangefinder   Two opposing thin wedges mounted on a reflex camera's focusing screen which displace the image laterally when it is out of focus.

Spotting   Removal of blemishes on prints caused by dust, dirt or scratches on the negative.

Spot metering   Taking a reading from a very small part of the scene being photographed.

Squeegee   Rubber-jawed tongs used to wipe the water from a film before it is dried.

Standard lens   Lens whose angle of view corresponds closely to that of the human eye.

Stop bath   Weak solution of acetic acid used to curtail development.

Stringer   Journalist representing a newspaper which does not have a full-time reporter in the locality.

Studio electronic flashgun   Large mains-powered unit with high output used for pictures indoors.

Sub-editor   Production journalist responsible for editing copy and laying out pages.

Substantive film   Film in which the colour-couplers which react with the developer by-products to form the dyes in the final image are in the emulsion. These films can usually be user-processed.

Subtractive printing   Colour printing technique which uses one exposure through a combination of yellow, magenta and cyan filters.

Synchro-sunlight   Flashlight used to illuminate the shadows in a picture, thereby reducing the contrast to a level the film can handle.

Tabloid   Newspaper with small or half-size pages.

Teleconverter   Lens put between a camera and its prime lens to increase the size of the image.

Telephoto lens   Generally a lens with a focal length greater than the standard lens. More precisely it is a lens whose optical layout means that its physical size is shorter than its focal length.

Through-the-lens metering (TTL) Exposure measurement made by measuring the light coming through the lens. This can be done before the exposure by light-sensitive cells in the pentaprism housing and, on some cameras, during the exposure by cells measuring the light reflected by the emulsion of the film.

Thyristor Solid-state switch in electronic flashguns used to turn on the current through the flash tube, and off after the subject has received the correct exposure.

Time and temperature Two linked criteria for correct processing.

Trade names Registered names of products – which must not be used to describe all similar products.

Transparency film Film whose processing steps produce a positive image, by fogging and redevelopment.

Trespass To enter another person's property without permission – for example, to take a picture. Usually a civil, rather than criminal, offence.

Tripod Rigid three-legged camera support of variable height.

Tungsten light Light from an incandescent bulb – usually warmer (i.e. redder) in colour than daylight.

Twin lens reflex camera (TLR) Camera with two matched lenses: the top one is used for viewing, focusing and composing and the bottom one for taking the picture.

Umbrella reflector Collapsible reflector frequently used with studio flashguns.

Upgrade An improved version of a programme, computer or ancillary device.

Variable-contrast papers Black and white printing paper with two layers of emulsion, each of different contrast and sensitive to light of a different colour. The contrast of the paper can be varied by using different-coloured filters between the enlarger light source and the negative.

Videograbbing Acquiring an image from a television broadcast. It can be done photographically or electronically.

Viewfinder Aid on camera to enable photographer to compose and focus a picture.

Wetting agent Chemical to reduce the surface tension of water and so prevent drying marks on negatives.

Wide angle lens Lens with a wider angle of view than a standard lens.

Windows A graphical interface for users of PCs – similar to that found on Macintoshes.

Wire machine Electronic apparatus to transmit a picture along telephone lines. Some require a print, others a negative.

Yellow Complementary colour to blue; the colour of one of the filter sets used in subtractive printing.

Zoom lenses Lens whose focal length can be varied within a specific range.

Bibliography

A visit to a good bookseller will demonstrate the wide range of books available about photography. Some are highly technical – and others are more anecdotal. Books relating to newspaper and magazine photography are a little scarcer, but do try to scour every secondhand bookshop until you have your own copy of Harold Evan's *Pictures on a Page*. The books I have, and find useful, include:

Tom Crone, *Law and the Media*, 3rd Edn, Focal Press.

Philip Dunn, *Press Photography*, Oxford Illustrated Press.

Harold Evans, *Pictures on a Page*, Heinemann.

Terry Fincher, *Creative Techniques in Photo-journalism*, Batsford.

Focal Encyclopaedia of Photography, Focal Press.

Vic Giles and F. W. Hodgson, *Creative Newspaper Design*, Butterworth-Heinemann.

Tom Grill and Mark Scanlon, *Photographic Composition*, Fountain Press.

John Hedgecoe, *The Photographer's Handbook*, Ebury Press.

F. W. Hodgson, *Subediting*; *Modern Newspaper Editing and Production*, 2nd Edn, Focal Press.

Brian Horton, *The Picture – A Guide to Good News Photography*, The Associated Press.

Ralph Jacobson, Sidney Ray, Geoffrey Attridge, *The Manual of Photography*, Focal Press.

Herbert Keppler, *The Nikon and Nikkormat Way*, Focal Press.

John Larish, *Understanding Electronic Photography*, TAB Books.

The Book of 35mm Photography, Curtin & London/Van Nostrand Reinhold.

Tom Welsh, Walter Greenwood, *Essential Law for Journalists*, Butterworths.

Appendix:
Code of Practice for the Press

The Press Complaints Commission are charged with enforcing the following Code of Practice which was framed by the newspaper and periodical industry and ratified by the Press Complaints Commission in April 1994.

All members of the press have a duty to maintain the highest professional and ethical standards. In doing so, they should have regard to the provisions of this Code of Practice and to safeguarding the public's right to know.

Editors are responsible for the actions of journalists employed by their publications. They should also satisfy themselves as far as possible that material accepted from non-staff members was obtained in accordance with this Code.

While recognising that this involves a substantial element of self-restraint by editors and journalists, it is designed to be acceptable in the context of a system of self-regulation. The Code applies in the spirit as well as in the letter.

It is the responsibility of editors to co-operate as swiftly as possible in PCC enquiries.

Any publication which is criticised by the PCC under one of the following clauses is duty bound to print the adjudication which follows in full and with due prominence.

1 ACCURACY

(i) Newspapers and periodicals should take care not to publish inaccurate misleading or distorted material.

(ii) Whenever it is recognized that a significant inaccuracy, misleading statement or distorted report has been published, it should be corrected promptly and with due prominence.

(iii) An apology should be published whenever appropriate.

(iv) A newspaper or periodical should always report fairly and accurately the outcome of an action for defamation to which it has been a party.

2 OPPORTUNITY TO REPLY

A fair opportunity for reply to inaccuracies should be given to individuals or organizations when reasonably called for.

3 COMMENT, CONJECTURE AND FACT

Newspapers, while free to be partisan, should distinguish clearly between comment, conjecture and fact.

4 PRIVACY

Intrusions and enquiries into an individual's private life without his or her consent including the use of long-lens photography to take pictures of people on private property without their consent are not generally acceptable and publication can only be justified when in the public interest.

Note — Private property is defined as any private residence, together with its garden and outbuildings, but excluding any adjacent fields or parkland. In addition, hotel bedrooms (but not other areas in a hotel) and those parts of a hospital or nursing home where patients are treated or accommodated.

5 LISTENING DEVICES

Unless justified by public interest, journalists should not obtain or publish material obtained by using clandestine listening devices or by intercepting private telephone conversations.

6 HOSPITALS

(i) Journalists or photographers making enquiries at hospitals or similar institutions should identify themselves to a responsible official and obtain permission before entering non-public areas.

(ii) The restrictions on intruding into privacy are particularly relevant to enquiries about individuals in hospitals or similar institutions.

7 MISREP-RESENTATION

(i) Journalists should not generally obtain or seek to obtain information or pictures through misrepresentation or subterfuge.

(ii) Unless in the public interest, documents or photographs should be removed only with the express consent of the owner.

(iii) Subterfuge can be justified only in the public interest and only when material cannot be obtained by any other means.

8 HARASSMENT

(i) Journalists should neither obtain nor seek to obtain information or pictures through intimidation or harassment.

(ii) Unless their enquiries are in the public interest, journalists should not photograph individuals on private property without their consent; should not persist in telephoning or questioning individuals after having been asked to desist; should not remain on their property after having been asked to leave and should not follow them.

(iii) It is the responsibility of editors to ensure that these requirements are carried out.

9 PAYMENT FOR ARTICLES

Payment or offers of payment for stories, pictures or information, should not be made directly or through agents to witnesses or potential witnesses in current or criminal proceedings or to people engaged in crime or to their associate — which includes family, friends, neighbours and colleagues — except where the material concerned ought to be published in the public interest and the payment is necessary for this to be done.

10 INTRUSION INTO GRIEF OR SHOCK

In cases involving personal grief or shock, enquiries should be carried out and approaches made with sympathy and discretion.

11 INNOCENT RELATIVES AND FRIENDS

Unless it is contrary to the public's right to know, the press should generally avoid identifying relatives or friends of persons convicted or accused of crime.

12 INTER-VIEWING OR PHOTO-GRAPHING CHILDREN

(i) Journalists should not normally interview or photograph children under the age of 16 on subjects involving the personal welfare of the child, in the absence of or without the consent of a parent or other adult who is responsible for the children.

(ii) Children should not be approached or photographed while at school without the permission of the school authorities.

13 CHILDREN IN SEX CASES

1   The press should not, even where the law does not prohibit it, identify children under the age of 16 who are involved in cases concerning sexual offences, whether as victims, or as witnesses or defendants.

2   In any press report of a case involving a sexual offence against a child —
   (i)   The adult should be identified.
   (ii) The term "incest" where applicable should not be used.
   (iii) The offence should be described as "serious offences against young children" or similar appropriate wording.
   (iv) The child should not be identified.
   (v)   Care should be taken that nothing in the report implies the relationship between the accused and the child.

14 VICTIMS OF CRIME

The press should not identify victims of sexual assault or publish material likely to contribute to such identification unless, by law, they are free to do so.

15 DISCRIMINATION

   (i)   The press should avoid prejudicial or pejorative reference to a person's race, colour, religion, sex or sexual orientation or to any physical or mental illness or handicap.
   (ii) It should avoid publishing details of a person's race, colour, religion, sex or sexual orientation, unless these are directly relevant to the story.

16 FINANCIAL JOURNALISM

   (i)   Even where the law does not prohibit it, journalists should not use for their own profit, financial information they receive in advance of its general publication, nor should they pass such information to others.
   (ii) They should not write about shares or securities in whose performance they know that they or their close families have a significant financial interest, without disclosing the interest to the editor or financial editor.
   (iii) They should not buy or sell, either directly or through nominees or agents, shares or securities about which they have written recently or about which they intend to write in the near future.

17 CONFIDENTIAL SOURCES

Journalists have a moral obligation to protect confidential sources of information.

18 THE PUBLIC INTEREST

Clauses 4, 5, 7, 8 and 9 create exceptions which may be covered by invoking the public interest. For the purposes of this code that is most easily defined as:
   (i)   Detecting or exposing crime or a serious misdemeanour.
   (ii) Protecting public health and safety.
   (iii) Preventing the public from being misled by some statement or action of an individual or organisation.

In any cases raising issues beyond these three definitions the Press Complaints Commission will require a full explanation by the editor of the publication involved, seeking to demonstrate how the public interest was served.

> *Comments or suggestions regarding the content of the Code may be sent to the Secretary, Press Standards Board of Finance, Merchants House Buildings, 30 George Square, Glasgow G2 1EG, to be laid before the industry's Code Committee.*

Index